SINGLE &

Soulfully Celebrating

SEX

UALLY

the Dance of the Sexes

WHOLE

SINGLE &

Soulfully Celebrating

SEX UALLY

the Dance of the Sexes

WHOLE

DR. DOUG ROSENAU

SEXUAL WHOLENESS
RESOURCES

Single and Sexually Whole: Soulfully Celebrating the Dance of the Sexes
An updated edition to material formerly published as Soul Virgins: Redefining Single Sexuality
Doug Rosenau, Ed.D.
Digital (eBook) format published by: © 2023 by Doug Rosenau

Published by Sexual Wholeness Resources, Suwanee, GA.

ISBN: 979-8-9885256-1-5 (Paperback)
       979-8-9885256-2-2 (eBook)
       978-0-9858107-9-5 (Limited Edition Hardback)

All Scripture quotations, unless otherwise indicated, are taken from the Holy Bible, New International Version®, NIV®. Copyright ©1973, 1978, 1984, 2011 by Biblica, Inc.™ Used by permission of Zondervan. All rights reserved worldwide. www.zondervan.comThe "NIV" and "New International Version" are trademarks registered in the United States Patent and Trademark Office by Biblica, Inc.™

Scripture quotations marked (CEV) are from the Contemporary English Version Copyright © 1991, 1992, 1995 by American Bible Society. Used by Permission.

Scripture quotations marked (MSG) are taken from The Message, copyright © 1993, 2002, 2018 by Eugene H. Peterson. Used by permission of NavPress. All rights reserved. Represented by Tyndale House Publishers..

Scripture marked (NCV) are taken from the New Century Version®. Copyright © 2005 by Thomas Nelson. Used by permission. All rights reserved.

Scripture marked (NKJV) are taken from the New King James Version. Copyright ©1982 by Thomas Nelson, Inc. Used by permission. All rights reserved.

Scripture quotations marked (NLT) are taken from the Holy Bible, New Living Translation, copyright ©1996, 2004, 2015 by Tyndale House Foundation. Used by permission of Tyndale House Publishers, Carol Stream, Illinois 60188. All rights reserved.

Scripture quotations marked (NASB®) are taken from the New American Standard Bible®, Copyright © 1960, 1971, 1977, 1995, 2020 by The Lockman Foundation. Used by permission. All rights reserved. lockman.org.

Scripture marked (BSB) are taken from The Holy Bible, Berean Standard Bible, and is produced in cooperation with Bible Hub, Discovery Bible, OpenBible.com, and the Berean Bible Translation Committee. This text of God's Word has been dedicated to the public domain.

Cover by Seismic Creative .

OTHER BOOKS BY
DR. DOUG ROSENAU

Slaying the Marriage Dragons

A Celebration of Sex

A Celebration of Sex after 50

A Celebration of Sex for Newlyweds

Soul Virgins: Redefining SINGLE Sexuality

Total Intimacy: A Guide to Loving by Color

A Celebration of Sex Guidebook

TO MY BELOVED CHRISTIAN SINGLES:

Please forgive our Christian culture for the way we've treated single sexuality:

- For not initiating honest conversations and building a helpful theology.
- For not creating a sex-positive culture that celebrates sexuality.
- For not helping you embrace "horny" and steward such feelings wisely.
- For simplistically banning behavior rather than appealing to your heart,
- For not guiding you in cultivating a godly sexual wholeness.

Let me encourage you to boldly and courageously:

- Challenge the current and confusing "hook-up" culture with God's love and truth.
- Create a sexual ethic based on valuing, celebrating and protecting sexuality—not just abstaining from certain behavior.
- Cultivate intimate friendships and communities to help you embrace and steward your sexuality.
- Reclaim God's sexual economy of chastity and soul virginity with the freedom and intimacy that only such attitudes and behavior can bring.

"Learn the sexual truth and never reject it. Get sexual wisdom, self-control, and understanding." (NCV "sexual" added)

Dr. Doug

CONTENTS

PREFACE

This book contains Doug's unedited words.

The book you hold is the life work of a caring man with a great passion. Dr. Douglas Rosenau cared deeply for those who hurt and he was devoted to helping them live in healing and freedom.

In an ideal world, Dr. Doug would be here to help you wrestle with the concepts in this book. He would be online personally, explaining the transformative truths and the difficult-to-accept principles. He would be rejoicing with you as you grasped the complexity and interrelationship of the beliefs he sets forward here. This book is, after all, the culmination of a lifetime of thinking, praying, discussing, and wrestling with these truths. He had thought through it well.

What you are about to read is the unedited version of the book he left on his laptop. He had it marked as edited and "final." I chose to leave it as he wrote and edited it. *These are his words.*

I believe these words can be transformative for any reader who wants to be sexually whole. Whether you are single or not, the values and principles he taught, such as true chastity and soul virginity, draw us to Christlikeness. Some of these principles were first published in Doug's book, *Soul Virgins,* written with colleague Michael Todd Wilson. That content —and the content here – was woven together over many years with in-depth input from many single students, clients, and friends. This content provides a guide for those wrestling with sexuality in singleness and also lays out truths on sexuality and sexual integrity that go far beyond singleness.

Watching Doug teach these principles in class was fascinating. His enthusiasm and conviction were solid, as was his compassion for those who misunderstood or disagreed with him. He valued lovingly challenging boundaries that kept people confined. Using phrases like "righteous flirting," he could draw out your biases and presuppositions and invite you to see the *value* he was highlighting. His gentleness, combined with a true gift of encouragement, made his invitation to consider his concepts even more appealing. I hope you experience that same openness arising in yourself as you read.

Doug's commitment to singles and sexuality was drawn from his own experiences with singleness as a young man and following an unwanted divorce, before marrying his precious Cathy—a marriage that grew for 35 years. Decades of mourning, wondering, guiding, and rejoicing with singles in his office and students in the classroom kept him personally engaged with these principles.

Doug went to dance in the presence of his beloved Lord on Palm Sunday of 2022. *He is sorely missed.* His teaching continues in the lives of hundreds of his students, many leaders, and in written works like this.

While there are teachings in this book that may be challenging, I pray you will not dismiss the whole because of a part. Lean in to discover the heart of a man who loved people and loved the Lord. Doug wanted you to know his Lord better through God's creation of sex and sexuality. Press in to glean truths from a man who wrestled with these concepts for a lifetime. You will find nuggets that will challenge you to grow. May what God taught Doug take root in you.

Michael Sytsma – One of the many friends of Doug's.

INTRODUCTION

Single adults are sexually whole.

I hope by the end of this book you can add a resounding, "Yes!" to this conviction. It is at the heart of every chapter. Christian singles can value, celebrate, and protect their sexuality—not just repress, tolerate or misuse it. They can enter fully into an intimate sexual celebration the Creative Trinity planned, an amazing "Dance of the Sexes."

God didn't design singles to be stuck in some holding pattern, waiting for marriage in order to find intimacy and sexual significance—singleness is not a synonym for an asexual existence. All humans begin as and are ultimately single people. Even Jesus was a single person. That being said, the concept of being "single" seems to have a negative connotation, especially in the Christian culture. For some it means: "I'm alone and missing something important," or, "I will never find true intimacy unless I get married," or, "I can never be content unless I am having sex." But this couldn't be farther from the truth! You have a special place and role to fulfill in the Body of Christ.

That's what this book is about: giving singles a wide-angle lens through which to see the bigger picture of their identity in Christ, and of their sexual identity—To help you create a positive sexual theology that goes beyond mere "do's and don'ts," and provides practical explanations of why and how to live within the Creator's awesome plan for human sexuality as a single adult.

God deliberately created you uniquely sexual. You are

one-of-a-kind, a man or a woman with an alluring sexual power and eroticism all your own. Your masculinity or femininity, and your ability to experience sexual feelings, adds a new dimension and potential to all your intimate interactions. Your sexuality gives you an amazing ability to experience intimacy in a fulfilling dance of the sexes with your sisters and brothers. While writing this book I've prayed for you — the reader — that *Single & Sexually Whole* would guide, motivate, heal, and enrich your sexual journey in a deeply personal and practical way.

CHAPTER ONE

God's Intimate Design in Sexuality

with Michael Todd Wilson[1]

The almighty Trinity was on a creative roll, having fun planning out their human being love adventure. They'd decided to create a world and populate it with human beings, but were still discussing how to help these finite creatures understand the infinite Jehovah. Ultimately, they would accomplish this through the living parable of Jesus —"God with us." But they also wanted to create *illustrations* and experiences that would reveal God's character and his relationship with them. As a wise theologian so beautifully stated about humanity and the creative Trinity, God wanted to make the "invisible" spiritual mysteries "visible" to his creation so they could experience him.[1]

> *"For since the creation of the world God's invisible qualities— his eternal power and divine nature—have been clearly seen, being understood from what has been made." Romans 1:20*

Nature (the created heavens and earth) is a marvelous part of that revelation. How the Trinity must have enjoyed creating each reflective metaphor! (Metaphors are figures of speech where we use a different

---

[1] Michael Todd Wilson is a Licensed Professional Counselor, Certified Sex Therapist, and Professional Certified Coach with Intentional Hearts, Inc., offering specialized Christian coaching for men around all areas related to sexual integrity recovery. He is co-author of *Preventing Ministry Failure: A ShepherdCare Guide for Pastors, Ministers and Other Caregivers.*

1

concept or representation to help us picture or explain something we might not otherwise understand.) In the Bible, God is portrayed as a solid rock, Jesus as a living stream, and the Holy Spirit as a gentle and powerful wind. Mountains reveal the strength of God's creative power, and sunsets evoke an appreciation for his artistry.

> *"The heavens declare the glory of God and the firmament shows His handiwork." Psalm 19:1 (NKJV)*

The Creator also wanted to demonstrate his love for his creation. After all, the Godhead has enjoyed perfect love and fellowship in eternity past through the relationship of the Holy Trinity. God desired his creation to understand that they could find true happiness and fulfillment only in intimate relationship—first with God, then with others. At this point, divine creativity reached its peak:

> *"Then God said, 'Let us make man in our image' … Male and female he created them." Genesis 1:26–27*

Scholars tell us these verses are poetic in style and use a form of parallelism that equates the "image of God" with "male and female." God created our sexuality to display his very image, suggesting that both masculinity and femininity are required to fully mirror and reflect the divine character

God's Grand Demonstration

God is deeply relational. He created humans to experience and reflect his own image of love and creativity—making the invisible visible. Our sexuality is his grand demonstration of intimacy. He chose to do this by creating wonderfully different but complexly interactive genders (male and female) with two important aspects of sexual relating: social or gender and erotic or romantic.

God gave us a glimpse into his very nature with our masculinity and femininity – the magnetic way they attract, complement, and relate to one another. Creating gender produced such concepts as father and mother, brother and sister, initiating and responding, strength and softness, charm and allure. Adam and Eve were created by God to begin the first family, and are the father and mother of us all.

How fun to watch men and women bring out the best in each other with character traits and accomplishments that could only occur as they interact with the opposite sex. How special to see same-sex friendships as women create those intimate and fulfilling girlfriend relationships—as men come together in a "bromance" with an intimacy often deepened through mutual activities. The Creator was amazing in instituting community and the importance of gender-based social sexuality (and what we will develop in Chapter 8 as "righteous flirting").

The Almighty also made Adam and Eve the first lovers, each with erotic longing to connect with and complete the other. Can you imagine the excitement and awe Adam felt the first time he gazed upon his Eve and she alluringly touched his total being? They deeply desired each other spiritually, emotionally, mentally, socially, and physically. But that's not all. Their "naked and unashamed" sexual relationship set the stage for a beautiful illustration that would tell the most remarkable story of all. God artistically formed the marital relationship to display the personal, *exclusive* love relationship God desires with each of us.

Even though our culture tries to divorce the two, erotic sexuality is so much more than "getting some" and creating sexual arousal with a willing partner—it's about intimacy and God's creative covenant relationship of marriage, mysteriously designed for sexual celebration.

> *"A man leaves his father and mother and is joined to his wife, and the two are united into one.' This is a great mystery, but it is an illustration of the way Christ and the church are one." Ephesians 5:31.32 (NLT)*

Perfect Intimacy: Reflected and Retold

In some sense, this divine story is retold every time one falls in love. In its purest form, a young man passionately seeks a bride; when he finds her, she is awakened by his love and desires to embrace his strength. He is enthralled with her beauty and longing for him. They've never quite known what they were missing before this moment, but now they must have what the other possesses. They want to know and be known as never before.

He invites her into a relationship, and their journey begins. They pledge their lives to one another, and look forward to their wedding. It will be a time when two wonderfully matched hearts and bodies will unite under the blessing of their friends, their family, and their God. Those in attendance will agree to hold the couple accountable to fulfill the vows they've made to each other—"for better or worse." When the ceremony and the reception are over, the couple seals their wedding vows by sharing what is meant only for the other—their "true sex." They have agreed to share this special relationship with no one else for the rest of their lives. Their sexual intimacy distinguishes their relationship from all others, and echoes the beautiful imagery found in Song of Songs 8:6: "Place me like a seal over your heart, like a seal on your arm; for love … burns like blazing fire, like a mighty flame."

Marriage is a metaphor for Christ's love for his bride, the Church. Jesus became human to reveal and fulfill the Father's plan for salvation and union with his people. Jesus seeks out his Bride and finds her, awakening her to something she's never known and inviting her to join him. She eagerly follows. This is where we currently find ourselves in this marvelous story of redemption: pledged to Christ and awaiting his return, when he will take his bride to the grand wedding feast to be with him forever.

Telling the Story through Broken, Imperfect Reflectors

Does that imagery stir something deep within your heart? This metaphor of *exclusive* intimacy and marital fidelity is often not fully developed for Christian singles. Humans are an immature and selfish people, so much interferes with our ability to play out romantic, sexual relationships as God intended. We struggle making "visible" human sexuality truly mirror the "invisible" intimate Creator of that sexuality.

> *"Now we see things imperfectly, like puzzling reflections in a mirror, but then we will see everything with perfect clarity. All that I know now is partial and incomplete, but then I will know everything completely, just as God now knows me completely." I Corinthians 13:12 (NLT)*

Quite often, our actual experience is a poor *reflection* of God's ideal. He knows that our reflection of his divine nature will always be imperfect until we get to heaven. Nonetheless, this ideal is the

Creator's intention for the genital expression of sexuality—the goal of an exclusive, intimate marital relationship.

This provides a good backdrop for your journey into single adult sexuality. We so easily wander off track and forget that our sexuality is intended to mirror the heart of the Trinity—created to reflect the value God places on intimate connection and love. His sexual verbs are "value," "love," and "connect"—not "score," "hook up" or "get off."

God wants not only our romantic commitments to reflect his character, but also that of our broader sexual identity and intimate friendships. If single adults want to mirror the Divine they must understand that God is always: *Creatively Intimate* in a way that adds (not takes) something to each relational encounter; *Mysteriously Beautiful* with the truth that men and women will regularly be surprised at how masculine and feminine beauty reflect the Creator; *Passionately Present* with a Trinity full of feelings and the ability to be fully present and focus that love on an individual; *Confidently Gentle* with an assured sense of self that can interact compassionately with others; *Intentionally Holy* with boundaries honored and unexpectedly eliciting a true freedom; *Wonderfully Good* and fulfilling.

Though God isn't physically sexual, he chose to reveal himself and the way he loves through human sexuality—making his invisible self *visible*. We could describe God as transcendently (supernaturally) sexual with the desire to be pursued, known and loved (by us). He designed his creation to experience and understand him through sexual intimacy, and to let our sexuality reflect his divine nature. Our intimate Creator wants his awe-inspiring character reproduced in all of our sexual interactions, as our hearts, minds and bodies reflect his love.

"But the Holy Spirit produces this kind of (sexual) fruit in our lives: (sexual) love, (sexual) joy,(sexual) peace, (sexual) patience, (sexual) kindness, (sexual) goodness,(sexual)

faithfulness, (sexual) gentleness and (sexual) self-control."
Galatians 5:22 (NLT) (sexual parenthesis added)

Placing God at the Center

The process of becoming sexually whole cannot be undertaken in your own strength. You'll need to rely on the power of God in your life and the presence of an intimate community of brothers and sisters. Without God providing purpose for your life and sexuality, none of this will even make sense. Unless you recognize God's claim on your life—especially your sexual life—you'll find little reason to buy into or even consider the concepts of this book.

However, if you recognize your place in the universe as God's creation, and the importance of his guidance in your life, you'll see that there's a Creator God responsible for our existence, who knows best how we were designed to function. Understanding this, it only makes sense to follow his "blueprint" for our lives—especially when it comes to the area of sexuality.

A three-dimensional (body, mind,heart) soul virginity, a lifetime commitment to sexual purity and integrity, then, becomes a lifestyle, regardless of the presence or absence of your physical virginity. The Creator joins us as we find our way sexually, enabling us to value, celebrate, and protect his *gift*. Yes, that's right, your sexuality is a great gift! The Bible talks about God's gifts to his children as valuable "pearls." Our ability to be sexually attracted and aroused, to create intimate sexual relationships, is indeed a valuable *pearl*. But, we need to heed Christ's warning,

"Don't give to selfish, uncaring people what is sacred; If you throw your sexual pearls in a pigpen, they'll just get trampled and your heart torn apart." (Matthew 7:6 paraphrase)

Note to Reader: I know some of you reading this book have been the victim of rape and sexual trauma. Your "sexual pearls" were trampled and you had no control over what was perpetrated on you. I am so sorry and my prayer for you is that you can allow God to lift your shame and the violation, as you become one of His beautiful, sexually whole soul virgins.

I hope by now you have a taste for the passion behind the writing of this book. God wants to start a positive sexual revival and revolution among Christian singles that can help them achieve true sexual purity and a fulfilling intimacy. I hope the following chapters will help you see the beauty and sacredness of your sexuality and all that God would like to bless you with. We desperately need a larger purpose for our sexuality, to give it life-changing meaning.

The Road Map to Sexual Wholeness

Catching God's vision for the larger story of your sexual journey will not be easy. You face many challenges, living in a culture indifferent to and often antagonistic to Christian values. The average age of marriage is advancing toward thirty, and casual premarital sex is widely accepted and encouraged—unfortunately, even among evangelical Christian singles. God's Word has so much to teach us as we create a new road map for sexuality.

> *"Do not let anyone fool you by telling you things that are (sexually) untrue…live like children who belong to the light. Light brings every kind of (sexual) goodness, right living, and truth. So be careful how you live. Do not live like those*

who are not (sexually) wise, but live wisely. So do not be
(sexually) foolish but learn what the Lord wants you to do."
Ephesians 5: 6a, 8b, 9, 15-17 (NCV Parentheses added)

In thinking about a new road map for single sexuality, I ran across a story of a young lady who'd been driving around Pennsylvania for some time, lost, and with a growing sense of exasperation. Upset that her every effort led nowhere, and at the onset of a migraine, she stopped for directions.

"Where am I?" she asked in frustration.

"You're in Greenville," replied a kindly old man.

"How do I get to Nazareth?" she inquired.

He reluctantly replied, "I wouldn't try to get there from here."

So it is with trying to get to sexual wholeness from the backdrop of dating apps, reality dating shows, and many other pop-culture influences. It's equally difficult finding direction from a Christian culture more defined by what not to do than what the Bible teaches and celebrates in terms of sexuality. In the chasm between a distorted but vocal Hollywood and an often judgmental, silent church, many Christian singles aren't sure (like the lady above) where to turn for direction. Deep down, they know they're lost and confused, but they aren't quite sure which direction to take to reach a godly destination.

So many Christian singles begin this journey hoping for only slight changes in direction, just to realize they need a completely new map—a radically different route to reach the destination God desires for them. Dear reader, more than you realize, your internal map/values and the way you live out your sexual story has been influenced by your surroundings. You try to live out what you believe and feel is right, but often the values shaping you come from a distorted culture and ungodly wisdom.

Creating a new road map and an understanding of sexual

wholeness is about discarding ineffective thinking and creating a new heart attitude and a more thoughtful sexual culture. This positive Jesus-culture will begin to ask the right questions. Not "How far can I go?" but "How can I steward my own and my partner's sexuality and develop our true potential to become all God wants us to be?" Or, "How can I value, celebrate, and protect myself and others, as we work to write our own unique sexual stories in a healthy, godly and effective way?"

Have you ever thought about all God wants you to express and experience through your sexuality: the ability to be intimately known and accepted, the thrill of the pursuit, the mystery and excitement of being a man or a woman and the power of gender interaction, pleasure and play, righteous flirting, the possibility of a profound "one flesh" union, and so much more?

How sad that our selfish, immature culture has so warped and idolized sex. I challenge you to ask God to give you a new map for your single-adult sexual journey—providing you with profoundly different values than the influences of secular culture on one side and the cries of "just don't" and ineffective prohibitions on the other. You need a road map of godly principles that will *revolutionize your hearts, minds, and behaviors.*

> *"You give me a better way to live, so I live as you want me to sexually." Psalms 18:36 (NCV "sexually" added))*

CHAPTER TWO

One is A Whole Number

Unfortunately, most people, married or single, have a difficult time seeing singleness as a good thing. ONE can truly be a whole number. Sure, Christian singles hope (if they can) to get to a place in life where they can endure singleness with godly contentment, but most don't see it as something to be celebrated. Yet I believe that single sexuality celebrates a three-dimensional intimacy that not only instills discipline and godly character, but also casts a vision of exciting potential and fulfilling relationships in a whole different venue than marriage.

Defining the Concept of "Single"

The word *single* can convey many misconceptions: like the idea that something is missing and incomplete. Single is often seen as a *deficit* model with single never as good as double. Singleness is not a "less than" life, and can be a place of abundance and great personal fulfillment.

I see Christians sometimes overemphasizing marriage as the ultimate goal and missing the unique intimacy of married and single people. We have much to learn from each other. We are all children of God, conforming to His sexual guidelines with a desire for deeply intimate relationships. We are all called to chastity and to love and be loved.

We must recognize that being single or married are just two different ways of living out lives and sexuality. But rather than make these two opposing forces with singles one down on the status rung, why can't we help both lifestyles prosper, personally and sexually? Both married couples and singles have a unique style of loving and serving that can help the Body of Christ flourish. The truth is that *none of us are complete without Christ* and a relationship with him.

Remember that Jesus was single. There is a rich tradition in the Christian church of singleness, celibacy and service. This goes clear back to the Apostle Paul and his encouragement that singles have a unique and special place of ministry and outreach.

> *"So I say to those who aren't married and to widows—it's better to stay unmarried, just as I am. I want you to be free from the concerns of this life. An unmarried man can spend his time doing the Lord's work and thinking how to please him." I Corinthians 7:8, 32 (NLT)*

Singles then, are not in a holding pattern, waiting for the plane to land at the destination of "marriage", so they can have sex and build the only relationship that promises true intimacy. Unfortunately, it is easy to feel this way, and many do. Yes, the majority of people do get married. Having an intimate lover and building a family is a common heart's desire. To move through life with your peers getting married and having children can feel incredibly isolating and confusing, even if you're living life as a godly single woman or man. Singleness is definitely not an alternative plan. It can be a beautiful season!

The divine Trinity purposefully created the state of unmarried, celibate adults to demonstrate love and creativity in unique and vital ways. Singleness can be a fun and meaningful state of being, a place to build deeply intimate relationships. It is also a place of costly obedience, experiencing sacrifice and learning to grieve. For quite a few, it will be a profound final destination. But Christian communities without singles will never be complete. Single adults have a critical role to play in a vibrant church community. And, singles cannot achieve sexual wholeness without living in community and having intimate friendships.

Many concepts are critical to doing "sexual" well as a single adult. Always keep in mind the *truth* that "Single Adults Are Sexually Whole." Christian singles can value, celebrate and protect their sexuality; not repress, tolerate or indulge it. Yes, they choose to place appropriate boundaries around the genital, erotic part of their sexuality; but as you will see throughout this book, that can actually enhance their sexual wholeness and freedom. Singles can fully enter into the social sexual celebration God planned, with an energy from their erotic sexual feelings—an enter into an amazing Dance of the Sexes.

A Tale of Two Dinner Parties

Imagine two dinner parties: Brad, a married man, sits in a small private dining room. A delicious steak dinner is brought out and he eats his fill, sharing his meal with his wife. He sits and talks with his "Eve" seated across from him and is enthralled with her presence. The two spend the evening in conversation and feel they are deepening their relationship in special, *exclusive* ways. At the end of the night, Brad has had a wonderful time and built a deeper knowledge of his lover.

At the second dinner party, Molly, a single girl, arrives to find herself at a large buffet with numerous finger foods, and chairs scattered around to encourage mingling. She's actually glad, because she is a vegetarian and there are plenty of meatless offerings. She has fun crafting a meal out of hummus, a variety of nuts, vegetables and desserts—returning to the buffet several times before the evening ends.

Some might throw up their hands and complain about not being served a sit-down dinner. Yet Molly finds herself enjoying the variety of the buffet and moves around the room freely, talking *inclusively* to many different people. Some are old friends, some are newer friends, and some she is meeting for the first time. She meets several interesting men and gets to know familiar ones a little better. At the end of the night, she has had a wonderful time. If she chooses to extend the evening with a coffee date, no permission is needed, and she will raise no eyebrows by simply conversing with a member of the opposite sex at a café late into the evening.

Both of these were great dinners and intimate experiences. Clearly, they are socially different, each with their drawbacks and benefits. A neuroscientist friend of mine, Bill Struthers, likes to define the sexual interactions available to married couples and singles as different kinds of *protein* with one eating meat and the other a vegetarian. To see one of these social or nutritional experiences as inferior is shortsighted. Singles should joyfully take pleasure in their buffet and recognize that their married friends sometimes grieve what they will never again have in a buffet. Yet both married and single have their own unique feast with special treats and privileges with wise sexual boundaries and choices. Both expressions of sexuality are meaningful, life-enriching, and provide insight into the love relationships of the divine Trinity. God loves *exclusively* with a covenant intimacy (a quiet dinner a deux) and *inclusively* with a communal intimacy (a buffet). In the end, it comes down to developing a graceful maturity and sexual discipline whether married or single.

Myths and Simplistic Assumptions about Singleness and Single Sexuality

Yet doubt remains for many about the purpose of their ongoing singleness: "I can't believe I'm still single in my mid-thirties! What's wrong with me?" "Maybe I need to find a different dating app and try harder." "I want sex." "If God loves me, why am I still single?"

Please don't look at singleness, single sexuality and finding a mate too simplistically. While it's possible your singleness may be due in part to poor dating skills, unhealed trauma, walls you put up, or unrealistic expectations, it's often much more complicated. Below are some myths and assumptions about singleness and single sexuality.

- "If I stay sexually pure, God will give me a mate, and guarantee amazing sex after we are married." God doesn't look at singleness as something He must rescue you from, nor does a great sex life occur without communication and practice.

- "I had sex and an abortion before committing to sexual purity. God must be punishing me by keeping me single." Sin always has a cost, but the Lord chooses to redeem our past if we turn to Him. What is often punishing us is the guilt and shame we haven't let him forgive and heal.

- "Marriage is the only committed, deeply intimate relationship I can enter into—where someone truly has my back." No, as will be developed later in this chapter, singles need "covenant" spiritual friendships that are much like a marital commitment with the ability to experience love and intimacy without genital expression.

- "I'm horny and need to have sex. I don't want to be celibate the rest of my life." Genital sex is a desire *not a "need."* Nothing

15

will explode or shrivel up if you don't have sex. That is an important part of this book: "What do I do with my horny feelings? How is remaining sexually chaste even possible?"

Our heavenly Father doesn't withhold good things from his children to be mean, to punish them, and certainly not because of his lack of love for them. He desires to give good gifts to his children (Matthew 7:7–11). Perhaps his desire is to give you an even greater gift.

Finding Intimacy, Contentment and Joy in the Single Journey

As much as some singles believe differently, marriage will not meet all your needs. In fact, a healthy intimacy doesn't depend on marriage at all. Having your deepest needs for intimacy does not begin with sex and a mate. It begins with God and the people in your life who love you.

God and You—Alone, Special and Loved

Here's the truth about loneliness: ultimately, everyone is lonely and alone. However, this is not a curse. Marriage, or finding a partner with whom to have sex isn't the antidote to loneliness, nor does it create wholeness in an individual. Real intimacy begins with the One the metaphor of marriage was intended to be a reminder of: God himself, through Jesus Christ, and the power of the Holy Spirit.

"See I have written your name on the palms of my hands."
Isaiah 49:16 (NLT)

"He will take delight in you with gladness. With his love, he will calm all your fears. He will rejoice over you with joyful songs." Zephaniah 3:17 (NLT)

God loves you, knows you personally, and sings special songs over you! Meaning and contentment stem from your relationship with him. Only Jesus can fill your "God-shaped vacuum"— your ache for loving connection. He can help turn your "loneliness" into a contented "aloneness." As a follower of Christ, I always emphasize that our relationship with God is what makes life worth living to single and married alike. Your vertical relationship with the Holy Trinity is what brings the potential for real intimacy in your horizontal relationships, with your community of friends and perhaps, a mate.

Think with me a moment. Since Adam and Eve brought sin and "Stupid" into the world, all of us have entered into a selfish, unfulfilling quest to be happy and fulfilled—personally and sexually. Our sinful natures prevent us from being all that God intended us to be. But, when we come to Jesus as Savior, and let him break the power of sinful Stupid in our lives, God then helps us find our true identity in that love relationship with Him, as we experience all that we were created to be as uniquely sexual men and women.

Note to Reader: I have sought to find words that describe how selfish sinful mistakes can painfully distort our sexual journey. I will often refer to sin as "stupid", as it never works for our good. Anything God creates as beautiful, Satan wants to destroy. The forces of evil especially want us to commit sexual stupidity and get confused and hurt.

Maybe you aren't sure what a love relationship with God looks like. It begins with Jesus as the One who can give you that connection with the Creative Trinity. Explore and learn: What does God care about? What pleases him? What saddens him? With a human lover, one way to express your thoughts and feelings is through a variety of communication. You might email, or chat in various ways. God has chosen to communicate with us primarily through the Bible—and those wise people who can help you apply Scriptural principles to your life.

If you're new to studying Scripture, check out the different translations of the Bible for yourself. Attending a Bible class at a local church, finding a daily devotional in paper or online, and listening to sermons, podcasts or praise music on the radio, television, or the Internet all serve to deepen your relationship with God. Music, in particular can touch your heart in a profound way.

Understanding Scripture is the primary way God talks with us, and prayer is our primary way of communicating with Him. Prayer is simply having a conversation with God, much like you'd have with another person. Sometimes a conversation with God doesn't even have to involve an exchange of words. Many find their most meaningful times with God are spent in silence and solitude while in nature or watching birds at a feeder through the window. Quiet your heart and mind, allowing God's Spirit to commune with you in the stillness. A love relationship with Jesus is the foundation for true meaning and fulfillment in your life and sexuality.

Growing into a Mature Wholeness

I think all of us want to become the best person we can be. As a selfish sinful person, I will never be the man that God designed me to be without Jesus's help. But, as I enter into a relationship with him, I can mature into a man who lives out Christ's gentle, wise character.

Maturity in marriage only comes through maturity in singleness—both relationally and sexually. Singles must first learn who they are independent of a spouse; otherwise, they'll forever be looking to their mate to "complete them." Singleness is not simply a training ground for a great marriage, but those who have learned to be fulfilled and contented singles make the best mates. It takes two mature, self-confident, unselfish people to make a whole, healthy marriage—or a healthy and whole friendship. Do the math: ½ X ½ = a ¼ of a great relationship.

Grow Sexual Character: Whether we are single or married, we learn and practice wise stewardship of our sexuality through our relationship with God. The sexual skills and disciplines He teaches us in the crucible of singleness apply for a lifetime. For example, McKenzie appreciates her husband Jim's ability to enjoy other women as whole people rather than seeing them merely as sex objects.

When they were dating, Jim explained to McKenzie that this was a more recently acquired skill for him. At a seminar, he'd been challenged to treat women as three-dimensional, with a mind and heart as well as a body. Now, when he notices a sexy woman at the mall, he looks more closely at her. He looks at what she is carrying and wonders what her life is like. He thinks about her God-given desire to love and give herself to a man who loves and protects her, knowing fully it isn't him. Jim might even pray for her, that she would come to know Christ if she hasn't already. This helped McKenzie feel safe as she understood the maturity God had brought about in Jim in his season of singleness.

Growing old is mandatory, but growing up is optional. Both before and during marriage, the "grown-up" who achieves

Christ-like maturity and virtues (Colossians 3:12–14) and learns to live alone is the one who thrives in so many ways, especially sexually.

Love the Skin You're In: Self-esteem ultimately comes from accepting God's decree that you are "fearfully and wonderfully made," independent of other's opinions about your looks, personality, strengths, and weaknesses. Quit comparing! You are special, deeply loved, and can be excited about being you. This includes your sexuality, gender, and body image.

> *"For you created my inmost being; you knit me together in my mother's womb. I praise you because I am fearfully and wonderfully made; your works are wonderful, I know that full well." Psalm 139:13, 14*

As a Christian counselor, I am continually amazed at how few people really believe God loves them. This, my friend, is a true starting point. Please accept the fact that God loves you and created you, an awesome, one-of-a-kind sexual human being.

Learn the art of self-affirmation. Create a list of a dozen things to thank God for in the person he created you to be. As you become more self-confident and comfortable in your own skin, you are more likely to forget about yourself and reach out to enjoy friendships in more meaningful ways. Becoming a 3-D soul-sexy man or woman is extremely difficult when you aren't comfortable in your own skin or have a poor body image. Focusing on "thanking the Lord" allows you to own what he has invested into you, his unique and special child.

Nurture Yourself: Whether we're single or married, God gives us personal responsibility to love and nurture ourselves as we delight in our relationship with him. Nurturing yourself and learning to enjoy your own company isn't the same as being self-absorbed. It's taking responsibility for enjoying your life and not comparing yourself to others. It's a healthy independence.

"But each one must examine his own work, and then he will have reason for boasting in regard to himself alone, and not in regard to another." Galatians 6:4 (NASB1995)

People who find contentment in being alone make great friends and mates. Encourage variety and novelty in your life; develop an appreciation for hobbies and adventure; cultivate the enjoyment of flowers, leisurely baths, or art galleries; force yourself to relax; take hikes in nature, allowing God to restore your soul beside "quiet waters" (Psalm 23). As you practice healthy self-nurture, you will be less likely to engage in unhealthy behaviors like porn and masturbation or excessive gaming. Being *lonely* and being *alone* are quite different.

Stay Childlike: As adults, we tend to forget the natural curiosity and playfulness of childhood. Jesus said we would learn about the kingdom of heaven by observing and imitating children—creatures who possess an awe of the world around them and live to play. Let God inspire the child in you, motivating attitudes and activities that turn your loneliness into daily adventures. Stay full of curiosity. Express your feelings. Laugh. Play games and have fun as you free the child within. Allowing yourself to be childlike will, when God brings you your mate, make you a much more interesting lover.

Serve Others: Author Gary Thomas wisely writes for married couples, and we can apply his words to every relationship. "When my heart gets filled by God's love and acceptance, I'm set free to love instead of worrying about being loved. I'm motivated to serve instead of becoming obsessed about whether I'm being served. I'm moved to cherish instead of feeling unappreciated."[2] Reaching out and serving is critical to being whole as a single person and so vital to creating much-needed community.

> *"Don't burn out; keep yourselves fueled and aflame. Be alert servants of the Master, cheerfully expectant. Don't quit in hard times; pray all the harder. Help needy Christians; be inventive in hospitality." Romans 12:11-13 (MSG)*

There are so many inventive options for serving: play an instrument in the praise band, teach in a Sunday school class, serve at a local homeless shelter, participate in hospital or nursing home visitation or evangelistic outreach, go on a short-term missions trip, or help at a summer youth camp. Whatever you do, remember you're building your relationship with God as you serve others. You'll be amazed at how reaching out beyond yourself can give you perspective and help alleviate your loneliness and self-preoccupation—actually make you less horny.

Heal Your Wounds and Learn to Love: Most adults have traumatic relationship baggage that can cause us to put up walls and prevent us from a deeper dive into intimate friendships. Often the wounded child inside of you is running the show and speaking for you. Our heavenly Father so wants you to heal and freely give and receive love.

Many have had sexual traumas that affect the way they view sexual relationships. What can you do to be whole and heal wounds? Get some counseling, become more self-aware, trust and discuss your fears with safe friends, take some personality inventories (like the Enneagram) to learn about your tendencies and needs for growth. God can help you heal, even from sexual trauma and guilt, as you get wise counsel and allow a caring community into your life.

Love Relationships: Filling the Intimacy Vacuum

Perhaps you've noticed that building intimacy with God is much like building intimacy with another person. That's because our human relationships are reflections of our relationship with God. He is by nature a relational being and created us with the same capacity for intimate connection. We shouldn't be surprised that when Jesus was asked what he considered to be the two greatest commandments, he responded, "Love the Lord your God with all your heart" and "Love your neighbor as yourself" (Mark 12:30–31).

I will keep repeating this, "Singles cannot achieve sexual integrity and wholeness apart from a loving community!" Singles need intimate friendships and community to flourish and keep their sexuality in its proper perspective. A relationship with God is primary, but deep connections with godly brothers and sisters is also critical.

> *"No one has ever seen God, but if we love each other, God lives in us, and his love is made perfect in us. And God gave us this command: Those who love God must also love their brothers and sisters." I John 4:12, 21 (NCV)*

> *"My children, we should love people not only with words and talk, but by our actions and true caring." I John 3:18 (NCV)*

> *"As iron sharpens iron, so a friend sharpens a friend." Proverbs 27:17 (NLT)*

> *"And let us consider how we may spur one another on toward love and good deeds, not giving up meeting together, as some are in the habit of doing, but encouraging one another..." Hebrews 10:24-25a (NIV)*

Creating Community

God and God's people—for Christians, this is where it all begins. These two relationships must represent your greatest investment of time. Having an intimate relationship with God is of highest importance. However, God knew we would need some representation of him here on earth through which he could love us and demonstrate his presence with us—people who could smile with us when we're happy, cry with us when we're sad, and hold us when we feel lonely or afraid.

I remember one young man whose mother had died. He just needed someone to hold him while he cried. He wanted a woman to do that with a nurturing presence, but was afraid to ask, for fear that he would make her uncomfortable, or that her expectation would be that their relationship would become sexual. We all have needs as human beings: touch, affirmation, support, to feel special and chosen, to be known and loved. This is why God encourages us toward community—real relationships with men and women—with whom he designed us to connect deeply in genuine, non-erotic intimacy. It's the purpose of the Church, the place where soul virgins (those who are single or married, who practice 3-D purity in their minds, hearts and physical lives) gather to develop relationships with others to help meet their need for intimacy.

We all know that just hanging out together does not necessarily create a supportive community. Community as God designed it will always include:

1. Laughter, fun, fulfilling activities that bring out the best in each other. God created humor and a childlike playfulness that can only be experienced as we interact with others. We need nurturing playgrounds and playmates. Sometimes we think we are tremendously horny when we're actually just lonely,

24

bored or selfishly preoccupied. Singles can create outings and times of fun fellowship that meet these non-sexual needs for connection in non-sexual ways.

Pay attention to the ways that singles can become touch-starved. Horny, sexually attraction and arousal will always be there. BUT, healthy single communities can learn to give safe and nurturing touch, both same-sex and opposite sex. You need those 20-second hugs, backs scratches, hand holding, roughhousing and other ways that satisfy the need for touch without thinking you're gay or using your sisters and brothers as sex objects.

2. Honesty and trust without manipulation or pettiness. Being genuine and transparent builds trust and safety. These are so critical for intimacy to flourish. God hates games and those who defraud their brothers and sisters. An important part of openness in building healthy relationships is engaging in those critical DTR's (**D**efine **t**he **R**elationship). Whether in good friendships or romantic dating, singles must be up front with their intentions, feelings, and boundaries as they define the meaning of a particular relationship.

3. Sexual integrity, chastity and accountability. Lauren Winner, author of *Real Sex: The Naked Truth about Chastity*, stresses that we live out our sexual discipline and chastity in community— we are responsible and accountable to each other. "Chastity, then, is a basic rule of community, but it is not a mere rule. It is also a *discipline*. Chastity is something you do, it is something you practice. It is not only a state—the state of *being chaste*—but a disciplined, active undertaking that e *do* as part of the Body. It is not the mere absence of sex but an active conforming of one's body to the arc of the Gospel."[3]

Note to Reader: Sexual chastity or purity (soul virginity) is not a destination or a goal to achieve. Sexual integrity is a daily and life-long journey of making wise choices and practicing sexual wholeness within your community. It is a process. It remains the same whether married or single, and isn't something that once lost is never regained.

4. Outreach and being a conduit for God's love and mercy. The Holy Spirit wants to use us to bless others. Healthy communities provide opportunities to minister into the lives of others. This could be missions trips, small groups of various kinds, volunteering, or leading classes. If Christians don't allow God's love to pour through them, they not only miss out on great opportunities for growth, but can become spiritually stagnated.

    "God's love has been poured into our hearts through the Holy Spirit, who has been given to us." Romans 5:5b (NLT)

    "Anyone who believes in me may come and drink! For the Scriptures declare, 'Rivers of living water will flow from his heart.'" John7:38 (NLT)

5. Righteous flirting (see Chapter 7) and affirmation of men and their masculinity and women and their femininity.

6. Deeper, more exclusive relationships without creating cliques or outcasts. Healthy communities possess an ability to allow deeper friendships to bless communal interactions. This could

include dating couples as well as best friends who choose not to isolate but to also have fun in a larger group of friends.

God not only designed you to flourish in community, he designed caring relationships to vary from the more casual to closer to the deeply intimate. As you progress up the continuum, the fewer and deeper they will be. You can enjoy a Sunday school class (casual), or a small group or friends you do activities with (close)—but deeper friendships take too much time and emotional investment to be committed to more than a few at a time. We need these. Those that know and love us enough to confront us and to provide comfort.

| Casual | Close | Intimate |

A Band of Brothers and the Sisterhood

"Behold, how good and how pleasant it is for brothers [& sisters] to dwell together in unity." Psalm 133:1 (NASB)

Men need deep friendships with other men—a close band of brothers who encourage them to reach their potential and walk in sexual integrity. Men need more "bro dates", time with other men with the intent of forming deeper relationships. Maybe we fear loving relationships will lead towards or be mistaken for same-sex attraction? Maybe we fear rejection and vulnerability? We men can be protective of our privacy, unwilling to disclose any information that could come back to haunt us. We don't easily open up and reveal our inner selves or express love to one another.

God created us with the need to be in relationship with other men. I worry when men are embarrassed by their desire for closer friendships and resist their God-given need to love and be loved. We hate to admit it, but we get a little emotional at those movies where men band together and support a brother who needs a hand. It is what we need, but is so counter to what usually plays out in our friendships. We must find those brothers who can love us, fight at our side and hold us accountable. Sexual integrity takes a team effort!

Women need a few close girlfriends—a healthy, fun sisterhood. Yes, they also need and thrive on men's support and affirmation, but men can never be your girlfriends. Women understand each other, and grow through sharing disappointments, making astute observations about relationships, going shopping, and just spending time hanging out. There also can be a negative propensity for comparing and gossiping, but it's amazing what a women's Bible study or a girl's night out can do for self-nurture and emotional contentment.

Why doesn't this happen more often? It takes time and intentionality. Like any good friendship, there needs to be trust and forgiveness for any inevitable misunderstandings. But girlfriends need girlfriends who can love and confront them as they encourage maturity.

Building BFF's

In his fascinating book, *Spiritual Friendship*, Wesley Hill reveals how important it is that singles have intimate friendships with many of the qualities of the covenant relationship of marriage. A meaningful community is not enough. Singles will need Best Friends Forever— these friendships can model love, transparency and commitment for the entire community of which they are a part.

"But Ruth replied, 'Don't urge me to leave you or to turn back from you. Where you go I will go, and where you stay I will stay. Your people will be my people and your God my God." Ruth 1:16

"After David had finished talking with Saul, Jonathan became one in spirit with David, and he loved him as himself. And Jonathan made a covenant with David because he loved him as himself." I Samuel 18:1, 3

Wesley Hill points out that biblical scholars see "the language of nonsexual friendship and romantic love are vocabularies that overlap and intermingle. Probably David borrowed the language and imagery of spousal love, just as Ruth did before him, to describe a relationship that wasn't sexually active but was, nonetheless, more intense, more committed and irrevocable, than most moderns consider friendship to be."[4]

Tim Keller summarizes the mission of a good marriage as: "Deep character changes through a deep friendship."[5] This should also be the goal of committed friendships—a crucible for helping you grow into the person God designed you to be. So many obstacles get in the way of deep, intentional friendships for singles. A busy lifestyle and work obligations can hinder them. With education and job relocations, the transient nature of the single life gets in the way of pursuing these committed relationships. Sometimes same-sex attraction interferes. Committed friendships among singles do not get the respect and honor they deserve and need.

How can Christian singles attain to the level of intimate friendship that their hearts long for? Hill suggests, "We might choose, as a few friends have done with me, to seek a more formal acknowledgment of our friendship by making public promises to each other. Or we might, less dramatically, choose to invite friends to become more regular fixtures of our lives."[6] It takes time and many intentional choices to coax these fulfilling friendships to life, but they are so valuable for carrying out God's command to live in love and sexual wholeness.

As you build loving friendships, you may wonder if something sexual exists because of the trust, love, physical affection and transparency in evidence. Sometimes these relationships, both same-sex and opposite-sex, can slip into sexual connecting that can jeopardize the whole relationship. God will not bless "friends with benefits" unless they are married. Keep those boundaries clear as you build those committed, deeply intimate friendships

We can confidently believe that through our personal relationship with Christ, the Holy Spirit is orchestrating an awesome sexual dance with our brothers and sisters. "Try and develop a holy life in private, and you will find it cannot be done. Individuals can only live the true life when they are dependent on one another."[7] Jesus will help you create a healing, growth-inducing community and develop intimate friendships. God will usher you into a place of maturity and sexual wholeness through your community and friendships. Singles are blessed with a unique opportunity and freedom to enjoy deep friendships and a significant communal intimacy that their married friends cannot.

> *"I have learned the secret of being content in any and every situation...." Philippians 4:12b*

CHAPTER THREE

Your Sexual Identity and Story

with Mark Yarhouse[2]

From birth, all of us begin to write our sexual story from our experiences. This story, our narrative, evolves over our lifespan. Pre-puberty, adolescence and early adulthood are all critical points in the creation of our sexual story and our sexual identity. The range of experiences and attitudes among single adults—with respect to their sexual narrative— is varied and complex, fulfilling and frustrating. Consider these examples:

"Since high school, I've typically had sex with guys I was dating and 'loved.' My present boyfriend was recently divorced and is grateful to be in a healthier relationship now. We both go to church, and have recently started to feel guilty about our sexual involvement. But why would God give us these desires if He only wanted married people to have sex? We're committed to each other—and seriously considering marriage at a more appropriate time—so why can't we make love?"

"My dad was special to me the night we discussed sexual boundaries and I agreed to stay sexually pure until my wedding day. The promise ring he placed on my ring finger, and his confidence in

---

[2] Mark Yarhouse (Psy.D.) is a professor and Chair in Psychology at Wheaton College. He specializes in struggles tied to religious identity and sexual and gender identity. He assists people who are navigating the complex relationship between their sexual or gender identity and Christian faith. Mark is the author of many books including: *Homosexuality and the Christian*, *Understanding Gender Dysphoria*, and *Sexual Identity & Faith*.

me, have helped me keep my resolve despite some very tempting and romantic moments with guys. I'm so glad that my dad encouraged me to maintain my values with every boyfriend I have had. I love the freedom I have with the boundaries I set. It's not always been easy, but the payoff in my relationships with the opposite sex has been special."

"I grew up in the era of the Purity Movement and felt a burden to stay sexually pure in my behaviors—but never had real teaching on what chastity was all about. I wasn't certain what the purity ring actually represented beyond the fear and shame it created for me. Girls had to be modest and boys fought not to be sex fiends. It has taken much healing and gaining new perspectives for me to grow more healthy sexual values and appreciate my sexuality in romantic relationships."

"I've never been sexually attracted to women, but having sex with men doesn't seem like the right answer, either. I'm so confused, and don't know where or how I fit in. Is there any place for me to express my sexuality as a Christian? I want someone to love; to express these feelings with someone special."

"I was sexually abused by my uncle, and had an abortion at sixteen. None of my relationships with men have been good. I pick all the wrong guys! So, I've decided to avoid them altogether. I've put on a lot of weight over the past few years—so I don't get asked out a lot—but that's probably just as well."

"I am not sure if I am a woman or a man. I have a man's body but my feelings and desires seem so much more feminine. This confusion has existed for so long, and I just don't know what the answer is."

"Since my divorce, guys aren't willing to keep dating me if I don't have sex with them. It's expected after we've been out for a date or two. I don't think I can change this."

"Women today are so aggressive! I don't think of myself as insecure, but it's harder to bite the bullet and ask a girl out without knowing what she expects. It's so much easier to fantasize about a relationship and take care of my own needs, thanks to Internet porn. But, I have to admit that my life feels lonely and incomplete like this."

These represent a few examples of the sexual journeys of single adults just like you — men and women full of hope, despair, with a desire for an intimate relationship and who are often confused. Precious friend, I wish I knew your story. Your sexual and relational struggles, confusion and victories, have so much in common with the stories of other singles—and have *often* been shaped by your circumstances, culture and accepted behaviors, rather than by your values and feelings.

Thinking Through Your Sexual Identity

So how do your sexual story and sexual identity differ? How are they both lived out? Your sexual story is the ongoing narrative that began at birth, that you are living out today like the stories above—and will continue to unfold throughout your life. Your sexual identity develops out of your sexual story but is more about creating meaning and direction for your narrative with a deeper understanding of your sexuality as you develop values, character, body image, attitudes and ways of relating that will guide your story.

If I wanted to get to know you on a less surface level and asked, "What does being a man or a woman mean to you?" "Who are you sexually attracted to and how will that shape your relationships?" "How will you live out your sexuality in relationships?" "How does faith influence your sexuality?" How would you answer me—what would you tell me? How would you describe this deeper sexual identity?

Most likely, you'd start with a particular piece – perhaps an experience, a value or a label – that you feel defines you as a sexual being: "I'm a man or a woman." "I get horny and want to hook up with someone." "I feel guilty about some of the choices I've made." "I'm gay (or trans)." "I'm a Christian." "I was sexually molested." "I am/am not a virgin."

In this chapter (and book) let's go deeper in exploring who you are as a sexual person. Let's get complex and look at identity without restrictive labels or shame. This means exploring and understanding your multifaceted sexual identity from different aspects. If we graph it as a pie, there are at least six pieces that form your sexual identity. In their own way, each of these pieces are critical in helping you develop and live out your sexuality with *meaning, authenticity, and freedom.*

SEXUAL IDENTITY

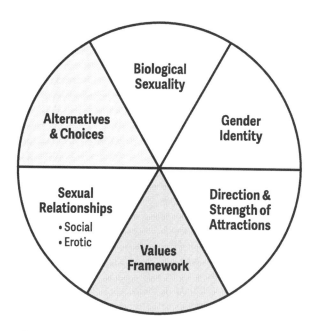

This chapter will help you begin to understand how each of these six areas of your sexual identity serve as catalysts to becoming sexually whole—becoming comfortable in your skin and enjoying satisfying intimate relationships with both the same and opposite sexes. Your sexual identity can guide your sexual journey.

Since this book is directed at Christian singles, it's important to think through a spiritual reality that can get in the way of experiencing your true sexual identity. After Adam and Eve brought sin and "stupid" into human existence, everyone has what Scripture calls the "flesh" (Greek work "sarx"). This is not your physical body, but what might be better translated as a "sin nature" or your "false self." Jesus so strongly warned his followers about Satan, and that the greatest destructive characteristic of Satan is his ability to deceive: "He has always hated the truth, because there is no truth in him. When he lies, it is consistent with his character; for he is a liar and the father of lies." (John 8:44 NLT)

In his tender book, *Abba's Child,* Brennan Manning devotes an entire chapter on how everyone can miss God's love, peace and joy by living out an "Impostor" existence. "The false self causes us to live in a world of delusion. The imposter is a liar. Our false self stubbornly blinds each of us to the light and the truth…the impostor proclaims his darkness as the most luminous light, varnishing truth and distorting reality."[8]

With everything beautiful that God creates, Satan's desire is to distort and warp. This includes your sexual narrative and identity. In living out a false imposter identity, you have developed ways of coping that have helped you survive. But these survival techniques, ways of trying to protect yourself and make sense of relationships and your sexuality, have often drawn you away from the beautiful person God intended you to be—and toward a *false self and distorted sexual identity.*

Jesus, through the power of the Holy Spirit, invites you to understand and abandon your false "imposter" self and help you grow into your true sexual identity. With God, your true self can then emerge, and your sexual identity will mature, free of misleading distortions. The divine Trinity will assist you in choosing wise alternatives— becoming the authentic and whole sexual person he intended.

> *"So letting your sinful nature (flesh) control your mind leads to death (of God's true sexual identity for you). But letting the Spirit control your mind (and sexuality) leads to life and peace." Romans 8:6 [parentheses added]*

> *Throw off your old sinful nature and your former way of life, which is corrupted by lust and deception. Instead, let the Spirit renew your (sexual) thoughts and attitudes. Put on your new (sexual) nature, created to be like God—truly righteous and holy." Ephesians 4:22-24 (NLT)*

As you consider your sexual identity, some aspects of the Sexual Identity Wheel may seem more consequential to you, and others less important. Consider how each of the pieces contributes to and defines who you are as a sexual person—how each is involved in determining the quality of your intimate relationships and how you live out your sexual story. And—how each part of your sexual identity may have some distortion through your false self.

Your Biological/Physical Sexuality

God created you a man (with a penis) or a woman (with a clitoris and vagina) with the ability to engage in genital sexuality. You also have hormones (testosterone, estrogen, etc.) that give you the ability to be sexually attracted and aroused – to feel horny! As human beings, you have a biological body that is always interactive with your mind with emotions and a will, and a spirit/heart longing for love. But, it is your amazing body that gives you that direct ability to be sexual.

In more indirect ways, your body was also formed with hands, arms, mouths, skin and with the ability to express love in a multitude of ways. You can touch, kiss, hug, and caress. Your bodies also provide the capability of sexually uniting to create life – sperm and egg joining to make babies. In fascinating three-dimensional ways, the body and mind express the desires of the heart.

Your biological brain/mind includes emotions (centered in the amygdala), sensuality (communicating with touch), and the ability to visually appreciate sexually attractive people. Your minds have a sexual circuit that awaits ignition, and hormones and nerves that build attraction and arousal. Your mind and imagination with mental imagery and fantasy are another critical aspect of enjoying your sexuality.

Your brain also helps you make choices and gives you the freedom to set boundaries within your sexuality to protect intimate relationships. All human beings have a prefrontal cortex in their brain that helps them determine their values and make wise choices. You were meant to be much more than out-of-control "sex-seeking missiles" – chasing the buzz of sexual arousal and casual hookups.

But, in a wonderful God-given way, it is your immaterial heart that has the most profound influence on the physical piece of your sexual identity – helping you discipline your desires and rightly express the gift of your sexuality. You can safely look, experience excitement, and intimately connect, if you allow your heart to guard your physical sexuality. I will develop this more in the Values Frame work of your sexual identity.

"Guard your heart above all else, for it determines the course of your life." Proverbs 4:23 (NLT)

37

One more observation about on your biological sexuality. It is also the place where a healthy or unhealthy body image resides. Many people simply cannot accept that God created them to be uniquely who they are. They fear, rather than revel, in the special body the Creator gave them. Very few men have "abs of steel" and few women have the body image du jour. Please affirm your brothers and sisters in Christ and help them appreciate their own bodies and shapes.

In astounding ways, we're all physically sexual with masculine or feminine bodies and hormones – visually alluring and created for intimacy. Now, let's look at how the biological piece of your sexual identity interacts with the other five pieces of your pie graph.

Your Gender Identity

This is how you identify yourself – as a man or a woman. As we study the brain and psychology, we realize that some things are hardwired. Women access both left and right brain hemispheres more readily, allowing them to multitask, to more easily express themselves, and helping them identify sexual cues. Some of your gender characteristics are learned or cultural, as you identify with masculine or feminine models in your environment and family of origin. Gender is different than orientation. One can be a particularly masculine man or a feminine woman and still be attracted to the same sex. Your gender identity and how you express your masculinity or femininity is a separate part of the pie from the direction and strength of your sexual attractions.

God wisely chose to make us male and female. Both genders reflect different aspects of the Trinity and help us elicit certain qualities in each other. Human beings are not unisex. We are designed to complement and lift each other up in our gender interplay and righteous flirting.

> "So God created human beings in his own image. In the image of God he created them; male and female he created them." Genesis 1:27 (NLT)

Yes, your gender is complex. In reflecting the Trinity, each of us carries both male and female traits. I'm a gentle, nonaggressive man, and my wife is a logical problem-solver. Even within the genders, there are often more differences among men or women than between them.

Your minds and hearts influence your gender identity, too. Though gender identity may seem mixed up in our current cultural climate, as you read further, you'll be challenged to think through God's plan for your sexual journey as a unique man or woman. The goal is not to stereotype gender differences but to help each person find and form their own masculinity or femininity and enjoy how that enriches their intimate relationships.

Note to reader: Some men and women experience a deeper level of gender incongruence. While it's not within the scope of this book to explore gender dysphoria and the transgender experience, we need to demonstrate compassion and wisdom with each person we encounter. God is loving and even in the midst of a confused and broken world, he uses us to provide support and a healing community as these precious children of God work through the perplexity and pain of their unique sexual and gender identity.

The Direction/Strength of Your Sexual Attraction

Who are you attracted to and how strong is that attraction? To men, to women, or to both? We use labels like gay, straight, bisexual or queer, and can get so confused or obsessed with this one piece of our sexual identity that it dominates our sexual expression and identity. This can happen in regard to gender identity but especially happens in dealing with sexual orientation and the strength of sexual attraction. The following diagram may demonstrate how this distortion has occurred in your life.

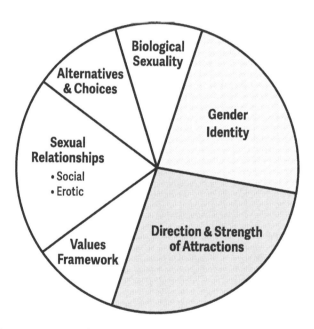

When we consider the direction and strength of our sexual attraction, several truths must be emphasized. One is that the direction of our attraction is not sinful. It is not a sin to be LGBTQ or to be straight with a strong sex drive. The problems arise with how we act out such attractions. Many may disagree with the statement that marriage is meant for a man and a woman, as well as with the concept of sexual chastity or abstinence unless one is married. But based on my understanding of Scripture and God's sexual economy, I believe these theological concepts to be true.

My friend Richard (for whom God has not changed his same-sex attraction) and I regularly remind each other that it is not a sin to notice men or women. We laugh about our mutual friend who says that "the first look is on God, the second look is on us, and the third look is probably starting to lust." Richard's looks are at men while mine are at women—and we both can slip into selfish lust.

We don't know exactly what causes the direction and persistence of sexual attraction. We can look to a variety of influences including the culture in which we were raised, any sexual trauma or distortion we've experienced, our family of origin and the effect of those relationships, as well as genetic propensities. Naturally, the *choices* we make will have an influence, too. For some, their sexual orientation remains the same, yet others experience some fluidity and are able to change and experience new alternatives.

Ginger has read that women can be fluid and may migrate in the direction of their sexual attraction over time. Her same-sex attraction hasn't changed nor has her love and appreciation of her redemptive Jesus. She presently is hanging out in perplexity of her attractions and developing other pieces of her sexual identity.

Sexual attraction can be so complex with the strength and direction of one's sexual attraction varying widely from person to person. You aren't simply born one way with no ability to choose *alternatives* as you create your sexual story and identity. Labels restrict us, and we can make many false assumptions that limit our options. God often doesn't perform miracles, but helps us make genuine changes and shows us how to live fully with imperfect solutions.

Carlos is living out his sexual journey with confusion and a determination to keep God's love and presence at the center of his life. He has always been more attracted to men, but then he met Kaylie, whom he surprisingly found attractive. He decided to take a risk and begin exploring a possible romantic relationship with her. He has no idea what the outcome will be or how Kaylie will process the complex person he is. But their common values and interest in each other are a good place to start.

The values piece of our sexual identity is critical in guiding our responses to our sexual attractions. A central theme of this book and sexual wholeness as a single Christian is the practice of "chastity" as a way of life. This value comes from the understanding that God created genital sexuality to be disciplined and expressed only in the covenant of marriage between a man and a woman. The state of singleness and practicing chastity or celibacy is a high calling, no matter what your sexual orientation might be or who you are dating. This call to be a celibate Christian single will be a costly form of obedience and a powerful testimony to the Creator of sexuality.

Your Values Framework

I strongly believe that the most foundational part of sexual identity is your values. Like building a house, your values frame the structure for every other piece of your sexual identity. A central foundation of our values as a Christian are the truths of Scripture and our Creator's purpose for sexuality.

> *"Joyful are the people of (sexual) integrity, who follow the (sexual) instructions of the Lord. As I learn your righteous (sexual) regulations, I will thank you by living as I should (sexually)!" Psalm 119:1,7 (NLT, parentheses added)*

Many Christian singles have given up on the many guiding principles regarding sexuality in God's Word. Maybe this is due to the Church having taught them so poorly. Values are formulated from various sources of authority. Your faith and Scripture are key, but values can also be influenced by Christian tradition and learned wisdom, from your ability to reason, and from your experiences with role models, peers and culture.

Please don't underestimate the way your Christian values may have been more strongly influenced by the surrounding culture than by godly influences and wisdom. Secular culture has sadly permeated Christian single communities, disregarding chastity in particular.

Your values provide the ability to make wise choices and set appropriate boundaries for a healthy sexual identity and intimate relationships. In developing your sexual values, five principles will be evident throughout this book:

1) Sexual feelings are God-given and good. God deeply loves each human being and created you for intimate relationships enhanced by your sexuality. Erotic sexual expression is not designed to create intimacy but to flow out of intimacy.

2) God has a sexual economy based on his character and truth as revealed in Scripture. Chastity, celibacy, and fidelity won't make sense if you don't believe there's a God who loves you and gave you guidance regarding sexual truth in Scripture. The choices you make will often hinge on whether your godly values or your sexual feelings hold the trump card. Your sexual values will always reflect the relationship you have with Jesus.

3) The third principle is simple: your values go much deeper than what you choose not to do. Yes, it is important to stay away from sinful STUPID, but all of us need to recognize that each of us are just a few bad choices from Stupid. If you make your values only "what you choose not to do," you will miss God's bigger picture and often live in shame and fear.

Sadly, Christianity has created a shallow "Carrot or the Stick" (reward or punishment) sexual values framework based on prohibiting behaviors—and this values system has proved to be quite ineffective. Engage in sinful sexual behavior and God will punish you (and hit you with a stick). Keep penises out of vaginas until you are married and God will reward you with a great sex life (that "carrot" isn't always true.) Carrot or the Stick morality breeds fear, repression and shame, and won't help you create the sexual journey God has for you. This value system depends on "external" rewards and enforcement. Your values should be personal; "internally" built and motivated in order to be effective. Your Christian values must be deeper and more thoughtful than what you do or don't do. They should help you value, celebrate and protect your sexuality and the sexuality of your Christian brothers and sisters.

4) Christians can work through to a positive celebration of their sexuality. We can embrace and enjoy horny. We can help each other revel in our gift of sexuality. So much false guilt and shame exist in working through a godly values framework and living out a sexually healthy narrative. As was stated in the first principle: Sexual feelings, whether towards the same-sex or the opposite sex are not a sin. What you choose to do with your feelings may be counterproductive and sinful. Let's get beyond simplistic statements like: "Sex is for marriage"

or "Jesus is the answer." With no explanation of how these concepts can *positively* impact your sexual narrative, they are unhelpful and often guilt-evoking.

5) Every special person is much more than their sexual mistakes, and redemption is always possible. Shame and fear of punishment won't foster the positive sexual values God desires for you. Each of you, with God's help, can create a transformed and meaningful new sexual story. Psychologists might call this "a transformative counter-narrative"— Amen!

"But among you there must not be even a hint of sexual immorality, or of any kind of impurity, or of greed, because these are improper for God's holy people. Nor should there be obscenity, foolish talk or coarse joking, which are out of place." Ephesians 5:3-4

What an interesting observation the Apostle Paul makes regarding godly sexual values. In the above passage, he emphasizes: Be moral, with no little gaps or self-deception in your sexual integrity; don't let any sexual impurity slip in and contaminate your sexuality; don't objectify and use those God wants you to protect. Finally, watch how you talk and joke about sex. These sexual values Paul lays out can help set the guidelines and guardrails for becoming sexually whole as a single Christian. The following chapters will also help to do this. Precious reader, you are responsible for developing a values framework and sorting through the differences between embracing your sexuality and stewarding it wisely, versus repressing or letting your sexual urges run your life. I hope you can see how foundational your "values framework" is!

Sexual Intimacy: Social and Erotic

The Christian philosopher Thomas Merton said so profoundly, "Love is our true destiny. We do not find the meaning of life by ourselves alone—we find it with another."[9] We are designed for intimacy, and sexually intimate relationships include both **social** and **erotic** sexuality. The concept of social (gender and familial) and erotic (genital and romantic) sexuality are based on the two ways God loves: inclusively, with a communal intimacy, and exclusively, with a covenant intimacy. We desire both of these types of relationships. Everyone needs to give and receive love!

Social Sexuality: God is inclusively relational. He loves all. Social sexuality demonstrates God's *inclusive* love as we arrive in a world with the same and opposite sex parents who love us in ways expressed through their unique genders. I take my masculinity into every relationship, and my gender weaves a vital thread into the tapestry of all of my interactions. We live most of our lives in social or gender sexuality, where being a man or a woman adds a rich dimension to all of our relationships.

Erotic Sexuality: Everyone also has an ability to experience sexual arousal and attraction, and this, with romance, creates erotic relationships. God wants to create an *exclusive* relationship with his children through Jesus Christ. Marriage and the genital, erotic expression of becoming "one" with our spouse is a profound metaphor for the love Christ has for his bride, the Church. God isn't humanly sexual, but uses our erotic feelings and the covenant of marriage to reflect and reveal the way he pursues and loves us.

> *"Here I am! I stand at the door and knock. If anyone hears my voice and opens the door, I will come in and eat with that person, and they with me." Revelations 3:20*

The tricky part comes as Christian singles deal with the erotic feelings within their social sexuality and are tempted to engage in casual hookups. In the same way that we always take our gender into all of our relationships, our libido or sex drive adds energy and complexity to our social interactions. These concepts are so important that Chapter 6 is devoted to exploring the social and erotic intimacy piece of your sexual identity pie.

Alternatives and Choices .

Everyone has willpower and the ability to make intentional choices. The prefrontal cortex of your brain allows you not only to hold values, it enables you to set boundaries and act on those values. This piece of your sexual identity pie, along with your values, will grow and shape all the other aspects of your sexual identity and story. In staying true to your sexual identity with all of the available alternatives and choices, remember that the Holy Spirit can help motivate and guide you. God wants to lift you out of your false sexual identity and into your true self.

> *"So I say, let the Holy Spirit guide your lives. Then you won't be doing what your sinful nature craves. The sinful nature wants to do evil, which is just the opposite of what the Spirit wants. And the Spirit gives us desires that are opposite of what the sinful nature desires. These two forces are constantly fighting each other, so you are not free to carry out your good intentions." Galatians 5:16,17 (NLT)*

I've observed that people have more *alternatives* than they realize. Sometimes it may seem that there are no good alternatives and you are boxed in by your trauma, consequences of previous immature

47

or stupid choices, or your sexual preferences. Please know that these assumptions are not true. Owning the privilege and responsibility for exploring alternatives and making wise choices can be life-altering and ultimately produce fulfilling outcomes. Your alternatives may not be perfect solutions but can still bring greater peace and freedom.

As we talk about alternatives and choices in staying true to your sexual values framework, we encourage much more than just regulating your behavior. Your sexual identity is so much more than what you do—it is who you are. Your values combined with wise choices create a disciplined, effective way to live out your sexual story.

In her book, *Sex and the Single Girl*, Dr. Juli Slattery wisely reminds us, "Sex is never just about sex. Our sexual opinions and choices ultimately reveal something much deeper about us and our relationship with God....The Bible distinguishes human beings from all creation in that we have moral choices in all areas, including how to express our sexuality. ...Your sexual choices are spiritual choices. ...You make sexual choices *not* based on how you are feeling in the moment, but by who you've chosen to become."[10] Godly values and sexual choices are intricately woven together for Christian singles.

The concept of positive and negative freedom is interesting. *Negative freedom* conveys the idea that a person does not have outside restraints on his or her thinking and behavior. They can do whatever they want. *Positive freedom* is best described as possessing the power to make wise choices—choosing restraints that can help us become all that God intended us to be. As Christians, we acknowledge and value guidelines (restraints) and believe God can guide our hearts and minds so we can experience true freedom. It's counterintuitive, but choosing to manage your sexual feelings with wise choices actually gives you greater freedom than indulging them.

Sacrificial obedience, thoughtful choices and healthy boundaries aren't popular concepts in our current culture. Christians singles, like all singles, want to have are fun, which sometimes means pushing the boundaries and just giving in. Doing things God's way won't always seem as fun or fulfilling at times. Allowing the Holy Spirit to help you make wise choices and choose healthy alternatives is not easy but can help you blossom sexually.

"Who are you as a sexual person?" and "What does sex mean to you?" are complicated questions. You have a complex and exciting sexual identity to explore and evolve. The following chapters will help you continue to write and re-write your sexual story as you develop your unique sexual identity.

CHAPTER FOUR

Soul-sexy Masculinity

Many men and women wonder, "What does it mean to be a "real" man or woman?" Like many men, I've had an interesting journey growing into my own masculinity. I've had friends tell me, "Doug, you have many wonderful qualities, but being macho isn't one of them." My gentle nature and lack of aggression have troubled me at times. My tenor voice and what my colleagues call a "cute personality" aren't exactly awe-inspiring. A friend told me he and his wife were thinking through people they would define as "sweet" and I made their Top 10 list. The other day I was shopping with my wife, and the sales clerk called me "adorable." Darn. I was hoping for "striking" or maybe "dangerous."

I have appreciated I Peter 3:4 that speaks of "a gentle and quiet spirit that is precious to God", but then I realized that this was addressed to women! A conversation that helped me become more comfortable in my own skin occurred many years ago with a female coworker. With all sincerity she told me, "Doug, I know you struggle with your masculinity, but you don't know how sexy a gentle man is to women." Since then, I've reveled in being a sexy, gentle man.

The Complexity of Gender

God chose to reveal himself through gender sexuality—the interplay between masculinity and femininity. Maleness and femaleness, with their complex interactivity, provide us with insight into the Almighty and his love of mystery and intimacy.

> *"So God created human beings in his own image. In the image of God he created them; male and female he created them." Genesis 1:27 (NLT)*

Trying to understand masculinity and femininity raises some fascinating and complex ideas: As fellow human beings, men and women are more alike than they are different; there are often more differences within the genders than between the genders; and each man and woman possesses at least some masculine **and** feminine traits. But, men and women truly differ and their gender differences add an energy to all relationships. The ways they magnetically attract and intimately complement each other reflect the relationship between the three persons of the Trinity

Beware of Stereotypes and Prejudices

We are all children of God. As three-dimensional beings, we're exactly the same.

> *"There is neither Jew nor Gentile… nor is there male and female, for you are all one in Christ Jesus" Galatians 3:28*

In our sexuality, personality, and human needs, more similarities than differences exist. At the core of our being, we all need God. He must be allowed to reign over our sexual desire as it pushes us toward intimate relationships.

In each of us, facets of God's image in masculinity and femininity coexist. My wife, Catherine, makes logical decisions, while I tend to appeal to my emotions and sensitivities. Our culture, family backgrounds, personality, and our personal traumas all affect the manner in which we express our masculinity or femininity within our individual genders.

So, when a conversation about gender differences and interactions comes up, try to go beyond simplistic answers. Our Creator reveals himself through these complex differences. Don't use gender to gain power, manipulate, or to box someone in. Gender differences have nothing to do with status, equality, or worth. The strength and allure of our genders should be enjoyed and celebrated as we employ them to maximize our relationships, not to manipulate or control.

The Harm of a Genderless or Unisex Culture

Currently, society has blurred the lines between the sexes. Although many motives may exist for doing so—like avoiding stereotypes, there is a risk involved. We're created male or female with a unique gender identity capable of synergy with the same or opposite sex. Like magnetic fields, we attract and create forces that would not exist apart from gender differentiation.

Gender creates a musical harmony—a veritable symphony. Men come alive in response to traits only women bring out in them, and women feel more secure as they relax in the pursuit and attention of a man. And, men bring out in their male companions greater integrity and a fun camaraderie. While women need girlfriends to empathize and relate in ways their Brothers can't. Even within the Christian community, we tend to downplay gender differences, rather than understand and celebrate them.

The "soul-sexy" concept of this chapter is important. In the

Bible, "soul" can be best defined as three-dimensional personhood. Men and women have a body, mind, and spirit. This human soulfulness is three interacting dimensions, not separate parts. Our bodies with arms, legs, hands and a brain, help the mind and heart express themselves. Our minds allow men and women to let feelings and values infuse their relationships with heart-felt love and playfulness.

Soul-sexy emphasizes that masculinity goes beyond strong bodies, deep voices, or the stereotypes of what's "hot." The qualities of men are more complex than our culture tends to embrace. Having a "cut" physique, being strong, and having sex appeal doesn't adequately define soul-sexiness for a godly man. Guys, a woman is often attracted to your mind and personality as you pursue her, or your heart as you exercise your strength to help those in need. Allowing God to let you live out a total soul-sexiness will revolutionize your relationships.

A Soul Sexy Man—Traits of Masculinity and the Male Operating System

In our brains and psyches, God made us unique and complementary on purpose. Gals, men can't be your girlfriends, but they can meet that need for strength and pursuit. Guys, unless you're hanging out with brothers who exercise integrity, affirmation and authenticity—you will never be all that God intended you to be.

1. Men value and desire an influential strength—to be significant and praised.

Men want to "man up" and have an impact in their sphere of influence. Recognition as competent is important as is that need to get the job done and solve that problem. Men are motivated by praise, admiration, and affirmation. It's amusing how simple men can be. I know I am being manipulated when my wife says, "Could you get that box down from the attic?" I have seen her get that same box down by herself, but I go get it and she says, "You are so strong, thank you." I am so proud of her praise, that I ask if there are any more boxes she needs brought down.

Men also want to exhibit honor in their interactions and earn the respect of those around them. Maintaining honor is a part of God's image in the masculine. Winning battles and keeping one's word creates self-esteem in men. There is a zeal for accomplishment and a craving to have a positive influence on those around them. God created "Adam" with strength and the ability to have a positive impact on the "Eves" in his life—to affirm in a way that only a man can accomplish.

Example: Kevin, a middle child with an older and a younger brother, can't remember a time when he didn't feel insecure. Then, two incredible things happened over a six-month period. He started a new job, uncertain of how to perform for his new (female) boss; but she became the best mentor he ever had! She encouraged him to trust his instincts and believed in him. Kevin also joined a small group at which the men and women truly enjoyed him, and even more important, they helped him see how special he was to them and to God. His masculine strength blossomed.

2. Men pursue adventure and challenge.

Man's warrior heart tackles new ventures and wants causes to champion. This male trait can also create a success-driven mentality and the need to compete and achieve. In positive ways, men can courageously risk rejection in pursuit of love, and crave an affirming feminine response. In exchange, men can meet the feminine need for pursuit and focused attention.

Unfortunately, there is a downside to this male desire for adventure and challenge. He can make the pursuit of Eve and sex his adventure, rather than making his quest a meaningful intimate relationship. Guys can sometimes get preoccupied with the challenge at hand, becoming defensive or withdrawing, especially when they fear failure. Men are also prone to sexual addiction when an errant need for adventure uses sex as an antidote to boredom.

Men get excited and grow through challenges. They more easily bond through activities. Sometimes this needs to be men bonding with their buds in a meaningful adventure. Gals, men also enjoy sharing their adventures and accomplishments with you. Friendships with men can be started and deepened by participating in a mutual activity—or one of his passions. This is much more likely to succeed than simply trying to begin a conversation.

Example: Jake loved the outdoors and enjoyed hiking and fishing. Twice a year, he and his buddies went deep-sea fishing in Florida. Taylor wanted more close male friends. She was pleasantly surprised when she organized a rafting trip with some of the men and women in her church singles group. The men came alive; they enjoyed the women and their own horseplay. The conversations before, during, and after the rafting were refreshing and honest. Taylor started a friendship with Jake that lasted even after they both married.

3. Men are predictably simple and more task-oriented.

Brain research shows that men tend to be more left-brained and analytical, with less connectivity to the creative right brain. This may be part of their hyper-focus and lack of ability to multitask. They gain identity through accomplishments and can become engrossed in whatever catches their attention at that moment.

Sexually, men can also be simple and focused. They're more hormonally-driven, less in tune with their feelings. Men have more testosterone, the primary hormone for sexual desire. They tune in visually to the specific physical attributes/sexual parts and respond more immediately to the sexual stimulation of their senses. In the dance of intimacy, men are often more assertive in their sexual desire. They will be more likely to think erotic thoughts and seek to meet intimacy needs through erotic behavior.

They can easily compartmentalize their lives as well as their feelings, which is both a blessing and a curse. A common misconception is that men need to cultivate the sensitive feminine part of themselves. No, they need to cultivate their masculine feelings. They may have greater difficulty accessing feelings other than anger, but they have a deep yearning for relationships with the women and men in their lives. Sports, projects, walks, and other forms of recreation can help men create a context to practice other intimacy skills, such as verbal conversation and the expression of their feelings.

Example: Teri was regularly getting her feelings hurt by Josh, and wondered if perhaps they were incompatible. Josh seemed selfish and insensitive to her needs – focused on his new job and seemingly uninterested in any in-depth conversations. One day, a friend of Teri's suggested that she talk to Josh while they accomplished a task; while doing so, asking for his advice, and praising him afterwards. Teri was bowled over by Josh's transformation and laughed as she realized how easy it was to motivate Josh once she understood his operating system more.

4. Men need to initiate and protect others.

Men's greater muscle mass and size help them to safeguard what they value. But men's initiative goes beyond the physical to deeper soul issues. Men love to be counted on and validated, both internally and externally. Stability in the midst of a crisis is a part of this masculine strength. Men exert influence by being courageous, sheltering others from harm, and showing that they're a force to be reckoned with in a crisis.

The chivalrous knight in shining armor who arrives just in the nick of time to defend is a common feminine fantasy adapted from these masculine aspects. Men are meant to step into the chaos of our broken world and make a difference. Initiative and proactivity are important male qualities which single women often lament they see too little of these days.

> *"The Lord is my rock, my fortress and my deliverer; my God is my rock, in whom I take refuge. He is my shield and the horn of my salvation, my stronghold." Psalm 18:2*

A man's strength in relationships is more than "slaying dragons"; it's an inner steadiness and ability to protect those in his life. In some ways, this is a reflection of God himself. As a rock of strength, a man has in his heart a need to provide — to care for the women and children God places into his life. Men can focus on the task at hand, and creating solutions can get in the way of being sensitive to what the women in his life need. Both men and women benefit from his ability to be a strong provider – to step into situations and create a place of safety.

Example: At a family function, Lance defended his friend, Gina, who was verbally attacked by her mom. He brought a strength and perspective to the situation that even her mom acknowledged, and she backed off with an apology. In response to Lance's behavior, Gina almost felt like her (divorced) dad was back in her life; that someone strong was in her corner. When she told Lance as much, he grinned.

5. Men come alive as they pursue and partner (dance) with women.

Adam was created to confidently affirm Eve's feminine beauty – in so doing he affirms his own masculinity. But some men neglect the pursuit of women, fearing rejection or not measuring up. Men can also be infatuated with women's erotic appeal and miss their deeper soul-sexiness. Women want to be valued as special. Having a man pursue her brings out surprising qualities, responses, and benefits to both sexes.

Example: Jane felt like the ugly duckling in her singles group. Justin, the guy all the girls saw as cute and successful, sensed this, and saw an inner beauty in Jane that was often overlooked because she was overweight and shy. He asked Jane to help him throw a party – giving her an opportunity to showcase her creativity, her playful nature, and her ability to make people feel comfortable. Jane saw Justin's encouragement and that party as a major turning point in her life.

Men often don't realize or understand how God designed the Eves in their lives to bring out the best of their masculinity. Without meaningful relationships with women, they'll miss out on important parts of who they were meant to be and become. An affirming and inviting Eve can have an astounding impact on the men in her life. This begins with the mother-son relationship and continues throughout life. Men mature in opposite-sex relationships.

Example: Tripp loved his sisters and the fun family times he had experienced with them. They doted on him and sought out his involvement in their lives. Last year, he took his younger sister to prom. The women he dated probably never knew what a debt of gratitude they owed to the close relationships he had with them. His girlfriend Erica often commented to her friends how lucky she was to have a man that brought out the best in her. They both attempted and accomplished things they never would have without the synergy of their gendered relationship.

Metaphors for Masculinity

I love metaphors and how they can give us a descriptive picture of important concepts. The Bible tells of "streams in the desert" or Jesus as the "living water." Remember metaphors are figures of speech where we use a different concept or representation to help us picture or explain something we might not otherwise understand. Here are two descriptive metaphors for maleness

1. A Chest of Drawers. A man is like a chest of drawers, with separate compartments for everything and nothing much self-disclosing on top. Men tend to be private, and are not as self-revealing as women. They often view life as a competition and a challenge. Their conversations reveal less because "knowledge is power" and they are careful about who they empower.

They often organize their lives with a work drawer, a "family and friend" drawer, a recreation drawer, and a God drawer. Everything has a separate space, with hopes that nothing spilling over to the next. This masculine trait serves men well in times of growth, stress, or crisis. And, can be unrealistic if men think they have a "sex drawer" that is separate from their "God drawer"—that the character and scent of one drawer doesn't permeate the other drawers as well.

2. A Sensitive Rock. It seems an oxymoron to put sensitive and a rock together. But, God calls men to be solid, a rock, as he empathetically listens to a range of feminine feelings, but does not mirror them. Oh, the blessing and the curse of having a narrower range of feelings and the capacity to contain them! With this emotional stability comes the challenge of being self-disclosing and self-aware of the broad range of his and her emotions. If you're a man, the women in your life will feel lonely and excluded if you don't develop the skills to access and express your emotions--to be that sensitive rock.

To the ladies, in general, "bottom-line" communication is the rule of the day for men. When they ask questions they want answers, not details. Men aren't usually interested in "chatting." "Don't tell me the whole story" and "Just cut to the chase" are men's mantras. They ask questions designed to elicit simple, factual answers. This is quite unlike their female counterparts, who ask questions as a means of connecting. When he asks, "Do you want to invite your roommate to the party?" Answer "yes" or "no". Sometimes, that simple response can motivate him to listen to the rest of the story.

Interesting (and Sometimes Frustrating) Male Characteristics

Men's operating systems can be both fascinating and at times, tremendously annoying. Below are just a few characteristics of our brothers that we may need to dig deeper to find those interesting qualities.

1. Focusing on the task at hand (often this is a priority of his). This perceived selfishness is actually a strength (e.g. when it comes to fixing something or accomplishing a task), yet many women see it as a negative (e.g. when they're so engrossed in a ballgame that they ignore everything else). Women sometimes wonder why men have a tendency towards arrogance, preoccupation, defensiveness, and selfishness. These are simply insecure distortions of the God-designed strengths of masculinity—a strong, proactive confidence and an ability to focus on the task at hand.

2. Providing has definition and limits. Men often want to take initiative and be a provider. However, once they believe they've fulfilled that role, they have a tendency to kick back and relax. "I grilled the steaks! What do you mean 'help clean up'"? Sometimes too great a distinction exists between what men consider men's and women's work: "I moved the couch like you asked. Could you bring me a cold one while you finish cooking dinner?" Guys beware: women usually won't let you get away with this limited involvement.

3. Believing sex is a need with a high sex drive. In most relationships (about 80 %), men will have the higher sex drive. Women may be astonished at the amount of time men spend thinking of sex during the course of a day. "Sisters" can't understand how difficult it can be for their men friends to discipline peeking up or down their dresses. But sex should never be seen as a man's "need." Sex can be a desire or fantasy, but nothing will explode or fall off if a man doesn't have a sexual outlet. Married or single, it is not a need.

Another distortion of this sex drive is men can see hooking up as validating their masculinity and a way to instantly get close to someone. Author Paula Rinehart warns men, "The easiest and most sure way to feel like a man is to have sex. It is the quickest feedback loop, a deep physical dose of masculine validation. The experience of sexual virility is so potent for a guy that his lifelong temptation is to turn it into a god and to make the woman the center of his existence rather than a person herself and his partner."[11]

Unfortunately, in our present culture, women are falling into the same sexual traps as men and seeing casual sex as a shortcut to intimacy, too. God's design is for erotic sexuality to flow out of intimacy, not be a shortcut to intimacy. Sexual hookups will never truly meet a person's yearning to be known and loved.

4. Leading or being laidback. Is there a part of the male operating system that wants to step in and make a difference? Yes. But, the majority of men are laid back and go with the flow. For the woman who's looking for a decision maker, a man can sometimes prove frustrating: "If it made a difference to me, I'd have told you. I don't care whether we have Chinese or Italian for dinner." Men often have a more casual approach to life unless a true priority or crisis is involved. They prefer to avoid conflict and do what's easier except when it truly matters. Women—take men at their word. Believe it or not, most of the time he really doesn't care. If, after the fact, you find out that he really did care, that's a great opportunity for a conversation about the importance of honest communication in relationships.

Women often say they want a spiritual leader in the man they date or marry. Men aren't always sure what that "dude" looks like. One young couple, being coached on their upcoming marriage, tackled this issue. He knew she wanted a spiritual leader, but he was a relatively new Christian; she had grown up in the church. In frustration, he finally confessed, "You want me to get us a devotional book to read together, but I've never been in a Christian bookstore and have no idea what you want. If you go get the book, I'll make sure we make the time to read it together." This young man truly stepped up and demonstrated spiritual leadership. As a couple, be willing to seek compromises.

One of my single friends wrote me about her desire for spiritual leadership in a future husband. "I'm not looking for someone who's an expert on the Pentateuch or went to a bible college. I'm a smart gal, and can figure most things out. What I do look for is someone who prioritizes faith; who budgets time to meaningfully talk and pray together; and who considers how we can love our community, giving and serving together."

God calls men to sacrificial initiative – resting confidently in their weight as men, valuing and pursuing women in ways that make a difference. A real man securely and non-defensively rests in his personal strengths. He knows who he is and has nothing to prove. This is where true humility begins, being confident in all God made him to be. Such confidence allows a man to forget about himself and simply enjoy others.

With godly self-esteem, a man can encourage feminine initiative and even follow her intuitive lead in the dance of intimacy. A real man is strong enough to wash feet and become the force behind the maturing of others. He doesn't fear being upstaged by her beauty and power but celebrates it. The ballerina steals the show, and he is able to follow her cue while providing strength for the lifts and compelling dance movements. Both "Adam" and "Eve" elicit and affirm each other's strength and beauty.

I'm painting with a broad brush in describing masculinity and femininity. The examples above are generalities, and not each description will fit every man. God designed each of us to embody a unique mix of masculine and feminine traits. In general, men will have a greater mix of masculine than feminine traits, and vice versa for women. Understanding the uniqueness of each gender can be tremendously beneficial to successful relationships with the opposite sex. Now that we have a better understanding of the masculine, let's take a closer look at the other half of God's sexual metaphor: soul-sexy femininity.

CHAPTER FIVE

Soul-sexy Femininity and the Dance of the Sexes

Most women can recall an early memory of when they felt feminine and special. Often this was a time when they wore a special outfit for an important occasion, or someone important in their life told them they were beautiful. When asked to describe this event, women recall how they felt, how their femininity had been emphasized, and maybe were even photographed. They felt wonderfully attractive, valued and uniquely "Eve."

Sabotaging Soul-sexy Femininity

Cultural pressures seek to deny women's God-given femininity, preventing them from fully celebrating their sexuality. Wonderful differences set them apart from men. Poor definitions, unfair comparisons, and cultural distortions often block women from embracing God's gift of an awesome sexuality and femininity. These cultural distortions exist in both the secular and Christian cultures.

Poor Definitions and Stereotypes

So often we look for gender models in all the wrong places. An example of a poor definition is the common cultural stereotype of touting actresses and models, with great sex appeal and much plastic surgery, as standards for feminine beauty and sexuality. Although women want to be admired for their external beauty, true sexiness extends beyond their physical attributes. Unfortunately, the media reinforces the stereotype that a sexy body trumps inner beauty and character.

Women in Western societies, especially in dress up occasions, often dress to emphasize the body, making it all the more difficult for a man to pay attention to a woman's three-dimensional sexiness. Guys, women appreciate men who don't objectify them and can focus on their total personhood, not just on the size and shape of their bodies. But women, let's face it—men can take their cues from the clothing (or how little of it) you choose to wear and the way you conduct yourself.

This opens the door to a concept that is often poorly defined in Christian culture: modesty. In Christian culture, women are often seen as the gatekeepers of chastity and modesty—so they squelch their sexuality. They can be shamed for having sexual desires or dressing in ways that complement their figure. Jeans and sweaters aren't meant to be baggy. Women have curves and the Creative Trinity meant for these to be celebrated--not create shame.

It's interesting though that when God created Eve, I believe he created her with some innate modesty that our present culture tries to eradicate. The Creative Trinity knew that Eve's beauty could become an idol to Adam. Men might not see the total package a woman is, but simply objectify her erotic sexiness.

Guys, let's be honest, much of your objectification of women is truly your responsibility. Men are responsible for controlling their lustful thinking regardless of what our Christian sisters are wearing. Women who are devout Christians also get turned on by men's bodies. Men are equally commissioned with the responsibility of stewarding chastity and modesty as we help our sisters live out sexual integrity.

Another harmful stereotype in Christian culture is that Eve was created to serve Adam's desires—to primarily be his helper and cater to his sexual desires. No! Eve was created in God's image, with power and appeal and purpose much beyond her relationship with Adam. When men and women interact, they complement each other and bring something special to those encounters. Even sexually, the interaction is meant to be mutual, not Eve servicing Adam. God made women with strong sexual desires too, and in marriage a turned-on wife is often the strongest turn-on to her husband.

Comparisons and Cultural Confusion

Women have the terrible habit of comparing themselves with other women. This diminishes their unique identity and self-worth as well as that of their sisters. The comparisons women draw create a rather constricted view of what it means to be feminine. For example, if a woman upholds motherhood as the pinnacle of femininity, she may, as a single woman, not accept opportunities to develop other aspects of herself apart from having and raising children. Or, she may miss the opportunities to use her maternal instinct to nurture and "mom" in a variety of ways, not just parenting.

Note to Reader: I don't want to minimize the yearning that women have to be married and raise children. The roles of both single and married women have limitations that must be grieved and sorted out to reach a greater acceptance. Having no children of one's own is one of those places where Jesus wants to enter in as you grieve and find comfort.

"Blessed are those who mourn, for they will be comforted."
Matthew 5:4

Being feminine and embracing the truth of who you've been created to be as a woman, definitely applies to body image. Tall, runway models who weigh 115 pounds, rather than the more typical 5'5" and 140-plus pound woman, lead to even more distorted perceptions and comparisons. Women, like men, must "take their thoughts captive" as they choose to rule out external influences and refuse to let them dictate how they define their femininity and sexuality.

Women experience an internal tug-of-war between the secular world and the Church. The world communicates impossible messages about femininity that combine a "Barbie" sexiness with a "successful woman who plays like the boys" in the corporate arena. Meanwhile, the Church sometimes leans too heavily to the other extreme, overly emphasizing a femininity expressed through service-oriented roles such as wife, mother, teacher, and childcare. A femininity that must be subservient to and revolve around masculinity. Somewhere between these exhausting messages, godly soul-sexiness gets lost. Men need to better understand how to relate to feminine sexuality in ways that honor both women and God. Women need not only to understand but also to embrace all that their femininity has to offer.

A Soul Sexy Woman—Traits of Femininity and the Female Operating System

In their book *Captivating*, Stasi and John Eldredge thoughtfully develop the idea that divine beauty is fashioned in all women. "Can there be any doubt that Eve is the crown of creation? Not an afterthought. Not a nice addition like an ornament on a tree. She is God's final touch, his pièce de résistance. She fills a place in the world nothing and no one else can fill."[12]

The pervasiveness of impossible standards makes women retreat in discouragement: slender, tall, smart, talented, successful, submissive, self-confident, etc. But, the pronouncement of Eve's status as the "crown of creation" can give hope—beauty is truly inherent in all women.

> *"Charm can mislead and beauty soon fades. The woman to be admired and praised is the woman who lives in the Fear-of-God. Give her everything she deserves! Festoon her life with praises!" Proverbs 31:30-31 (MSG)*

1. Beautiful and Powerful

Women want to be seen and known. They contain a power in their beauty that can never be fully understood. They're energized by attention and feeling special – especially attention from their own Adam. But, their beauty comes from their total feminine psyche, not just their bodies. Eve was designed in such a way that Adam will notice and attend to her, as she adds a richness to all their interactions.

God gave women *allure* that draws men into levels of emotional intimacy they might otherwise struggle to reach on their own. Women can use body language, touch, gazes and nonverbal communication to convey deep messages without uttering a single word.

With all this beauty and power, God also gave women an innate modesty that is lost in our modern, hookup culture. Modesty is more of an attitude and who a woman is rather than what she does or wears. It could be described as refusing to use her sexuality to manipulate but rather to exercise sensitivity in the way she dresses and acts. God made Eve with a self-confident and humble modesty that protects her power and beauty. Her allure was not for her own gain but rather to empower her to bring out the best in Adam, her companion, and everyone in her sphere of influence. This unselfish stewarding of her influential beauty gives Eve a mysterious appeal.

> *"It is not fancy hair, gold jewelry, or fine clothes that should make you beautiful. No, your beauty should come from within you—the beauty of a gentle and quiet spirit that will never be destroyed and is very precious to God." (1 Peter 3:3, 4 NCV).*

Does this mean modesty clashes with being soul-sexy and alluring? Author Wendy Shallit, in her best-selling book *A Return to Modesty*, says sexual modesty might squelch a superficial type of allure, but that's the stuff of which one-night stands are made. The true feminine allure doesn't squelch a woman's sexuality. As Shallit writes, "In fact, it is more likely to enkindle it."[13] "Letting it all hang out" leaves little to the imagination, undermining the thrill that should accompany the gentle unfolding of feminine mystery.

Deep within the soul of a man lies honor—a need to pursue, earn, and provide for his woman. With a soul-sexy allure tempered by modesty, women elicit from their men patient respect, loving attention, and complete commitment. Abstaining from sexual manipulation or pretense, mature women encourage the men in their lives to man-up and prevent either from reducing their relationship to selfishly chasing erotic adventures. Because, within intimate opposite-sex relationships, women's beauty and power can also become distorted.

For example, some women learn early in life to wield sexual power in order to manipulate men. Rather than bringing out the best in men, they attempt to control them with their sexuality. In her book, *Sex and the Soul of a Woman*, Paula Rinehart encourages that, "True sexual power...rises out of the innate attractiveness God gave you as a woman, an allure that is incredibly attractive to a man. ...What a man is usually drawn to in a woman is two steps past her physical appearance. ... intuitively he knows he has stumbled on someone who can glimpse his heart, who seems to know him in ways he has longed to be known. ...Sexual power of this nature is really creative power—power that adds to both individuals and subtracts from neither."[14] Men are constantly attracted to and intrigued by their female friend's alluring beauty and power.

Examples:

Taylor, looking cute and sexy on a group camping trip after sleeping in a tent, with a ribbon in her hair and a passion for fishing.

Jodi's friendly winks and affirmations, as she laughs and feels special with her male buddies, energizing the whole party.

Jim couldn't believe the strength and staying power his friend Jocelyn demonstrated as she worked through the loss of her sister and a demanding boss at work. He could see why women are often the more resilient gender under stress. He found that staying power so attractive.

2. Mysterious and Surprising

Women call it mysterious. Men call it confusing! What a fascinating complexity the female gender is to men. God is always mysterious and full of surprises and it seems women are made in his image to reflect this part of His character. Therefore, we're not sure God ever really intended a total comprehension of women by men—their complexity is part of their mystery. Women add a lot of color and the unexpected to relationships. And, since men are always fascinated and drawn to challenges, women's unpredictability certainly catches his attention.

Men can give numerous examples of how feminine needs and responses remain elaborate and complex. Yet paradoxically, this trait also supplies the unexpected adventure men enjoy. A humorous example is a woman's tendency to pack for every occasion in one suitcase—to dress up or down, for warm or cold, and for rain or shine. Women call it "remaining flexible," often leaving their male counterparts bewildered: how can a five-day trip possibly require five pairs of pants, three skirts, three sweaters, six shirts, two dresses, and five pairs of shoes? Compared to the straightforwardness of men, women are indeed entertainingly complex.

However, men need a basic understanding of the female psyche to enrich their relationships with them. Although she may be full of surprises, the soul-sexy woman desires to be pursued—to be known and special. This can take courage and intention on a man's part. I remember one friend telling me his dad's advice on his son's approaching wedding, "Son, if you do nothing else, make sure she always feels special. Pay attention to her and keep pursuing her, and you'll be a happy man."

Examples:

Anna amused her male co-workers when she was asked by the waiter to choose between two items on the menu, "Why don't you surprise me?" This was certainly not their typical response.

Craig was frustrated. Just when he thought he had his friend Spring figured out, she would come up with an unexpected response or feeling. Eventually, he became intrigued and amused. The most recent was when she got upset because he hadn't asked her to go to the symphony, when he knew she didn't like classical music! She explained that the music wasn't important, but she had this new dressy outfit with no place to wear it.

3. Emotionally Aware and Socially Connected

Women are also emotionally full of surprises which can add a richness to relationships. Some of this can be attributed to hormones, particularly at certain times of the month. However, their emotional variability and awareness is much more than mere hormonal fluctuations. Women often experience and take pleasure in a wider range of emotions than most men. I'm not saying men don't express feelings, but women's brains seem to tune into feelings more readily. This can benefit a woman's relationships by enabling her to connect and bond more easily. Unfortunately, it can also allow her feelings to sometime override her common sense.

This might explain why many women follow their hearts when it comes to relationships. Her friend might ask, "Why are you dating him?!" Because she's so emotionally connected, she might not be able to see that from her girlfriend's point of view that he lacks some key ingredients for a long-term relationship. This emphasizes a woman's need for both male and female friends to give her greater objectivity when her emotions might cloud her own good judgment.

Casey surprised herself with her own emotional responses. She'd experienced no big traumas, like her friend Pat who could be easily triggered. She was a practical engineer. Yet, she was full of emotions: excitement, anger, sadness, arousal. It helped when a girlfriend made a comment, "Maybe it's just the woman in you, and that's a great thing. Don't try to emulate your male colleagues." Though it made her feel uncomfortable, Casey learned to appreciate the intensity of her wide range of feelings.

Women often have an intuitive feel for social connection. They possess an empathetic ability to respond to the feelings and needs of others. Their empathic responsiveness reflects the integration of their awareness of people, situations, thoughts, and emotions into almost a sixth sense. Therefore, women often have the ability to quickly size up a situation, the people involved, and their possible thoughts and emotions. Perhaps this is why some women enjoy hour-long phone conversations, and knowing the details of their friends' lives, which men generally find cumbersome and unnecessary.

Men see life as more of a competitive playground in which to share information cautiously. Men prioritize relationships; however, this can look quite different from their female counterparts. This difference can be illustrated with the following anecdote from a couple's marriage. The husband ran into an old friend at the airport. The two guys quickly pulled out their phones, updated each other on their plans, and were on their way. Afterward, the husband commented, "It was so good to see him." His wife replied, "See him? You barely looked up at him!"

Women have a gift for achieving deep degrees of social and emotional intimacy. Even in little ways like nodding their heads and making those soothing noises while talking. Intimate relationships help women find identity and a deeper meaning in life.

Examples:

Jenna felt so close to Craig, but knew he had a pattern of pursuing women and quickly ending the relationship. So she guarded her heart. Although she was disappointed when he chose to end their romance, she refused to settle for someone unable, or perhaps unwilling, to create a deeper intimacy. She was blessed to have a dad and brother who had taught her that men could learn to meet the emotional needs of a woman, so she refused to accept less.

Cat was so appreciative of the single's community she found when moving to Phoenix. To feel accepted, supported and valued was something she was afraid might not happen again after leaving her Dallas' group of friends. She got more in touch with how much she needed to give and receive love.

4. Uniquely Nurturing and Protective

Women are mother bears that protect the security of life and relationships. How fascinating that God made woman the one who creates life in her very body, nurtures it for nine months and protects it for a lifetime.

Though trauma and brokenness can interfere, nurturing comes naturally in relational settings for both married and single women. Maternal nurturing can be seen in a woman's interactions with those around her. This goes beyond a desire to have children to a deeper ability for fostering and protecting life. Even the way God chose to create life illustrates this. Men initiate by providing the seed, but women do the hard work. And this desire to nurture isn't just found in women who like children. When soul-sexy women are grounded in their God-given identities, they nurture and elicit the best from others.

> *"She's quick to assist anyone in need, reaches out to help the poor. ...When she speaks she has something worthwhile to say, and she always says it kindly." Proverbs 31:20, 26 (MSG)*

By design, women are gently nurturing and protective. As creators and nurturers of human life, women want safety, intimacy, and security. However, after the Fall, this protective, maternal trait often emerges in women as a nagging, controlling spirit. Women must work to understand that fine line between being an assertive Mother Bear and a micromanaging Nag.

Examples:

I was going out with some colleagues for lunch and as I got in the front seat to drive, my female friend said, "You haven't fastened your seat belt." Another friend warned me, "I wouldn't try to make a left turn here." I thought to myself, "Goodness, I have my wife in the car with me."

Kari had tremendous compassion for Justin as he grieved the loss of his business. He didn't feel very manly anymore. At first, Kari didn't realize that her empathy was healing more than the loss of a business, but also wounds from a mother who'd abandoned him. Justin needed that soft shoulder to cry on, and hopeful encouragement, as much as he needed a loving mother bear, encouraging him to eat right, believe he was an amazing man, and try another business opportunity.

5. Confidently Inviting and Openly Receptive

It wouldn't be accurate or helpful to say that women shouldn't or don't initiate activities and relationships. If you think back, many of the fun and meaningful experiences you've participated in were initiated by the women in your life. The feminine concepts of being inviting and receptive go deeper than simple initiating or passively receiving.

Every Eve has a unique and powerful "sexual" voice that goes beyond erotic attraction—to being a feminine facilitator. As she warmly responds to Adam's initiative, she becomes a catalyst and elicits hidden traits of strength from him. Eve is like a confident ballerina that can pull Adam into the Dance. She can use her feminine sex appeal and power to either manipulate men or to propel them into being a knight. As she appreciates and invites Adam's pursuit – as she is openly receptive to all he can add to her life, she brings out the best in him with qualities he wouldn't experience apart from her feminine presence. She can be a force his male buddies can't duplicate.

Example:

Mike never thought he could try a new career until he became friends with Caitlin. She reinforced his confidence and masculinity enough that he pursued a new job, one that payed significantly more, bought some new, more flattering clothes, and began to take some relational risks. Caitlin grew, too, as she saw her own transforming power, and valued the healthy relationship she and Mike enjoyed.

This feminine propensity for being receptive and responsive also can also reflect a woman's sexual desire. Women have a libido and enjoy erotic sexuality. Yet, often what turns them on is different from what turns on their male counterparts. Sex researcher Dr. Rosemary Basson states that women's sexual desire often differs from men's desires. Women aren't as hormonally driven and often have a more *responsive* sexual desire that needs to be triggered by some form of initiation.[15] A woman may often become excited by a man's attention to her, or to his masculine character, or his risking emotional connection. I sometimes refer to this female sexual attraction as an "emotionally horny" rather than a physical allure.

You might have heard the old adage, "women give sex for love, and men give love for sex." In its sinfully broken form, this statement can ring true. Some women do give their erotic sexuality to get what they believe is love. But even in healthy relationships, women who experience emotional intimacy are more likely to respond to their partners. Women typically don't think as much about sexuality as men, except in the dating or in the early years of marriage, with the emotional and hormonal cocktail of new romance and heightened sensuality very prevalent.

Example:

In their romantic relationship, Sara and Joel laughed at the different ways they were turned on by each other and how their boundaries had to be different. Sara thought of last weekend, and how turned on she'd been just watching Joel pay special attention to his 89-year-old grandmother, and how Nana enjoyed his attention. Joel found that same weekend arousing because of Sara's cute shorts, long legs and pedicure.

After almost 40 years of marriage, it still surprises me what turns my wife on sexually—and how her receptivity can get me going. As my special woman, I am so grateful for how she has invited and encouraged me to be the man God intended me to be.

Metaphors for Femininity

Once again, let me use a descriptive representation, a metaphor, to help explore and understand the feminine perspective. Eve could be described as:

1. **An Armoire**. If men are like a chest of drawers, women more closely resemble armoires. Throw open the door of an armoire and the items are visible. It has few compartments, and everything is openly visible: shelves of shoeboxes, sweaters, and underwear. This lack of compartments let's everything be interactive. You can create a whole outfit by easily pairing the items in the armoire that you are so clearly seeing.

Like the content of an armoire, a woman's thoughts and feelings all crisscross. They don't have all the separate drawers and compartments. Their relationships interact whether romantic, family, work, or friendships. Their past shelf and present shelf are seen and remembered—and brought up quite often. It can get a little overwhelming for their male counterparts, but an armoire is very cool piece of furniture.

2. **A Mother Hen or Mother Bear.** Women are typically in tune with the safety needs of those around them. Married and single women alike make comments such as, "Fasten your seatbelt" or "You're tired, get some rest." Women seem to have a hidden radar that detects danger and when her "alarm" goes off, she unleashes a litany of warnings about potential hazards. Security is vital.

As with Jesus, who likened himself to a protective mother hen, women want to keep their loved ones safe. Guys sometimes complain that their girlfriends nag a lot. But sometimes it's about a safety or health-related issue he hasn't paid attention to. I tell men to honor the Mother Hen in their girlfriends or wives, those protective injunctions from the women in their lives can save them from a world of hurt.

"O Jerusalem…how often I have wanted to gather your children together as a hen protects her chicks beneath her wings, but you wouldn't let me." Luke 13:34 (NLT)

Interesting (and Sometimes Frustrating) Female Characteristics

Below is a brief look at some of the commonly perceived differences between men and women:

1. A multi-tasking wonder. As previously noted, research supports that a man and a woman's brain differ. The tendency for women to multitask is facilitated by the greater connectivity between the creative side of the right brain with the more analytical left side. This enables most women to attend to more than one thing at a time. They can listen to the television, keep an eye on the party, and have a coherent conversation—all at the same time. The problem can be that they want us guys to do the same.

2. Soulfully spiritual. Like the armoire, a woman is less likely to compartmentalize her faith. The high population of women in churches demonstrates their deep, spiritual need to commune with others and with God.

Christian women long for men who can model, encourage, and initiate a strong faith in their relationship. God is the one who breaks the power of evil in the human heart and creates trustworthiness and stability, qualities dear to the feminine mind and heart. Women appreciate men who bring stability and trust to the relationship, especially when it comes to faith and values.

3. An amazing unpredictability. Women keep men on their toes. Men need to embrace these seemingly illogical shifts and women's fluid nature. They can get irritated with the surprising mysteriousness of the women in their lives or step back and accept and appreciate it. Women in their sexual attraction, intricate bodies, emotional awareness, and need to connect, are just more complex than men.

4. That critical connecting. Women connect through questions and conversations: What women call "connecting conversation" with their girlfriends, men call "idle chitchat." When women ask men questions, a man can feel interrogated and think, "I've got to fix it," rather than sensing her need to simply connect. "How was your day?" is rich with possibility for connecting conversation, until the typical male responses of "Fine" or "Why are you asking?" If you're a guy, and this is your typical response, ask the women in your life for suggested responses that might help you open the doorway to deeper connection.

5. Different values and priorities. One woman commented to me that her favorite Christmas gift from her boyfriend was a used book. Knowing that she'd also received expensive jewelry, this surprised me. She explained that the book had been hard to find. That "scored more points" than the jewelry because it showed he was thinking about her and cared enough to take the time to find a gift she valued. To her, it demonstrated that he valued their relationship by investing significant time and energy on her behalf.

Women are more attracted to how a man acts than how he looks. Manning-up with kindness and character scores more points than getting buffed and putting on a shirt and tie. I wonder if maybe I should back up some on this point? Women do care about what men wear, and often think to themselves, "Get some new clothes."

I hope you now have a better appreciation for the fascinating differences God wove into the very fabric of the genders. Often the differences that drive us crazy are the same characteristics that draw us toward one another.

The Dance of the Sexes

I love describing relationships as a dance. As a sex therapist, I work with couples that have some poor sexual dancing skills. The dance of the sexes affirms and enhances our gender differences as we learn to protect each other's total sexuality with a thoughtful chastity based on honoring who we are as three-dimensional people rather than what we do. A soul-sexy person is someone who embraces and celebrates his or her gender uniqueness; elicits, releases, and enhances innate traits of the opposite or same sex; confidently moving into resonating relationships with his sister or brother while valuing and protecting each other in this dance of the sexes.

Within the church, we need more opposite sex friendships. Unfortunately for some, avoiding the opposite sex may seem like the safest road for lessening the sexual ache or not engaging in Stupid. But by God's design, quite the opposite is true. Dancing with the opposite sex is actually an effective way to scratch the loneliness itch and build healthy sexual relationships.

In dancing, moves can be spontaneous or scripted; steps are coordinated so no toes are stepped on; boundaries are set, but the partners are invited into each other's personal space; the music and styles vary with line dancing, waltzes, ballet, tango, slow dancing, swing, and hip-hop. Wow!

You've experienced this dance in your own life. Chad and Ashley were thought of as an item in their singles group. They insisted they were just friends, but everyone wondered how they could enjoy each other's company so much and not be more interested. Though they'd explored a romantic involvement – they didn't have much chemistry when they kissed – they decided to continue as close friends. Chad's dates never realized how much they owed to Ashley, who'd coached Chad and helped him understand how women felt and responded to men. And Chad knew more clearly what he did and didn't want in a woman as he remembered how Ashley had made him feel strong and worthy of respect.

For her part, Ashley hadn't realized how smart and attractive she was until she met Chad. He brought out the best in her. Her femininity seemed to come alive, and she was surprised that she had somehow become more attractive to the guys in the church group. Chad and Ashley enjoyed the dance of the sexes and deepened a "social" soul-sexiness that affected each dimension of their personhood.

So the dance of the sexes goes on, men and women nurturing and inspiring one another through intimate relationships, understanding that God created us with fascinating differences meant to reveal diverse aspects of his character. So put on your dancing shoes as we explore social and erotic sexuality—you don't want to sit this one out.

CHAPTER SIX

God's Sexual Economy: Implementing Social and Erotic Sexuality

Penis, vagina, orgasm—some words are specific and don't need much of a definition. But when we get into concepts like gender identity, healthy flirting, horny with sexual attraction and arousal, and chastity— yes, they'll need more explanation. In fact, we'll need to develop a innovative new Christian vocabulary, as we give different meaning to old words and develop some helpful models to describe and define sexual concepts and relationships.

Much of the confusion in single adult sexuality comes from poorly defined concepts and inadequate road maps for the sexual journey toward wholeness and loving connection. In writing this book, it has been a challenge to find helpful terms and models to guide you in understanding the Creator's purposeful design for sex.

God's Sexual Economy

I often refer to God's view of sexuality as *God's "sexual economy."* The word economy comes from the Greek words: *oikos* (household) and *nomos* (rules, guidelines). In biblical times, a person working as a steward of a given area of household responsibility was expected to manage it according to an *economy*, or a wise set of principles or household rules. Similarly, the Creator has established human sexuality within an "economy" – principles and guidelines – to lead us into the full enjoyment of intimate relationships.

"God wants you to be holy, so don't be immoral in matters of sex. Respect and honor your body. Don't be a slave of your desires or live like people who don't know God. You must not cheat any of the Lord's followers in matters of sex. Remember, we warned you that he punishes everyone who does such things. God didn't choose you to be filthy, but to be pure." 1 Thessalonians 4:3-7 (CEV)

Valuing and Protecting Sexuality

Because the Lord intended us to enjoy our sexuality, his sexual guidelines are there to help us experience his best. No Christian wants to dishonor his or her body, or sexually confuse or take advantage of a Christian brother or sister. Although God chooses to forgive and not cripple our lives if we mess up sexually, he does expect us to steward our sexuality wisely according to his economy—not according to contemporary cultural values.

This book will never give you a legalistic list of sexual do's and don'ts and then use shame and fear to make sure you follow the rules. Chastity is positively defined as valuing, protecting and celebrating your sexuality. But, the Creator's gift of sexuality is precious and Satan wants to distort anything God sees as loving and valuable. Therefore, we need to be cautious and wise in understanding that there's a cost when we violate God's sexual design. Our sexual mistakes will have sexual and relational consequences.

"But people are tempted when their own evil desire leads them away and traps them. This desire leads to sin, and then the sin grows and brings death." James 1:14-15 (NCV)

The cost or "death" that sin brings seldom results in a physical death, but with sin (Stupid) something always is lost. More often what dies is we forfeit or distort *God's best for us sexually*. Therefore, protecting and stewarding your sexuality will have a great impact on how your sexual story unfolds.

The Meaning of Sexuality

Throughout this book I intentionally use the term *sexuality* because the word *sex* is often taken to mean intercourse. Sexuality is much broader and more inclusive that the narrow definition of genital sex. As you live out your sexual story, keep remembering the importance of developing your values framework and making wise choices. Many erotic sexual behaviors occur due to inadequate planning, spur-of-the-moment impulsiveness or giving into horny—rather than intentional values–driven decisions. As you consider the following models, remember: wise, deliberate choices will both create and guard genuinely intimate relationships—and create a positive sexual wholeness.

Now, let's further define the concept of "sexuality" and the human expression of sexual intimacy both socially and erotically.

God's Design for Sexual Expression: *Social* and Er*otic* Sexuality

Social sexuality is something we experience with all people, including friends and family. It's the large box we all live in that started with our early interactions with our mom and dad. This is sometimes described as gender, family or friendship sexuality. Whether in friendship or business settings, the fact that we're male or female affects all our relationships with others.

"Treat younger men as brothers, older women as mothers, and younger women as sisters, with absolute purity." I Timothy 5:1-2

"Keep on loving one another as brothers and sisters." Hebrews 13:1

Social sexuality can be seen as the place we dwell most often whether single or married—a place where we don't eroticize those around us, but treat them as brothers and sisters, sons and daughters. Christian ethicist Stanley Grenz states that social (affective, gender) and erotic (genital, romantic) sexuality reflect the two ways God loves people: inclusively and exclusively.

God loves everyone inclusively, and created humans with a need for community. God also loves exclusively, and invites us into a personal relationship through Jesus Christ that employs the metaphor of Christ and the Bride. Therefore, social sexuality is expressed in community while erotic sexuality always has boundaries that keep it exclusive. "The marriage bond is fundamentally *exclusive*....In contrast, the bond formed by single persons is less defined and as a result more open to the *inclusion* of others...In short, the single life can express the divine reality as characterized by a love that seeks relationship (community) *non-exclusively*."[16]

Inclusive and exclusive are great concepts to help us define an inclusive *social sexuality* that's enjoyed in community, and exclusive *erotic sexuality* that's designed for full expression only in the covenant relationship of marriage.

In social sexuality, no restrictions are placed on who we accept and love. God values this inclusive way of relating:

"For God so loved the world that he gave his one and only Son." John 3:16

"Come to me, all you who are weary and burdened, and I will give you rest." Matthew 11:28

But can you truly experience a deep connection, safety and to be truly known and loved without being exclusive? Jesus taught that a personal relationship with our Creator God comes only through an exclusive relationship with Him.

"I am the way, the truth and the life. No one comes to the Father except through me." John 14:6

Genital sexual expression and sexual fidelity were designed to be exclusively shared with a Covenant lover, husband or wife. I don't want to create confusion because, though I believe erotic genital sexual expression is for a marital relationship, I also can see within social sexuality that deeper friendships will evolve (BFF's) that mirror the commitment of a marriage relationship and become more exclusive—though remaining non-erotically sexual. God wants us to follow his example and learn to love inclusively and exclusively.

Our "protein" metaphor (from Molly's story of eating at the buffet) fits when describing the difference between social and erotic sexuality. Social sexuality has a unique type of protein that we could view as vegetarian, while erotic sexuality could be looked at as steak. Chaste singles choose to protect the erotic and refuse to eat steak while still finding fulfillment as a vegetarian. We live in and experience two different types of sexual expression and both are important. We can get confused and blind-sided by our masculine or feminine social interactions if we forget that erotic sexuality, the ability to be sexually attracted and aroused, is always present and provides an energy within social sexual relationships.

Erotic sexuality focuses on our ability to be sexually attracted and aroused by people and cues in our environment—and to fall in love. Erotic sexuality stems from your sexual desire, and is sometimes referred to as genital or romantic sexuality. In a simplistic way, it's feeling horny and attracted toward someone with a desire for genital sex, and in God's sexual design, a marital intimacy that goes way beyond just feeling horny. Erotic sexuality, like all of sexuality, is three-dimensional, with your minds and hearts involved with your bodies. If we unpack "horny" we can see a longing to be special, to be known, and for intimate connection beyond the physical. That's why God chose erotic sexuality to portray marital oneness and the relationship of Christ and his Bride, the Church. He made his invisible love visible through human lovemaking.

The Gift Boxes Model: Unpacking Social and Erotic Sexuality

Within the broader arena of *social sexual relating* you'll always have *erotic sexual feelings;* because you have erotic sexual feelings, you'll find yourself desiring *erotic sexual behavior* and a special person in your life with whom to sexually bond. And within erotic sexual behavior resides *true sex* (the act of sexual intercourse or any genital stimulation) within a marital relationship. Let me further explain these concepts with the following illustration:

With a big grin on his face, Vickie's husband Wayne brought her a large box one year for her birthday. She opened the package to find an assortment of jazz CDs, some of which were her favorites.

SOCIAL & EROTIC SEXUALITY

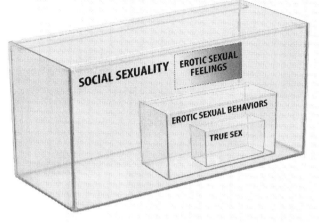

Music was something Wayne knew was important to her, and had known this before they even dated.

Inside the large box was also a medium-sized box. Upon opening it, Vickie found a number of personally selected gifts for the home Wayne knew she wanted. Before their marriage, Wayne learned to appreciate her taste in decor. His gifts showed thoughtfulness and that Wayne knew what was important to her.

Then, to her surprise, Vickie found a tiny box hidden within the second box. When she unwrapped this smallest box, she was thrilled to discover a blue topaz ring, more special and costly than the other gifts. The brilliant color of the topaz reminded her of their honeymoon and the beautiful blue Mediterranean Sea.

The Box of Social Sexuality

The big gift box that we all live in, especially singles, is the place of social sexuality. This place of communal living as sexual beings has special significance. "The single life is intended to serve as a picture of the expansive love of God and of the divine will to an inclusive community. Abstinence is crucial for the fulfillment of this purpose. Abstinence is an apt picture of and supports the nonexclusive nature of divine love. By abstaining from the act which celebrates exclusive bonding while remaining open to forming the bond of friendship with many people, the single person provides a picture of the God whose goal is the establishment of human community, which although intimate in a nonsexual way, remains expansive."[17]

> *"Love each other (sexually) like brothers and sisters. Give each other more (sexual) honor than you want for yourselves." Romans 12:10 (NCV) ("sexual" added to text for emphasis)*

Notice that the box for social sexuality is much larger than the others. This is not only because people live there most often, but it also emphasizes the beauty and complexity of living out a three-dimensional sexuality. Our sexuality describes *who we are,* rather than what we do. Your heart and mental attitudes about masculinity or femininity, soul virginity and erotic sexuality will have a profound effect on how you live in community with your brothers and sisters. It isn't possible for you to do anything relationally – including talking on the phone, going hiking, or enjoying worship – without expressing some aspect of your sexuality.

Below is a list of what it means to live out the joy and challenges of Social Sexuality as singles in community.

- Developing your *sexual identity* with masculinity and femininity, attraction, and critical values.
- Gender connecting with both sexes, and *righteous flirting* (explored more in Chapter 7)

- An inclusive sexuality—reflecting God's plan for *intimate community* and creating deep friendships that can flourish because a three-dimensional chastity—with genuine face-time and presence, activities, and fellowship.
  - Treating each other as "brothers and sisters," the singles' community can meet non-sexual needs in non-sexual ways.
    - *Safe touch* and 30-second hugs, women cuddling and men roughhousing, genuine affirmation of a three-dimensional sexiness, and same-sex interactions with no fear of labels.
    - Affirmation of each other's soul sexiness with no hidden agendas.
  - Practicing mutual accountability, encouraging and empowering each other to realize all God wants them to be.
- Recognizing and appreciating the energy of erotic feelings (with sexual desire and attraction)—while the erotic is stewarded with appropriate boundaries.

The church hasn't done well in dealing with the eroticism that's always present in relationships. Erotic sexual feelings within the box of Social Sexuality can create confusion and discourage us from engaging in meaningful community and vital relationships with our brothers and sisters. Because, YES, even in social sexuality, we're still sexual beings with sexual desires. Godly communities and friendships can't escape erotic sexuality.

In the Social Sexuality box, erotic sexual feeling goes from non-existent (no shading) to strong (darkest shading)—with the encircling dotted line illustrating that the erotic is designed to be exclusive, and will always need appropriate boundaries. In everyone's life there will be those who are more or less likely to trigger sexual attraction. Those relationships will require greater boundaries and caution.

I remember a young wife, married just eight months, coming into my office, anxious and distraught, because there was a coworker to whom she was attracted and thought was "hot." I asked if she thought that because she was married, choosing to practice chastity would come easy; that now, she wouldn't have to discipline her sexual attractions like she used to. Tearfully, she replied, "I hoped so."

The erotic component within social sexuality serves many purposes. Obviously, it creates an interesting tension/energy, and can be the motivation for exploring romantic relationships. It also encourages you to be disciplined and learn to manage your sexual feelings, rather than allowing them to control you. Wisely stewarding your erotic, genital sexuality is not an easy task. But, if you choose to discipline it, it will add a dynamic energy to your social sexual relationships.

The Box of Erotic Sexual Behaviors

Within the large box of social sexuality are two smaller boxes – gift boxes some singles may never experience, and others haven't yet, but may in the future. The medium-sized box will be opened and enjoyed only by those who deliberately choose to enter into an exclusive relationship. This box contains a variety of *erotic sexual behaviors and feelings* – activities considered romantic or arousing. Erotic sexual behaviors include the mental (such as composing love letters) as well as the physical (kissing and caressing). These behaviors designed to be indulged in simply because two people have a physical or emotional attraction to each other; they're reserved for 'confirmed' romantic relationships.

The following bullets explain what this gift box represents within a romantic relationship:

- Mental/heart actions (romantic fantasies, love letters, and intimate conversations).
- Physical actions (kissing, holding and caressing).
- A genuine erotic relationship that respects the bikini line (explained in Chapter 21) and preserves *true sex* (intercourse and orgasms) for marriage.

When couples are in love, they'll wonder how chastity works for them. Remember, healthy, mature relationships grow beyond the selfish question, "How far can I go?" They sort through what the erotic emotional and physical actions, with wise boundaries, mean for their unique relationship. How they can help each other grow into the amazing sexual man or woman God intended them to become.

I think it's helpful to employ colors when thinking about a couple's intimacy. Green Intimacy is becoming "Intimate Companions" with emotional involvement, physical affection and spiritual sharing. Green intimacy will be similar to the healthy intimacy we create with friends. Purple Intimacy is exclusive to lovers, where there is romantic and sexual attraction. Purple is becoming a couple, with a lot of flirting and connecting. The goal of this intimacy is not sexual arousal or foreplay for genital intimacy. Purple will be sexually arousing, but that's not the goal. It's about sensuous connecting (kissing, hugging, caressing) that doesn't have to lead anywhere. Purple intimacy—sensual connecting while managing sexual arousal, is keeping in mind that the person with whom you're enjoying erotic sexual thoughts and behaviors, may not be your future Adam or Eve. The Box of True Sex is being valued and protected. Orange Intimacy is the box of true sex with intercourse, orgasms and the commitment of marriage.

The Box of TRUE SEX

Inside the erotic sexual behaviors box is the smallest box of *true sex*. True sex involves the most intimate erotic sexual behavior. This special box was intended by God to remain unopened until a couple enters the most intimate of sexual relationships – marriage.

True Sex involves:

- Oral sex, mutual orgasms, as well as the ultimate expression of genital intercourse.
- A legal commitment and a vowing of one-flesh permanence that helps create the foundation and safety for true sex.
- True Sex seeks to recapture "the naked and unashamed" joy of the garden of Eden.

In God's sexual economy, true sex is, at minimum, defined as sexual intercourse (see Hebrews 13:4). Whether oral sex, anal sex, and mutual orgasms should be included is often questioned, thanks to Hollywood, political figures, and the media, which debate whether oral sex is really sex at all. For the thinking Christian, however, I strongly suggest that the only appropriate place for these behaviors is in the category of true sex. I am in no way endorsing all of these behaviors for every married couple. I'm simply stating that I believe *all oral, anal, and vaginal sexual behavior (as well as mutual orgasms) is biblically inappropriate outside of a committed marital union.*

True sex was given as a picture of the intimacy between Christ and his Bride, the Church. As such, all expressions of erotic sexuality should honor and derive their meaning from marital lovemaking, and the covenant relationship God created and blesses. The box of erotic sexual behaviors and thoughts in premarital dating relationships will always be incomplete, pointing toward true sex in marriage. Although true sex in marriage completes the earthly metaphor, it, too, remains an incomplete mirror of the ultimate intimacy our souls long for – an intimacy that will only be satisfied by God himself at the end of the divine love story in heaven (Revelation 21:1-7).

The Relationship Continuum BRIDGE: Defining Intimate Sexual Relationships

A continuum is a pathway along which things progress. To better understand God's design for sexual intimacy, the Relationship Continuum Bridge helps singles navigate their way sexually from single to married—and further illustrates how social and erotic expressions of sexuality fit into three different types of relationships: connecting, coupling, and covenanting. The ultimate purpose of the Bridge is to help singles build fulfilling intimate relationships and find sexual wholeness, guided by where they are have progressed on the Continuum.

The Relationship Continuum Bridge

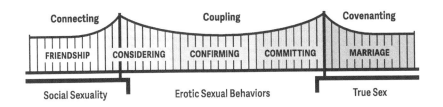

Let's explore the continuum and the three distinct relationships it represents: Connecting, Coupling and Covenanting. The first and third relationships on the continuum (single Connecting and married

Covenanting) are each important in their own right. One isn't godlier than the other; God uses each to teach and accomplish his purposes throughout our lives. The middle relationship (Coupling) is best understood as a "bridge" between Connecting and Covenanting. Only one Coupling relationship will eventually progress to Covenanting. All others will eventually return to Connecting. With this basic understanding, let's look at each one separately.

Connecting

Connecting relationships contain many familiar ideas, including friendships and casual dating. The term "connecting" helps us understand that sexual connecting begins from our earliest gender/social interactions with our parents. This place on the Continuum includes sexual desire and erotic urges; however, the emphasis of Connecting relationships is on friendship—not erotic sexual connecting. Here, in pairs and groups, same and opposite-sex connections develop that are designed for growth and companionship.

Single adults will have any number of connecting relationships at a given time, regardless of whether they're actively seeking a mate. Eventually, a potential soul mate may appear who prompts them to pursue group dates or even more deliberate one-on-one time together to get acquainted more intimately. Consideration of exclusive dating may take place in Connecting, but no decision about exclusivity has yet been made. Men and women can enjoy these relationships while intentionally maintaining healthy boundaries, guarding their hearts, and engaging in honest dialogue.

Looking at the Relationship Continuum Bridge, "Connecting" relationships are where Social Sexuality takes place. Erotic sexual behavior and true sex are inappropriate and outside of God's plan for these relationships. This site of connecting friendships becomes a safe place to explore and develop a comfortable masculinity or femininity—and the dance of the sexes.

Connecting friendships is also the place where romantic attraction occurs, but it is in the beginning stages of Consideration with no exclusive commitment yet.

Coupling

Coupling involves three unique decision-making stages: considering, confirming, and committing. Many couples are confused because they don't make deliberate choices or know exactly "where their relationship is." What initiates a coupling relationship is a mutual decision to become exclusive. That is the first vital Post as you get on the Bridge. Coupling begins the process that is intended to lead to Covenant marriage. Adult dating or courtship has a purpose and is designed to help you find your future mate.

The **Considering** stage of coupling actually begins in Connecting friendships. Always remember that in all three types of relationships, sexual energy and attractions (horny) will take place. But, erotic sexual behavior aren't helpful in this time of "getting to know you before we get on the bridge of exclusivity." The erotic can confuse the discovery process with too much value put on the intimacy and fun of the physical, while ignoring possible deal-breakers. Important evaluation of each other's suitability as a life partner is taking place—even in this beginning place of considering. At a point in time, an honest discussion should be had that leads to a deliberate choice to become an exclusive couple (Coupling and let's get on the Bridge) or not. The time it takes from the first date to when a couple deliberately defines their relationship may vary widely.

As an "item on the bridge," the couple begins more exploration as to whether the potential for marriage between them exists.

Physical romance, in the form of erotic sexual behavior, becomes a comfortable part of expressing affection and attraction. Each couple needs to negotiate which behaviors they will and will not allow, recognizing true sex as reserved for the relationship of marriage.

Confirming is the stage when a couple is "engaged to be engaged." From my experience as a therapist, this seems to be the most neglected element of premarital relationships. As the decision to marry settles on a couple, I *firmly believe* couples should seek premarital counseling and have open discussions about their future. Topics such as the desire for children, STIs and sexual histories, financial budgeting, gender role expectations, religious preferences, family skeletons, and other intimate issues should be shared in a trusting environment before a decision is made.

This is the time to put all the cards on the table, *before* commitments are made and wedding invitations are sent—before the pressure is too great to allow them to back out of a less-than-ideal marriage. For couples who stay the course toward marriage, those practicing this stage of coupling will find a greater freedom to delay their engagement and wedding plans for a short time (if necessary) to more adequately address any issues that arise in confirming. They'll also greatly reduce their risk of divorce in the early years of their marriage due to unrealistic expectations about their mates.

Committing is the engagement stage of coupling. It includes a formal proposal of marriage, though it may or may not involve an engagement ring. Specific plans evolve with wedding logistics and the practical preparation of joining two lives forever. If the couple has successfully navigated the confirming stage, they will likely find this stage less emotionally tense than those who didn't. A formal engagement may be relatively short, taking only as long as the practical elements of mailing invitations, planning the wedding and honeymoon and the financial decisions of where to live and how to combine incomes.

Covenanting cements the "two become one" partnering of marriage. With the final "I do's," the relationship is forever changed. This is the second big post on the Bridge. In God's eyes, soul mates have formed, and lovemaking (true sex) is shared within the safety of a lifelong commitment to each other—not simply living together. The high level of trust created by such a commitment becomes God's vehicle for true erotic fulfillment.

Though many in our society view marriage as a needless formality, God views marriage as a covenant between two lives that are forever bonded. All prior connecting and coupling relationships serve as preparation for this remarkable love relationship now being completed. Only in this stage is true sex appropriate; marriage provides the ability to truly be "naked and unashamed" both physically and emotionally.

So, the continuum progresses from connecting friendships to romantic coupling with appropriate erotic sexual behaviors, through to true sex and the covenant commitment of marriage. In your sexual journey, keep thinking through God's plan and the strategic place of erotic sexuality in each type of your relationships. Dear reader, keep thinking through how the human desire to be pursued, known and loved, accompanied by sexual attraction, can promote taking destructive sexual shortcuts in your quest for true intimacy. Getting naked may seem quicker than hours spent talking, but can lead you down a destructive path of blowing through boundaries the wise Creator put in place to guide and grow your intimate relationships. Please keep thinking through social and erotic sexuality and the relationship Continuum Bridge, as you understand God's sexual economy and His amazing plan for valuing, celebrating and protecting your precious gift of being sexual.

CHAPTER SEVEN

Friendship Sexuality and Righteous Flirting

Earlier, I described sexuality as God's grand strategy for creating and enriching deeply intimate relationships. God isn't humanly sexual, but the Creative Trinity chose to reflect how they love and relate by making us sexual beings. Your being a man or woman colors every relationship that you're in and assists you in fulfilling your need to love and be loved.

Social or Friendship Sexuality and the Importance of Community

The family is God's central unit for learning healthy gender relating. The nuclear family was intended to model God's family: the church. Moms, dads, sisters, and brothers—all sexual beings with desires—are meant to build relationships as a family. This social sexuality is more about intimate companionship, rather than being erotic or romantic. Dads and other men help sons learn things that men do, including how to initiate and protect. Moms and other women teach daughters about real beauty and their alluring femininity.

> *"Treat younger men as brothers, older women as mothers, and younger women as sisters, with absolute purity." I Timothy 5:1-2*

As we grow into adulthood, we're further tasked with creating new families (friends and communities) beyond our nuclear family, as we live out our sexual stories. Remember that even in healthy families, sexual surges occur. A dad or brother may notice his daughter's or sister's body, yet choose to maintain godly boundaries rather than objectify her. This sexual discipline prepares younger men and women for healthy erotic relating. Their satisfying social sexuality grows into romantic coupling and the dance of the sexes takes on a more sensual, erotic flair.

But, most friendships never become romantic. Both married and single adults need supportive male and female friends who can help them steward their sexuality. Opposite-sex friendships will look different for married couples than for singles. However, both are necessary to experience community as God intended.

Single adults especially value their married friends, who meet some of their needs for opposite-sex interaction. My wife and I have many single friends whom we nurture. Regardless of whether you remain single or someday marry, healthy connecting with both genders is critical to creating community and scratching the loneliness itch—to becoming whole sexually.

Unfortunately, you weren't born knowing how to relate with the opposite sex—it's learned. Even if you had excellent role models growing up, creating your own opposite-sex peer relationships as an adult takes practice. Sadly, I don't think we create and evolve same-sex friendships that well either.

The different settings that single adults find themselves in can create special challenges. Too often at Christian seminaries and churches, singles aren't given much opportunity and aren't encouraged to reach out and create opposite-sex friendships and engage in righteous flirting. The ever- present desire for romance, and the feelings that can quickly surface in friendships, also create challenges. So what can men and women do to build community and those important opposite-sex—and same-sex friendships?

> *"No one has ever seen God, but if we love each other, God lives in us. And God gave us this command: Those who love God must also love their brothers and sisters."* I John 3:18 (NCV)

> *"A friend is always loyal, and a brother [or sister] is born to help in time of need."* Proverbs 17:17 (NLT)

Women, Inspire Your Brothers to Connect

Ladies, you have no idea how important a role you play in bringing out the best (or the worst) in the men in your lives; whether he's dealing with sexual surges, working through sexual attractions, dealing with life's stressors, or trying to find a friend or a wife.

Show him respect. More than women, men need to feel competent and respected. Respect is shown in a variety of ways: praising his efforts, recognizing his strengths and accomplishments, asking him for help, and valuing his opinion. Do you want more sensitive responses from him? Respectfully ask for it and you'll be surprised how he mans up.

Communicate clearly. Men don't operate well under the assumption that they "should know what's going on." They value clear, bottom line communication. Being clear prevents many hurt feelings and gives his problem-solving brain good information to process and act on.

Receive and respond. Though they want to initiate, men may have difficulty risking rejection. Demonstrate appreciation for and encourage their initiation when they do. I still remember when my future wife enthusiastically accepted my invitation to take a country dancing class with me in the early days of our relationship. I took more risks initiating after that.

Men, Inspire Your Sisters to Connect

Make a conscious decision to protect, defend, and honor the women in your life. Women flourish with male attention and want to feel secure and special. Small courtesies, such as opening doors, and offering to carry heavy objects increase her sense that you care. Every woman welcomes someone who will stand up for her and defend her — her knight in shining armor. Honor her through small gestures.

Communicate more and more often. Women need to hear you speak from your heart. Being open and honest about your personal opinions and feelings makes such a difference. Risk self-disclosure, especially of your feelings.

Make her feel special. Give her your undivided attention. Try talking to her without engaging in distracting activities (like watching TV or looking at your phone). Noticing and responding to her needs goes a long way; but it doesn't count as much if she has to ask or remind you. One of my single women friends was feeling especially down. A male friend noticed and said, "You must have forgotten how beautiful you really are." His thoughtful attention immediately improved her mood and confidence in herself.

Men and Women Inspiring Same-sex Friendships

Girls need girlfriends who resonate with their feelings in ways that men can't. Men need other men to bond with through activities in which they affirm each other in masculine ways. An important part of Social Sexuality is same-sex friendships that can even spill over into righteous flirting.

Here are some observations on how same-sex friendships get sabotaged which could easily be prevented. Don't compare yourself to your friends, but learn to feel comfortable with who you are and what you've achieved. Don't gossip, but intentionally work at building each other up. Don't get scared when intimate friendships inspire unexpected sexual feelings—acknowledge and steward them wisely. Men, you can build close same-sex friendships without worrying about others thinking you're gay. Women, quit making comparisons and judgments about the women around you and just reach out and get to know them.

Additional Tips for Connecting Friendships

Below are a few more suggestions for making same-sex and opposite-sex friendships more rewarding—which helps keep those sexual feelings on track:

- Develop a supportive community. Be intentional and persistent. Great friendships aren't forged overnight. Best friends grow from casual friendships that develop further when you spend more time together.
- Invite your friends to help you with your insecurity, poor communication skills, weight loss, or guilt—and to join you

in fun hobbies, parties or even your daily life. Be transparent, vulnerable and real.

- A key to great communication is empathy. Learn to step back from your own feelings and opinions and make an effort to walk in someone else's shoes. Being an objective listener is not easy but can yield great rewards.

- Don't focus on your romantic relationship to the neglect of your other friendships. After the breakup, do you really want to come groveling to your old friends because you neglected them during your "hot and heavy" relationship? Even after marriage, your friends need you and you need them.

- God not only designed us to flourish in community. He designed community relationships to vary from casual to close to *deeply intimate*. Singles can enjoy a Sunday school class (casual), or a small group or bros (close)—but deeper friendships take additional time and emotional investment. Like Jesus, it is difficult to find the time and emotional space to develop more than 3 to 12 intimate relationships.

Casual	Close	Intimate

The Erotic in Social Sexuality

It's fascinating how the energy of the erotic adds color, spice and complexity to social sexuality and righteous flirting. Theologian Ronald Rolheiser expresses how sexuality is so much more than erotic behaviors. "Sexuality is beautiful, good, extremely powerful, sacred energy, given us by God and experienced in every cell of our being as an irrepressible urge to overcome our incompleteness, to move toward unity and consummation with that which is beyond us. ...Human sexuality is not just the act of sex. In a broad sense, it is the energy that drives us into community to find intimacy and completeness."[18]

A mistake the church has made is not helping singles recognize, embrace and steward their sexual energy—celebrate not fear it. We all have erotic feelings with sexual attractions and arousal whether single or married. And, we haven't as a Christian culture, realized that our sexual energy is much more useful than just propelling us to true sex and marriage. There are so many ways the loving Creator uses sexuality to teach and bless his human creation.

One important part of God's grand plan is that erotic sexual attraction lead to marriage and the creation of families. But he also blesses married and single people with a gender interaction that is fueled by sexual energy and the desire to be connected. I describe this as righteous flirting, which we have too little of. So, how can communities encourage righteous flirting? Or, maybe a better place to start is: "What is righteous flirting? Can I enjoy it and not be married?"

Righteous Flirting: Enjoying the Dance of the Sexes

I define righteous flirting as the enjoyment of gender sexuality, while appreciating and stewarding the ever-present erotic energy. Sexual feelings can be a confusing and enlivening component of social sexuality. When I describe the concept of righteous flirting, people often respond, "I thought flirting was manipulative; how can it be righteous?" I would agree that worldly flirting is about giving someone attention to get a particular (often selfish or dishonest) response. So, yes, unrighteous flirting exists. By contrast, the purpose of righteous flirting is building up our brothers and sisters and creating fun, fulfilling relationships.

Christian leaders often ask if I couldn't have conveyed my concept without using the word "flirt." One asked why I didn't call it "positive gender interaction." Not only does that sound dull and academic, it doesn't communicate the concept that there's something erotically sexual (God-designed) about righteous flirting and the interaction of the genders. Our human interactions may include almost none, some, or a lot of erotic attraction to be stewarded. If we unpack even more the concept of the sacred sexual energy God blesses his human creation with, we can embrace and celebrate the fact that social sexuality has a stimulating erotic energy that occurs when the masculine and feminine interact with love and support. Let's not fear horny—let's embrace all the good our sexual energy can create.

"And let us consider how to stir up one another to love and good works…" (Hebrews 10:24)

Some great examples of righteous flirting were the visits to my mother-in-law in her nursing home. One time I arrived to the home early and saw her primping as she fixed her hair and put on some lipstick. I was one of the few remaining men in her life, and my visits brought out her femininity, which in turn affirmed my masculinity. There was a sexual energy that was intimate, playful and meaningful for both of us.

Can righteous flirting take place in same-sex relationships as well as with the opposite sex? I would say yes, in the way I define the concept. When I hang out with my guy friends, sharing fun times of play or work, this interaction can be considered righteous flirting. My masculine self-image is validated.

A single friend recently told me about a recent weekend outing with his guy friends. One of the highlights was playing "King of the Mountain" on a large rubber raft in the lake by the house. They laughed and roughhoused, throwing each other off the raft. He shared that though he struggles with same-sex attraction, this had nothing to do that type of eroticism. He appreciated the wrestling (all people have a need for touch), and the bonding of being with men with whom he shares a common faith and meaningful friendship.

Our tendency is to recognize physical beauty, but going back to an important theme in this book, righteous flirting also involves affirming the mind and spirit, too. Righteous flirting reflects the integrity of your heart and has the opportunity to pour life into the men and women in your life.

> "And this is my prayer: That your love may abound still more and more in knowledge and depth of insight, that you may discern what is best." Philippians 1:9,10

The Art of Righteous Flirting

Righteous flirting makes social sexuality and the importance of community come alive. While many singles may theoretically understand what I mean by righteous flirting, some express difficulty, especially, in feeling free to truly enjoy the opposite (or same) sex. This may be especially true for those who (like me) grew up in a more conservative faith tradition with sexuality defined by what we didn't do. For those who need more reassurance, here are a few of the essential *elements* of righteous flirting that can fit so well in a Christ-centered community:

- a heightened sense of masculinity or femininity, becoming more aware of your gender sexuality and its power
- an awareness of God's image in men and women, enjoying the soul-sexiness of the other person
- stewarding sexual attraction and arousal with godly boundaries—not fear or guilt
- playfulness and uninhibited interactions, enjoying the feeling of attraction
- conversational bantering with playful give-and-take
- non-verbal connecting such as making eye contact, smiling, and appropriate touch
- holy hugs and kisses "Greet one another with a holy kiss" Romans 16:16 (I think the "holy" comes down to motive and manner of engaging in physical affection.) Singles can get "touch-starved" and need those longer hugs and tender caresses, handholding or a shoulder massage

Styles of Righteous Flirting with Connecting Friendships, Romantic Coupling and Marriage

Be careful and wise—your flirting could become harmful. Flirting to manipulate or merely to satisfy your own selfish desire or ego leaves a brother or sister feeling used and abused. Setting wise boundaries in Connecting, Coupling and Covenanting relationships will ensure that each person feels whole and enjoys the benefits of righteous flirting.

Connecting: I have two women with whom I really enjoy righteous flirting – my wonderful granddaughter and my 93-year-old mother-in-law (who during the writing of this book has gone home to Jesus). My granddaughter, Caitlyn, knows how to tug at her Papa's heartstrings with feminine wiles: her laughter, her playfulness, and her beauty. My mother-in-law grew up in the Old South, an only daughter with four brothers. She enjoyed men and made me believe I could walk on water.

Righteous flirting also can include actual sexual desire and attraction in Connecting friendships, romantic Coupling and Covenanting True Sex. The depth of the relationship will dictate how it's played out. Sometimes this flirting is just a friendly interaction with a single brother or sister turning on the feminine charm or masculine appeal, but having no knowledge of whether that relationship might progress into the romantic. The winks, smiles, flipping of the hair; all can create an attraction worth pursuing.

Chantal and Tyson met through their church. Their eyes locked when Chantal walked in that first night. Righteous flirting began by enjoying each other's laughter and experiencing opposite-sex companionship with innocent erotic overtones. They resisted fanning the flames of *eros* they felt and avoided instant Coupling. This was particularly healing for Chantal, who was raw from a breakup. Both sensed potential in their relationship, but instead created appropriate intimacy in Connecting through playful flirting without any further expectations.

Coupling: Righteous flirting takes on a richer tone when a couple's romantic interests are engaged. Sexual surges add zest, with conversations and looks more lingering and erotic—yet still respectful. Righteous flirting in Coupling builds a foundation of self-confidence and vulnerability. Chantal was used to men falling all over themselves, captivated by her cute figure and femininity. With Ty, she determined to clean up her dance of desire and to build him up as a friend, rather than manipulating him into having sex. She came to value healthy flirting as she focused on affirming him—and yes, sexual thoughts and behaviors grew more intimate.

Covenanting: Have you ever seen an elderly couple at your church as he opens the door for her and gently guides his bride inside? Their tender and enduring love truly inspires. Adams and Eves at any age are fun to watch, but older couples bring a special meaning to righteous flirting. They know each other's bodies and spirits well, yet the dance of the sexes continues to create meaning in their relationship. Probably the greatest danger to their relationship will be if they lose their ability to playfully flirt and forget to treat each other with love and lightheartedness.

Wow, so righteous flirting is honoring the Creator's gift of sexual energy with both masculinity and femininity reflecting his intimate nature. In social sexuality, it won't have the romantic, erotic intent that coupling relationships have. But, in friendship or marriage, righteous flirting cultivates a fun, affirming way to express love and build a positive sexual intimacy in the Dance of the Sexes

> _"Don't just pretend to love others. Really love them. Hate what is wrong. Hold tightly to what is good. Love each other with genuine affection, and take delight in honoring each other." Romans 12:9,10 (NLT)_

CHAPTER EIGHT

The Dance of the Sexes: Boundaries and Those Crucial DTRs

One single woman angrily spouted, "In all this talk about being modest so I don't tempt my Christian brothers, where does the man's responsibility come in?" It can be difficult to be our brother or sister's keeper. But, with love and courageous conversations, single adults can tackle the complicated task of placing appropriate boundaries around romantic feelings, sexual desires and attractions.

"Therefore let us stop passing judgment on one another. Instead, make up your mind not to put any stumbling block or obstacle in the way of a brother or sister." Romans 14:13

Protecting the Dance of the Sexes

I like the word "protect." It's a loving word, full of care and concern for another's wellbeing. It also means that there's something valuable worth preserving. So, how can we protect our brothers and sisters in the Dance of the Sexes?

Women Protecting Their Brothers

Gals, learn the difference between sexual seduction and feminine allure. Know your own sex appeal and what turns on your Christian brothers. In the dance of desire, men are more visual; when they see a red bra strap, they start to wonder if the panties match and if it's a thong.

You can more carefully consider your clothing and sit modestly. Sitting immodestly or leaning over so you're exposing underwear, cleavage or other skin is a sexual cue to your brothers more powerful than you know. Your feminine parts (navel, legs, breasts, waist, hips, genitals, undergarments) create mental images that excite them and require many deliberate choices on their part to maintain their sexual integrity.

I remember a mom who brought her fourteen-year-old daughter into my office. "Can you help me teach Jessie the difference between being feminine and being seductive? She wants to wear micro-miniskirts and clothes I think are inappropriate in public." I started by comparing Jessie's clothes to her mom's: "Look at your mom's sweater. It shows she has a nice figure but doesn't make your eyes go directly to her breasts. Her skirt outlines her hips and legs. As a man, I can appreciate that without wondering what else is under the skirt. Jessie, your skirt is so short that unless you keep your legs crossed, your panties show. Your low-cut top draws a person's eyes directly to your breasts." I can only imagine what effect young women's apparel like Jessie's have on hormonal teenaged boys!

It's important to emphasize that "modesty" is not repressing your femininity or making you responsible for your Christian brother's thought-life. The church can shame or judge women harshly and not hold men responsible for stewarding their thought-life. You might ask for honest feedback from close male friends about any clothing you have that may cause a problem for them. That's what a supportive community is all about. And as they're honest with you, will you be brave enough to throw out a favorite bikini or top? Men are always responsible for what they do with the thoughts in their heads, but women must take responsibility for the role they play in providing unnecessary erotic stimuli —while still maintaining their feminine allure. So, I'm not saying wear clothes a size or two bigger so your figure doesn't tempt your brothers and for goodness sake, throw all your bikinis away. God made you physically alluring.

Another area to consider are touches that could be friendly or erotic. What may be a friendly touch to you might be a turn-on to a man. You may say, "But I'm a touchy-feely person!" I'm not saying you should stop all touching. Everyone needs touch, especially single adults who are often touch-deprived. However, be aware of creating erotic arousal or sending messages you don't intend.

> *"Promise me, O women of Jerusalem, …not to awaken love until the time is right." Song of Songs 2:7 (NLT)*

Men Protecting Their Sisters

Men, know your own appeal and what might be a sexual turn-on to that Christian sister. Think through what could be perceived as sexual overtures or behaviors that might be interpreted as promises of deeper intimacy to her. Failure to do this can cause much confusion in your relationships. Women need you to be Jesus in their lives. Think of Mary, Martha, Mary Magdalene, the woman at the well, and so many other women that Jesus loved.

> *"Treat…older women as mothers, and younger women as sisters, with absolute purity." 1 Timothy 5:2*

Control your sexual desire and visual nature. Embrace but discipline horny. Keep from constantly scoping out breasts and other women's body parts. Honor women as people rather than treating them as sex objects. Think with your head and not your hormones. The most seductive women are often those who have deep unmet heart needs. God needs you to help them heal and grow—not get sexually involved with them.

Be aware when paying attention to your female friends. Such attention carries deep meaning and can unknowingly create erotic arousal and attraction in women. Two hours spent at Starbucks in deep conversation may give a mixed message and stimulate romantic interest. Just as visual cues turn a man on, genuine empathy and attentive listening from a mature Christian brother may mislead your female friend. Don't shy away from being empathic; just be intentional about protecting her heart by maintaining clear boundaries as to the nature of your relationship.

Monitor caring touch and affection. A masculine hug or gentle touch is a wonderful thing to a woman. However, some may interpret more than you intend from such a hug. Just as they respond to empathy and focused attention, women can be quite sensitive and cued in to touch as well. Guys, you can be careful as to how long, how often, and where you touch as you convey the correct message for that relationship.

Never forget that women have libidos and can lust, too. You can practice appropriate modesty and help them steward their sexual drive. Touches, looks, and too-tight jeans might trigger them. Sexual integrity and chastity are a communal goal in protecting each other as sexual beings.

> "Each of you should learn to control your own body in a way that is holy and honorable, not in passionate lust like the pagans who do not know God; and that in this matter no one should wrong or take advantage of a brother or sister." 1 Thessalonians 4:4- 6

DTRs: Defining The Relationship

Christian singles are often confused about the nature of their relationships because they seldom communicate openly about them. Assumptions, hidden agendas, and confusion abound with little Defining The Relationship. Eric gave Dana a wounded look. "You mean you aren't interested in dating me?" His intense blue eyes looked away as he nervously played with the napkin in his lap. They were two friends having a casual lunch on a lazy Saturday afternoon. His question surprised her.

Eric and Dana met at church and had been friends for two years. They had a deep friendship and spent a considerable amount of time hanging out in groups, or one-on-one, but Dana had always assumed that their relationship was platonic. Looking back, she hadn't given him a reason to think otherwise, had she? What should she have done differently?

Megan hadn't had a close friendship like she had with Janna since college. She couldn't understand when Janna started becoming less available. Megan finally got her courage up and told Janna how much her friendship meant. Janna revealed her preoccupation with a new work project. She also confessed that she had a difficult time opening up to people and being vulnerable. After this conversation, their friendship went to a new level.

Like the stories above, single men and women have a responsibility and privilege to protect their intimate friendships. Maybe the situation was more about Eric's unrealistic expectations and Dana hadn't actually done anything to lead him on, but perhaps she could have altered their dance to create a better understanding of her desire for a friendship and nothing more. Megan regretted not having cleared the air. None of these singles were practicing the three C's.

Practicing the Triple C's of an Effective DTR

Three critical elements are involved in effectively defining relationships and keeping them healthy: constant, compassionate and clear. I am not saying this is an easy process. So many variables get in the way: love and romance, attachment issues, traumas and culture. But, for intimacy to thrive, it takes these honest, courageous, loving conversations

> *"So you must stop telling lies. Tell each other the truth, because we all belong to the same body. When you talk, do not say harmful things, but say what people need—words that will help others become stronger. Then you will do good to those who listen to you." Ephesians 4:25, 29 (NCV)*

Constant

Constant can be defined as "continually occurring." A major problem with DTRs is that they don't occur frequently enough. I know part of the problem is the emotional energy they take, and the fear of rejection or hurt feelings. I encourage you to confront your negative feelings around DTRs because defining a relationship actually prevents hurt feelings, and fosters great friendships. Romantic involvements demand risks and tackling them directly reduces the uncertainty for both parties.

Compassionate

DTRs must express a real concern for the other person. They must reflect Jesus with a humble, kind and loving presentation.

One single lady told me that she thought she was very successful at clarifying a friendship or breaking up with a boyfriend. I asked how she did that and why she felt the men were okay. She replied, "I always build them up and tell them how lucky a woman will be to have them as a boyfriend. That the chemistry wasn't there for me, but that wasn't their problem, it was what I was or wasn't feeling. I think they were able to let go of me with their egos intact and feeling better about themselves."

The tone and loving concern in the delivery of a DTR is critical. Think of Jesus in his relationships and how he could love and confront others. We can learn to communicate with love and concern while still being honest.

"Speaking the truth with love" Ephesians 4:15 NCV

Clear

Mature singles must grow to a place of transparent dialogue. Clarity carries with it the idea of being easily understood, of being truly honest. Singles can learn to confront and push through their discomfort in discussing sexual chemistry and romantic topics such as "Okay, so it's clear that we're attracted to each other. I've struggled to maintain godly sexual boundaries in my past. I want to do something different this time." Or, "I've really enjoyed getting to know you. I'd like to explore the possibility of a more serious relationship as a couple. What do you think?" Or, "You're a wonderful friend, but I don't feel any chemistry between us. You're the brother I never had, and I wonder if we could keep this relationship a friendship?"

This transparent dialogue also applies to DTRs for any friendship and what you have to offer or want in a given relationship. I remember an awkward interaction I had when I asked a male acquaintance if he was willing to develop a closer friendship. He replied that he didn't have the time or the need for another male friendship. After I got over feeling rejected, I appreciated that I'd taken the risk and that he had been honest—though not very compassionate— in his response.

The Complexity of DTRs

"Speaking the truth in love" and creating effective DTRs isn't easy. Many factors can influence a comfortable and successful one. Some people prefer a direct approach and others need a softer approach with kindness thrown in with the honesty. Men and women can have very different ideas about what an intimate relationship and commitment looks like and the importance of a DTR. Men tend to be more commitment averse, and may need confrontation. Women may be more physically affectionate or emotionally open, and this can be misinterpreted.

Sexual feelings and attraction can come unexpectedly and create relationship dilemmas. Just because someone has a crush on someone doesn't mean a relationship has to begin or end. Maybe a DTR needs to take place with a close friend, not the person involved, discussing how to manage such feelings. Attractions may or may not be mutual, or may be more about being horny than wanting a truly romantic intimacy. I hope you are seeing how these discussions are so important, especially if sexual attraction is there.

This gets into another complexity of DTRs—they may be engaging in the delicate task of ending a friendship or dating relationship. This is definitely a time when both compassion and honesty must be present. Some friendships should never go romantic and some friendships may become toxic and need some adjustment.

Intentionally Creating DTRs

Single adults often create a mess in their friendships by not making deliberate choices to end or deepen a relationship. I hear this complaint so often, especially concerning single men: "He won't decide where we are in the relationship!" Singles don't have to be ruled by their emotions or lapse into a lazy "whatever." Depending upon your age and personality, the DTR may already be a common element in your interactions with opposite or same-sex friends. But for many, it's a new and important practice—and a powerful way to protect and grow relationships.

"Intentional" is an interesting word with its definition meaning that something won't come natural but involves a deliberate courageous choice. DTRs can be like jumping into a cold pool on a hot summer day—you have to grab your nose and jump. The more you practice them, the easier they are to have. And, as you see how they protect and grow the relationships you want, you will be motivated to risk more of them.

CHAPTER NINE

Three-Dimensional Soul Sexuality and Heart Attitudes

with Gary Barnes[3]

I love movies in 3D. Everything comes alive more vividly and the action seems more realistic. When the Godhead made humankind, it was like they were problem-solving: how to help their creation experience *love* more intensely. And making them three-dimensional with a body, mind and heart was an important part of that plan.

Intimacy theologian Christopher West refers to the Trinitarian Relational Godhead as the "Eternal Exchange of Love" and we as humans, created in the image of God, have been invited participants in this eternal exchange of love with God and one another in a full, rich and satisfying intimacy.[19] The Creative Trinity wanted men and women to experience their "invisible" loving nature by creating "visible" sexual three-dimensional beings that would reflect their God-given ability to form intimate relationships. Without the multi-dimensionality of our bodies, minds and hearts, we humans wouldn't have the ability to love and celebrate intimacy.

---

[3] Gary Barnes (Th.M., Ph.D.) is professor of biblical counseling at Dallas Theological Seminary. He is a licensed clinical psychologist, certified sex therapist and ordained Anglican priest. Gary is an editor of the book, *Sanctified Sexuality: Valuing Sex in an Oversexed World*, helped create a compassionate video on sexual identity (www.CompellingLoveFilm.com), and teaches graduate school sexuality classes.

Three-dimensional Soul Sexuality

The word "**soul**" is often defined as our immaterial self or inner being, but in Scripture soul more often refers to the total person—the self with a combined physical, psychological and spiritual nature. This fuller understanding of the *soul* melds the *material* and the *immaterial* dimensions into a unified whole. In *Care of Souls*, David Benner identifies the soul as "the meeting point of the psychological and the spiritual"[20] with the immaterial dimensions given expression through a physical body and brain. Benner encourages, "Let us understand soul as referring to the whole person, including the body, but with a particular focus on the inner world of thinking, feeling and willing."[21] I refer to this as "heart attitudes"—a God-transformed *heart* and *mind*.

So, you're not made of different parts, rather your soulfulness consists of different dimensions that interact and have a capacity for intimacy dependent on the whole personhood. One way of thinking about this is *not* that you have physical, psychological, spiritual "parts," but that you **are an** interactive physical, psychological and spiritual being. A three-dimensional personhood gives the concepts of sexual chastity, attraction and romance a much deeper meaning. You can look at yourself as a blend of a physical body, a thinking mind, and a spiritual heart that God can transform.

> *"Offer your bodies as living sacrifices…be transformed by the renewing of your mind…[appreciate] the measure of faith God has given [to each spiritually]." Romans 12:1-3*

These three interwoven dimensions, working together, give you the ability to live out your core values, build intimate friendships and — live as sexual beings with social and erotic sexual relationships. Your body wonderfully combines hormones, blood vessels, nerves, muscles, skin and genitals to create and express sexual attraction and desire. Your mind involves your imagination, your will and your choices, and your emotions. Your heart gives you the ability to experience true love and creates the ability to become "one" with another (Genesis 2:24).

Expanding your understanding of this will help you experience deeper and more meaningful social and erotic intimacy. The body component expresses what the mind feels and the heart desires. Jesus willingly took on a body so he could love and die for us. The more we study the mind/brain we see it as the center of our emotions and our capacity to make choices. Your heart is the deepest, invisible element of our personhood that God comes in and redeems, and the Holy Spirit fills. Your bodies, minds and hearts work together to help you be that whole intimate, sexual being. Human beings can't thrive without each of these dimensions being present in an interwoven and interactive way.

I appreciate the quote by theologian Oswald Chambers, as he stressed how Jesus always worked three-dimensionally to bring healing and maturity to the lives of those he touched. "We are apt to confine life to one phase only, the physical; there are three phases: physical, psychical and spiritual. Whenever Jesus touched the physical domain, a miracle happened in the other phases as well."[22]

Your Body

Your sexuality is lived out through your body. Your ability to touch, your hormones and sexual desire, your smiles and laughter, your eyes as the window to your inner being—all of these help communicate intimacy in the Dance of the Sexes. Our eyes see images, but it is our heart and mind that give them meaning. God opens our eyes through our minds and our hearts to experience all he desires for us relationally and sexually.

"The eye is the light for the body. If your eyes are good, your whole body will be full of light." Matthew 6:22 (NCV)

"He wants you to learn to control your own body in a way that is holy and honorable. Don't use your body for sexual sin like the people who do not know God." I Thessalonians 4:4-5 (NCV)

"Suddenly, their eyes were opened, and they recognized him." Luke 24:31 (NLT)

Your body also has a subtle sexiness that you may have noticed—things like hands, hair, mouth, and eyes; nonverbal expressions; verbal cues such as pitch, tone, and rate of speech; nurturing and protective gestures (opening doors, offering assistance in need, etc.). Your body helps you express many different feelings and behaviors, especially your social and erotic sexual interactions.

"If you use your lives to do the wrong things your sinful selves want, you will die spiritually. But if you use the Spirit's help to stop doing the wrong things you do with your body, you will have life. The true children of God are those who let God's Spirit lead them." Romans 8:13-14 (NCV)

"Who may go up on the mountain of the Lord? Who may stand in his holy Temple? Only those with clean hands and pure hearts…" Psalm 24:3-4ᵃ (NCV)

These three dimensions are often linked in the Bible, especially the heart and body, and the heart and the mind. I Corinthians 6:19 tells how our bodies are the temple of the Holy Spirit and Psalm 24:3-4 (above) explains how we can enjoy a close relationship with the Almighty. We must have a disciplined body (clean hands) and a pure heart to further that communion with God. The "clean hands" reference can certainly speak to your sexual integrity. Are you using your hands to click on godly websites, to make wise choices in self-stimulation, or to touch another unselfishly?

We must remember that: "Our spiritual life does not grow in spite of the body, but because of the body. When once we understand the bodily machine with which we have to work out what God works in, we find our body becomes the greatest ally of our spiritual life."[23]

> "There's more to sex than mere skin on skin. Sex is as much a spiritual mystery as physical fact. … Or didn't you realize that your body is a sacred place, the place of the Holy Spirit? Don't you see that you can't live however you please, squandering what God paid such a high price for? The physical part of you is not some piece of property belonging to the spiritual part of you. God owns the whole works. So let people see God in and through your body." I Corinthians 6:16, 19-20 (MSG)

As Christopher West explains in Our Bodies Tell God's Story, "the body is not only biological, … the body is also theological…" and therefore, "…sex is not just sex".[24] Your body's capability for sexual attraction is an important part of God's plan. The body is crucial to telling and experiencing the nature of becoming "one flesh." A major theme in the Bible is "Oneness not based in Sameness." We see it first in the Trinity (three separate persons, one being). Then, Adam and Eve becoming "one flesh." It's demonstrated in the relationship between God and his chosen people. It's in the redemptive work of Christ, restoring our loving relationship with God. It's the Church as the Bride of Christ. It's this "one another" dynamic of the many members of the Body of Christ, all one in Christ, and creating a community that reflects the divine. And in the final chapter of biblical history, all of those in Christ will be one with him in the eternal exchange of love of the Trinitarian Godhead. Sex and the body provide an experiential object lesson to lead us to the deeper mysteries of the universe.

Your Mind

"So letting your sinful nature control your mind leads to death. But letting the Spirit control your mind leads to life and peace." Romans 8:6 (NLT)

Your sexuality is psychological, not merely physical. In brain research, we see that the human brain is able to think and reason in ways that differ from animals. You have a prefrontal cortex that allows you to make choices regarding various alternatives in living out your sexual identity. You also have an amygdala, the feeling center of the brain, that allows us to experience anger, excitement, and love. Spiritual Director Dallas Willard explains that the connection between thought and feeling is so intimate that the "mind" is usually treated as consisting of thought and feeling together, as they are interdependent, and are never found apart.[25]

Your mind is truly a complex aspect of your personhood. Curt Thompson's profound book, *Anatomy of the Soul*, offers Daniel Siegel's definition, "The mind is an embodied and relational process...that regulates the flow of energy and information."[26] Your brain is capable of thinking and feeling. Thompson further expounds, "your mind is embodied, which means it is housed in your physical self and depends on your body to function. Of course, the mind includes the brain, but other parts of your body play a role in the flow of energy and information."[27]

Ask yourself, "Where in my body am I experiencing this feeling, generated by my mind?" Sexual relating depends on your ability to think, feel. imagine and choose. With your mind, you form attachments, you experientially *know* others and are known in turn by them. You are created with the desire to be pursued, chosen, known, valued and loved—in general, and as a sexual man or woman. In one of his sermons, Pastor Tim Keller spoke to all of our fears and yearnings:

> *"To be loved, but not known is comforting but superficial,*
>
> *To be fully known but not loved, is our worst nightmare,*
>
> *But to be fully known and fully loved, that is our deepest yearning."[28]*

Your mind thinks and provides willpower. Remember in Chapter 3 when we discussed your broader sexual identity and emphasized your values and the alternatives and choices you make around them? This is your mind at work. You choose to allow God to change your heart, and with willpower, you cooperate with God by obedience. Willpower alone won't bring sexual integrity and wholeness, but obediently choosing to be transformed in your heart and mind by God's sexual guidelines can work wonders.

> *"Don't copy the behavior and customs of this world, but let God transform you into a new person by changing the way you think..." Romans 12:2a (NLT)*

When our minds began to objectify a sister or brother, or to allow those sexual cues in the environment to lead us to selfish lust, we can choose what we want to think about. In adding the word "sexual" to the following biblical verse, you can more clearly see the importance of the choices you can make with your mind.

> "We demolish <u>sexual</u> arguments and every <u>sexual</u> pretension that sets itself up against the knowledge of God, and we take captive every <u>sexual</u> thought to make it obedient to Christ." II Corinthians 10:5 ["sexual" added for emphasis]

God wants us to enjoy our sexual feelings and appreciate our ability to be sexually attracted and aroused. God also wants to help us be wise and mature in how we allow ourselves to think when it comes to sex. Our memories have stored up sexual images and thoughts that impact our sexuality, and God can help us erase or change some of those sexual images (often gotten from porn). Our minds are conditioned by our sexual experiences and desires, so that our minds can be filled with distortions as well as godly images. The Great Physician can help heal traumas, forgive mistakes, get rid of a porn-riddled thought-life and help you mature sexually. Sexual integrity and wholeness isn't a destination, it's a daily journey full of choices you make with your minds and your hearts.

Your Heart

> "Above all else, guard you heart, for everything you do flows from it." Proverbs 4:23

> "My body and my mind may become weak, but God is the strength of my heart and my portion forever." Psalm 73:76 (NCV)

The heart is the most profound dimension of our human soulfulness—expressed through our minds and bodies. It becomes the dwelling place of the Holy Spirit and can have a direct impact on your values and how you live out your sexual journey. Christian philosopher James K.A. Smith emphasizes, "What if, instead of starting with the assumption that human beings are thinking things, we started from the conviction that human beings are first and foremost *lovers*? What if the center and seat of the person is found not in the heady regions of the intellect, but in the gut-level regions of the heart?"[29] Smith further explains that men and women aren't simply what they think, but are ultimately motivated to create a deeper meaning and identity by what they *love* because "it is our loves that orient us toward some ultimate end or *telos*."[30]

> "I give you a new command: Love each other. You must love each other as I have loved you. All people will know that you are my followers if you love each other." John 13: 34-35 (NCV)
>
> "God is love. Those who live in love live in God, and God lives in them. We love because God first loved us." I John 4:16b, 19 (NCV)

When we talk about the Creative Trinity emphasizing intimacy through the creation of sexuality, the stage is set for a dynamic within the heart - an interplay between identity and intimacy. The more confused or conflicted I am about my true identity and settle for a false self, the more difficulty I'll experience in my intimacy. The more barriers I experience in my intimacy, the more physically one-dimensional I'll tend to be in my sexuality. It is in the *heart* that one truly experiences the freedom to love and to love well sexually—and this must start with the experience of God's powerful love.

Poet-pastor Craig Barnes provides a favorite quote related to identity and intimacy: "The secret to intimacy with another person is discovering the sufficiency of God's love without that person. It is the only way we are ever free to give love to another human being who can never meet the needs of our souls."[31] Truly experiencing God's love, enables us to love others and to find our true selves.

So, if you want to experience God's gift of sexual wholeness and purity, you'll have to let him transform your heart and identity as you find your true self—and as you allow God's love to *transform* your social and erotic sexuality. A heart-motivated sexual purity can then emerge. Sexual purity often gets a bad rap because it's simplistically used as a goal to be attained by repressing one's libido and refusing to engage in sinful sexual behavior. Look up a better definition of what "pure" means. Actually, to be "pure" is to feel clean and free, to have healthy God-directed heart attitudes, to enjoy a clarity in understanding and incorporating godly values, and to be free from toxic heart attitudes and anything that might contaminate the enjoyment of your sexuality. It's a "heart" thing.

> "Blessed are the [sexually] pure in heart, for they shall see and experience God's [sexual] freedom and joy." Matthew 5: 8 (DER paraphrase)

Your sexuality can be contaminated by your heart. You were designed with a heart with a longing for completion. This is accomplished through your social and erotic sexuality. Ultimately, only God can fulfill those longings, but most singles yearn for special love in their lives. Satan, the master of deception, doesn't only employ your bodies when he tempts you to engage in harmful choices. He wants to distort your hearts and your loves, too. Pay attention to those intuitive "catches" in your conscience, indicating that something's wrong, and listen for the Holy Spirit's leading. When you seek a personal relationship with God through Jesus Christ, the Bible will help transform your heart and mind. Amazingly, we can become like Christ: kind, patient, unselfish and loving.

Heart Attitudes Shape Behavior

In a fascinating way, your heart and mind are interwoven and shape your behavior. Scripture speaks to this, calling it a "heart attitude" or the "spirit of your mind", often addressing the heart and mind together.

> *"Search me, God, and know my heart; test me and know my anxious thoughts. See if there is any offensive way in me." Psalm 139:23-24a*

> *"For the Word of God is alive and active…; it judges the thoughts and attitudes of the heart." Hebrews 4:12*

> *"I pray that the eyes of your heart may be enlightened…"
> Ephesians 1:18a*

Oswald Chambers writes, "Thinking takes place in the heart, not in the brain. …The expression of thinking is referred to the brain and the lips because through these organs thinking becomes articulate. According to the Bible, thinking exists in the heart, and this is the region with which the Spirit of God deals."[32]

"Be renewed in the spirit of your mind, and put on the new self, which in the likeness of God has been created in righteousness and holiness of the truth." Ephesians 4:23-24 (NASB)

God uses each of our dimensions to bring us to a sexual maturity and wholeness. Hebrews 8:10 tells us that in the new covenant that Jesus brought, things will be markedly different than with the Old Testament covenant God made with the Israelites. This time it won't be about their behavior. This new covenant was written in Christ's blood and results in a changed heart and a renewed mind.

"But this is the new covenant I will make…, says the Lord: I will put my laws in their minds, and I will write them on their hearts. I will be their God, and they will be my people." Hebrews 8:10 (NLT)

Jesus understood how distorted, sinful and immature our hearts can be, especially sexually. Think about how your heart and mind together provide a conscience that makes you uncomfortable when you aren't being Christlike. God wants to work in your *heart-directed minds.* If you invite the Redeemer, he will renovate your sexual self, beginning with your heart attitudes.

"And the peace of God, which transcends all understanding, will guard your hearts and your minds in Christ Jesus." Philippians 4:7

Sexual Relating and Our Three-Dimensional Selves

The concept of a three-dimensional "soulfulness" or personhood is crucial to understanding sexuality and the Dance of the Sexes. When the Apostle Paul encourages the Corinthian church not to seek simple sexual fixes with the temple prostitutes, he tells them that their bodies are the residence for their hearts and the holy Spirit. He writes:

> "But you can't say that our bodies were made for sexual immorality. They were made for the Lord, and the Lord cares about our bodies…. Run from sexual sin! No other sin so clearly affects the body as this one does. For sexual immorality is a sin against your own body. Don't you realize that your body is a temple of the Holy Spirit, who lives in you and was given to you by God? You do not belong to yourself. 1 Cor. 6:13, 18-19 (NLT)

Paul helps us begin to understand that we can't divorce our sexuality from our spirituality. They couldn't just run down and get their bodily sexual fix from a temple prostitute. We are designed to practice chastity in our bodies (what we do), our minds (what we fantasize about and the choices we make) and our hearts (our values and loves).

Jesus challenged us to be careful with our sexuality. The Bible's word for "sin" means missing the mark, or falling short of God's plan for loving human interaction—of doing "stupid." With compassion and sadness, he posed the question: "What can anyone give in exchange for their soul?" (Mark 8:37) He realized how easy we could be enticed by Satan to forfeit the joy and fulfillment he designed us to experience with our total personhood— bodies, minds and hearts.

Sexual lust misses God's mark as it objectifies a brother or sister. It covets something that isn't ours to enjoy and disrespects what is ours to enjoy. Our sexual thought-life can be so destructive to healthy relationships.

> *"Anyone who even looks at a woman with lust in his eye has already committed adultery with her in his heart." Matthew 5:27–28 (NLT)*

Our Lord knew people could misuse their bodies with sexual hookups. But, his revolutionary teaching to the religious leaders of his day demonstrated how their minds and destructive fantasies could adulterate and contaminate their relationships—as easily as physically acting out. He recognized how we can all sadly do Stupid with body, *mind* and heart. Scripture emphasizes that we are to be careful so that we "do not wrong or cheat another Christian." (I Thess. 4:6 NCV) We can hurt and cheat our brothers and sisters by playing with their bodies, their emotions and their hearts.

Let's pretend: You're at a party and are getting turned on by that sexy person across the room. What if God brought that man or woman to the party so he or she could experience sexual respect, and healing from their past sexual abuse—and all you did was visually hit on him or her? Sexual wholeness is a 3-D way of life that reflects Jesus' heart of love and compassion.

One young man complained that I had destroyed his ability to comfortably lust when I encouraged him to look at women as three-dimensional. When he saw a woman with eye-catching female parts, he stated that it was hard to lust after her body when he asked himself, "I wonder if she knows Jesus?" When he gave her a real life, and took the time to really look at her as a fellow human being, he knew what he needed to do with his thought-life.

Your Christian brother or sister is not just a body. Guys, she isn't just great breasts or beautiful legs. She's a three-dimensional person – and maybe with gorgeous legs – who wants to be cherished and to have someone special guard her heart. Gals, he isn't just a cute butt or sexy smile. He's a person – maybe with a cute butt – who wants to be valued, and to find a soul mate to complete a yearning in his heart for true sexual fulfillment.

If we take the time to see each other in 3-D, it helps the Dance come alive, and helps you value, celebrate, and protect your own sexuality as well as the sexuality of those around you. You'll begin thinking with your heart and mind, rather than being led by your hormones. This is the essence of growing in 3-dimensional sexual maturity and wholeness.

> "Let us purify ourselves from everything that (sexually) contaminates body **and** spirit, perfecting (sexual) holiness out of reverence for God." 2 Cor. 7:1 (parentheses added)

CHAPTER TEN

Living Intimately from Your Heart – An Inside-Out Lifestyle

with Dr. Gary Barnes

Wouldn't it be great if guilt, fear and "Stop it!" could motivate godly change? Most of us can empathize with the poor bird a young lady once bought for companionship. To her dismay, not only did her parrot know how to speak—his language was much too colorful. One day, in utter frustration, she threatened, "One more dirty word and I'm putting you in the freezer!" Sure enough, he used one of his choice words, and into the freezer he went. Within twenty seconds he was pecking and scratching to be let out. He squawked, "I'll never say another dirty word again!" The woman had pity on him and let him out. After three months with no bad language, she asked him, "What changed your attitude?" to which the bird replied, "What in the world did that chicken do?!"

Several years ago, I was conducting a singles' workshop on sexuality. As I shared the topic with a Christian friend, his immediate response was, "Two hours on single sexuality? How many ways can you say don't?" I sadly reflected on this response, realizing that simplistic "don'ts" and trying to manage behaviors, won't foster loving stewardship of one's sexuality or meaningful intimacy. While threats may work for a while, external constraints won't motivate healthy sexual behavior over the long haul. The fear of being plucked and put in the freezer, like the chicken, won't insure lasting change. Your heart attitudes—your internal motivations—are what really count.

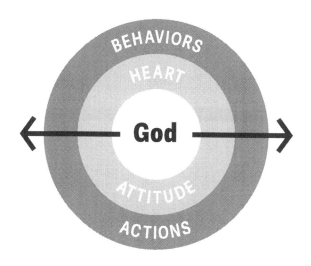

Living from the Inside Out

So often, Christians start on the outside circle of actions and try to abstain from assorted sexual behaviors so that they feel more "holy" and sexually pure and closer to God. This was the history of my own conservative Christian background. I had so many "don'ts" around various behavior—but not many practical guidelines. The Outside-In approach believes that regulating behavior will produce godlier attitudes that will hopefully bring us closer to God.

This approach doesn't necessarily produce sexual purity, as witnessed by our present Christian culture. Jesus confronted the Pharisees that a morality based on behaviors misses the deeper heart motivation of God's love and empowerment. Their values framework became legalism in which they were seeking to win God's favor. The sage theologian Brennan Manning pegs legalism so well: "The Pharisees falsified the image of God into an eternal small-minded bookkeeper whose favor could be won only by the scrupulous observance of laws and regulations. Religion became a tool to intimidate and enslave rather than liberate and empower."[33] Dear reader, I fear many of us grew up in a conservative Christian culture with our sexual morality based on sexual legalism centered mostly on what we didn't do.

Instead, God wants us to live from the inside out. Seeking God first will allow your heart to be transformed by the Holy Spirit, which over time, will produce more chaste behavior and the ability to value and celebrate your sexuality. Let's take a closer look at the three aspects of this lifestyle: God, heart attitudes, and behavior.

> *"Don't become so well-adjusted to your culture that you fit into it without even thinking. Instead, fix your attention on God. You'll be changed from the inside out." Romans 12:2 (MSG)*

God's Passion Power and "Belonging"

As with everything in the Christian experience, the process must start with your own personal relationship with God, found through Jesus as Savior. Jesus promises to transform your heart and life, giving you the power, through the Holy Spirit, to be sexually whole. We could call this passion power because in two powerful ways it will always trump simple willpower or guilt. First, passion power chastity is based on the belief that God wants what is best for us. Secondly, and just as important, the loving Trinity gives us the power to value, celebrate and protect our sexuality in a way that we never could without a godly passion power.

"So we tell others about Christ, warning everyone and teaching everyone with all the wisdom God has given us. We want to present them to God perfect (whole) in their relationship to Christ. That's why I work and struggle so hard, depending on Christ's mighty <u>power</u> that works within me." Colossians 1:28-29 (NLT)

For God is working in you, giving you the desire and the power to do what pleases him." Philippians 2:13 (NLT)

Jesus-followers must commit to understanding what God says is best for them. Sorting through and applying such questions as: "What does God say through the principles found in Scripture?" "What character traits and heart attitudes does he desire from you?" "How can those traits reflect his desire for you sexually?" You may never fully understand God's reasoning for all he asks of you, but pursuing God as a matter of first priority will help you learn to trust him—a trust that will anchor you, spiritually and sexually, as you move toward the outer circles of heart attitudes and behavior.

Our sinful nature leads us to adopt strategies for personal gain that prevent God's better intentions for us. C. S. Lewis wrote, "We are half-hearted creatures, fooling about with drink and sex and ambition when infinite joy is offered us, like an ignorant child who wants to go on making mud pies in a slum because he cannot imagine what is meant by the offer of a holiday at the sea ."[34]

"Wherever your treasure is, there the desires of your heart will also be." Matthew 6:21 (NLT)

Jesus always cut to the chase when he taught. Paraphrasing his teaching, "If your treasure is valuing, celebrating and protecting your sexuality, then the desires of your heart will enjoy the astonishing sexual economy I've designed for you." Theologian James K.A.. Smith emphasizes this inside-out personal transformation in his book, *You Are What You Love*: "Discipleship is more a matter of reformation than of acquiring information. The learning that is fundamental to Christian formation is affective and erotic, a matter or 'aiming' our loves, of orienting our desires to God and what God desires for his creation."[35]

This is so true with your sexuality. Smith further encourages that, "You can't think your way to new hungers."[36] The loving Trinity has to retrain your hunger and the desire of your heart. But the promise is there—if you build a relationship with God, he will take your selfish, disordered loves and give your heart and mind a passionate power, and you'll be able to fill your sexual story with integrity, love and wise choices.

> *"God did not give us a spirit that makes us afraid (of sex),*
> *but a spirit of (sexual) power and (sexual) love and (sexual)*
> *self-control." II Timothy 1:7 (NCV parentheses added)*

Another part of God's passion power is placing his children in community, where they can practice loving relationships. Singles cannot live out sexual integrity and fulfilling intimacy without their brothers and sisters. You need a safe place to experience love.

> *"Love is patient, love is kind. It does not envy, it does not*
> *boast, it is not proud. It does not dishonor others, it is not*
> *self-seeking, it is not easily angered, it keeps no records of*
> *wrongs. Love does not delight in evil but rejoices with the*
> *truth. It always protects, always trusts, always hopes, always*
> *perseveres." 1 Corinthians 13:4–7*

What a transformation God's love can bring: you become patient not pushy, not covetously lusting after and envying what is not yours; unselfishly seeking the best for those you're in relationship with, being honest about your sexual motives, and protecting the other person as you build trust and refuse to cast judgment for past sexual mistakes.

God begins your transformation with *belonging*. First, is a relationship with Truth with a capital "T"—Jesus Christ. He cares about helping you incorporate healthy sexual values in your lives that begins with Jesus and his "peeps." As you experience the love and testimony of a community (Belonging) living out God's truth, you'll stay on that Inside-out journey from the big "T" love relationship to incorporating his little "t" truths (Beliefs) into a transformed heart and mind.

Transformed Heart Attitudes and "Believing"

How exciting that an intimate relationship with God will transform your heart and mind. We move from "belonging" to Jesus and a Christian community into actively growing a belief system that guides us very practically.

> *"I will take away your stubborn heart and give you a new heart and a desire to be faithful. You will have only pure thoughts, because I will put my Spirit in you and make you eager to obey my laws and teachings" (Ezekiel 36:26–27 CEV).*

Your heart refers to the core of who you are, the control center of your three-dimensional self. Jesus tried to show the religious leaders of his time that actions like ceremonially washing their hands or the denial of certain foods wasn't as important as the need to change their hearts. He always stressed the importance of heart motivations—not just what you did or didn't do.

> *"Anything you eat passes through the stomach and then goes into the sewer. But the words you speak come from the heart—that's what defiles you." Matthew 15:17, 18 (NLT)*

Long ago, Saint Augustine gave us his personal story and his theological reflections on the human heart in his book, *Confessions*. After many unsuccessful attempts to manage his sexual urges, he understood that the human heart consists of conflicted loves, and that our hearts are restless until they find their rest in the God who made us for himself. He also emphasizes that the solution for our conflicted loves is not our own willpower but love itself. We must nurture, cultivate and protect a greater love that orders and displaces the lesser loves in our lives.

Here is where willpower comes in. We have to choose to believe and adopt God's value system. Remember in your Sexual Identity that an important piece of your pie was Alternatives and Choices based on the values framework you developed. If you ask God for his will, and seek his heart, he will honor you with a Christ-like attitude that will motivate effective sexual behavior. But, you must intentionally choose to follow God's sexual economy.

It's a collaborative process. You won't value and protect your brothers and sisters in Christ without passion power and a changed heart. And, God uses your ability to make choices to change your heart and steward your sexuality. Willpower must enter in and you must choose to accept God's invitation to follow his sexual plan. As you pursue Jesus, God's transformation of your heart will radically empower you to grow your desires into his desires.

"Work hard to show the results of your salvation, obeying God with deep reverence and fear. For God is working in you, giving you the desire and the power to do what pleases him." Philippians 2: 12b, 13 (NLT)

Alternatives and Wise Choices—"Behaving"

A heart motivated by God's desire will significantly impact your behavior. As you cultivate a more intimate relationship with him and become more intentional about conforming your heart to his, you'll be more successful at creating godly sexual behavior and become more intentional about making choices from your renewed heart.

This inside-out process works as you begin thinking with your heart and mind rather than being led by your hormones, emotions, and selfish desire. You'll become better at recognizing sinful behavior that keeps you from God's best. Your heart attitude and motivation can be profoundly changed and you'll be much less likely to find yourself one bad choice from sinful Stupid. Your Creator knows that your values are much more critical than your behavior. This inside-out voyage is the essence of growing in sexual maturity and wholeness.

"Create in me a (sexually) pure heart, O God, and renew a steadfast spirit within me." Psalm 51:10 (parenthesis added)

"A heart at peace gives life to the body…" Proverbs 14:30

If all you do is try to will yourself to abstain from certain sexual behavior and call that virginity, you'll end up without a true compass. That's why chastity and virginity are about so much more than physical behavior. Instead, virginity will become a lifestyle attitude from your heart that guides and protects you along your sexual journey – one that can truly impact your actions and behavior. Chastity and sexual purity are passion-powered by the patient, loving and self-controlled person you are in Jesus, not just what you do.

As Ronald Rolheiser wisely admonishes in his book, *The Holy Longing*, "sexuality lies at the center of the spiritual life. A healthy sexuality is the single most powerful vehicle there is to lead us to selflessness and joy. Just as unhealthy sexuality helps constellate selfishness and unhappiness as does nothing else. We will be happy in this life, depending on whether or not we have a healthy sexuality."[37]

The Slippery Slope of Sacred Sexuality

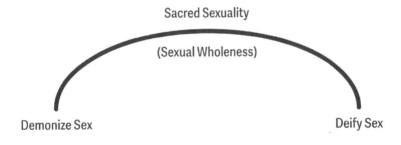

Sacred Sexuality

(Sexual Wholeness)

Demonize Sex   Deify Sex

The Slippery Slope of Sacred Sexuality

Let Dr. Barnes and I make some final observations on the inside-out process. This diagram, "The Slippery Slope of Sacred Sexuality"[38] demonstrates the difficulty of elevating our personal experience of sexuality to its designed love and sacredness. You will tend to slide in one of two different directions as you seek to achieve a balanced sacred sexuality. You may tend to demonize sex, or tend to deify sex. As sexual beings, if you demonize sex, you'll miss out on the greatness and goodness of sex. And, if you deify sex, you'll be in danger of making what God intended as a good thing, into an ultimate thing.

Let us explain: the first tendency is "demonizing" sex with legalistic repression, and in many ways making your sexuality something to fear. I grew up with a legalistic list of "do's and don'ts" that primarily consisted of "don'ts." It was sort of like this: "don't, don't, don't, don't, don't, do, don't, don't. . . ." And what was the one "do"? Something like kissing before marriage—but never after midnight. For me, the "don'ts" were externally imposed by the Church and the "sex police" (my parents, pastors, etc.). These "don'ts" weren't very effective in high school and college, especially as I gained more independence.

Advice such as "true love waits" is good; but without a practical explanation of how and why it waits, such encouragement will only last so long. It eventually breaks down without something deeper and more substantial driving it. This ineffective demonizing of sexuality brings shame and fear rather than godly discipline that promotes a healthy sexual wholeness.

Single adults with this approach to godliness are often surprised when their sexual urges overwhelm their genuine desire to make godly choices. Unfortunately, they've never learned to make godly choices motivated from God's heart and with his power. They've simply repressed their sexual feelings rather than accepting and disciplining them.

Think of repression as trying to choke your sexual desires into submission. Ultimately, this method is destined for failure. Stewarding your sexual drive means accepting them and learning to manage them, which is quite different than demonizing sex.

The second sabotage of a balanced sacred sexuality swings to the opposite extreme of "deifying" sex. This can result from attempts to meet nonsexual needs sexually. God gave us a need to be loved, touched, pursued, chosen, and accepted. Belonging to a believing community can help meet these nonsexual needs non-sexually. But so many Christian singles develop their relationships with nudity, orgasms, or mutual masturbation, but with little regard for the deeper issues of sacred sexuality. I cringe when people deify sex and call it a "need."

Deifying sex becomes an attempt to make a good thing an ultimate thing, and it can't bear the weight of that. These efforts to "elevate" sex and make it about pleasure and needs that must be satisfied, denigrates sex, as it misses the true purpose of sacred sexuality: intimacy. Deifying could be called "Christian hedonism," a lifestyle of indulgence in which everything but vaginal intercourse is considered acceptable behavior for unmarried couples. But this completely misses God plan for sexual wholeness

Another way to demonize or deify sex is to not have a deeper understanding of "social" and "erotic" sexuality (Chapter 6). God gave each of us erotic desire and the ability to be sexually attracted and aroused. To *demonize* this and repress your sexual energy is to forfeit a beautiful gift. But, to *deify* erotic sexuality is also limiting. If you deify the erotic, you won't experience "brother" and "sister" friendships with righteous flirting and the meeting of nonsexual needs. Jesus chided the religious rulers of his day for practicing a shallow, behavior-based morality that focused on outward appearances—entirely neglecting the more important matters of the heart. They weren't practicing an inside-out theology, and this would apply to all areas of their lives including their sexuality.

"What sorrow awaits you teachers of religious law and you Pharisees. Hypocrites! For you are careful to clean the outside of the cup and the dish, but inside you are filthy— full of greed and self-indulgence. … First, wash the inside of the cup and the dish, and then the outside will become clean, too." Matthew 23:25–26 (NLT)

Fellow Jesus-follower, in working toward a healthy inside-out sexual wholeness, you're going to face temptation on the slippery slope to either demonize or deify sex. It's important that you have an awareness of this, and that you're not on autopilot. To develop a personal sexual ethic, you must intentionally work with an inside-out approach to elevate sexuality back to its theological significance and to truly experience higher "sacred sexuality."

That's why an Inside-out approach is such good news: *A heart surrendered to God passion power produces godly behavior directed by him.* If the attitude of your heart is to please God and surrender ownership of yourself and your sexuality to his plan for your life, God's desire will become your desire. Your hearts will become one with an amazing sexual maturity and wholeness—a sacred sexuality that avoids slippery slopes.

"Then make my joy complete by being like-minded, having the same love, being one in spirit and of one mind." Philippians 2:2

CHAPTER ELEVEN

What Is a Soul Virgin and Why Become One?

I recently saw a magazine article that encouraged working with the two different parts of a single's social networking. The concept was that singles needed to set goals for their sex life and also for their dating life—sex as recreational and dating as romantic. One young woman related that in her college culture, you would sleep with a guy to determine if he was someone you wanted to date. How tragic! Sex has become recreation or a screening device. Our culture today, even our Christian culture, is sadly losing any type of meaningful sexual integrity, fidelity and genuine sexual intimacy.

We need a revolution, a dramatic change in values and attitudes, which champion God's guidelines for sexuality. In today's hook-up culture, a virgin is most often viewed as someone naive or missing out on something that's expected. But what if we viewed chastity as more than something to lose, or certain behavior we've chosen to abstain from?

Defining Virginity

Cassandra views herself as a virgin (technically). She's had oral sex with many former boyfriends and given hand jobs, but has never gone all the way.

John has hooked up with many guys, and wonders if that's a lesser sin than dating a woman and risking getting her pregnant.

Jimmy knows he's a virgin. He's never kissed or even intimately held his girlfriend, fearing the power of his sex drive, and not wanting to take advantage of her.

Mark and Tiffany have gone further than either intended. They've been naked together and had mutual orgasms, but feel good that they've never had "sex."

Kristi battles huge guilt over her sexual past, and wonders why a Christian guy would want to marry her. Her friend Jenny, influenced by pop culture, "doesn't see why virginity is that big a deal, anyway."

What do all these single adults have in common? They have distorted concepts of what virginity, sexual purity and godly celibacy, is all about. Like many singles, they've failed to understand God's design for true sexual intimacy through *soul virginity* and social sexuality. Remember the word "soul" is looking at humans as 3-dimensional with a body, mind and heart. So, "soul virginity" is a chastity that is lived out in the body, mind and heart with a godly discipline.

> *"No discipline seems pleasant at the time, but painful. Later on, however, it produces a harvest of (sexual) righteousness and peace for those who have been disciplined by it." Hebrews 12:11 (parentheses added)*

> *"Your love must be real. Hate what is evil, and hold on to what is good. Love each other like brothers and sisters. Give each other more honor than you want for yourselves." Romans 12:9-10 (NCV)*

The differing viewpoints about virginity are curious and bewildering. Many singles, having grown up in the post-sexual revolution of the 1980s and 90s, view virginity as old-fashioned. To many, having sex is a teenage rite of passage and more recreational. Others see chastity and saving genital sexuality till marriage as a standard to maintain, passed on from their parents or church, but never really grounded in their personal value system.

So much mythology and confusion exists. One young couple who maintained their physical virginity were upset when their friends accused them of making a big mistake. What if they got married and found out they were *sexually incompatible*? Shouldn't they find out before getting married? I asked if they had sexual chemistry, and they asserted, "Yes!" I looked at the young man and asked, "Do you have a penis?" "Yes," he stammered, surprised at such a direct question. So I asked the young woman, "Do you have a vagina?" to which she replied, "Yes." I reassured them that they were physically compatible and that true sexual compatibility was more about the state of their hearts and minds, rather than the size, shape, or utility of their bodies parts. I also encouraged them that great lovemaking could take time and effort to develop.

Our present sexual culture is difficult terrain for Christian singles to navigate. Many still believe God wants true love to wait, and that stewarding their sexuality within God's sexual guidelines is important. But, we need to go beyond "true love waits" to develop "why" and "how" true love waits. In this book, I want to help you embrace your sexuality and your capacity to be sexually attracted and aroused (horny)— to cast a broader vision of sexual single adults living in community and sharing a fun social sexuality and an heart-shaped chastity they never dreamed possible.

Chastity and delighting in your sexuality are, in some ways, tightly linked. In *Celibate Sex,* Abbie Smith writes, "Lust misuses sex for personal gratification, uprooting it from God's intended purpose. Chastity, then, should rightly involve a proper use of sex and stewarding of one's sexuality, rooted in God's intended purposes. My journey toward becoming chaste has been inseparable from my journey of becoming sexual…Understanding my sexuality has allowed me to be satisfied in my chastity, and understanding my chastity has allowed me to freely explore my sexuality."[39]

"I the Lord search the heart and examine the mind, to reward each person according to their conduct, according to what their deeds deserve." Jeremiah 17:10

Think with me, as the above Scripture emphasizes, our conduct and deeds reflect our hearts and minds. Physical virginity and sexual chastity in your *conduct* as a single person is important in God's eyes. But, it's a means to an end. Your chaste behaviors are based on and express your inside-out, heart and mind values; you are choosing to let God direct your conduct and guide you into true sexual wholeness and intimacy. Keeping penises out of vaginas is not some magic formula for sexual purity. Sexual Wholeness and chastity involve a much bigger picture.

Have you ever thought deeply about what virginity/chastity is NOT:

- NOT—God's method to ensure that single adults don't have sex
- NOT—An impossibility and unrealistic
- NOT—A goal to achieve
- NOT—Defined and maintained by refraining from certain sexual behavior
- NOT—Something that once lost can never be reclaimed

The Virginity Distortion and the Purity Cult

Often, when I ask a Christian couple who are dating, what, if anything, they're doing sexually, they reply with everything (often with oral sex, and mutual masturbation resulting in orgasms) *but having sex*. Wow, so much sexual hypocrisy and confusion exists even with Christian singles! One young woman felt so guilty about her sexual past. When her brother and future sister-in-law chose to wait until their wedding day to kiss, she was miserable. After the wedding, her new sister-in-law, seeing the guilt her husband's sister was feeling, confessed that she and her new husband had oral sex before their wedding day—but they'd never kissed.

A woman client told me that technically she was a still a virgin because no man had ever ejaculated inside her. She believed that she hadn't crossed that virginal boundary because becoming one flesh meant exchanging fluids and planting seed. In the early 60's, theologian Harvey Cox coined the word, "promiscuous virgins"[40] to describe those who did everything but have sexual intercourse.

Where did we lose a proper understanding of chastity? How has this promiscuous "virginity" come to exist? I think much of this is because our definition of sexual purity was built on the Virginity Distortion or what I have labeled the Purity Cult. Maybe it's an overstatement, but conservative Christianity has created a toxic distortion in the way it has dealt with sexuality, and in particular, the way it has chosen to make sexual guidelines simply about behavior, performance, reward and punishment. I deliberately call this a cult since a cult can be defined as a religious group with a belief system that is false or dangerous.

When I write about the Virginity Distortion or the Purity Cult, I'm addressing much more than the Purity Movement of the 90's—though that did bring to the forefront the flaws in the framework of our Christian sexual values. In their book, *Talking Back to Purity Culture,* Rachel Welcher and Scott Sauls points out the toxic effects of the purity morality with its idolization of virginity, downplaying feminine sexuality or overemphasizing modesty and the need for girls to take the lead in maintaining sexual purity. Men too were confused about sexual desire—were they sex fiends constantly fighting their own lust? And sadly, many populations were never addressed: those with same-sex attraction, infertility or sexual trauma, or those who'd lost their virginity.[41]

I'm reminded of Jesus's warning to the Pharisees,

> *"The things you teach are nothing but human rules. You have stopped following the commands of God, and you follow only human teachings." Mark 7:7b- 8 (NCV).*

Theologian Brennan Manning, writes of the danger of legalistically focusing on managing behaviors and missing God's love and creativity. "Instead of expanding our capacity for life, joy, and mystery, religion often contracts it. Pharisees invest heavily in extrinsic religious gestures, rituals, methods, and techniques, breeding allegedly holy people who are judgmental, mechanical, lifeless, and as intolerant of others as they are of themselves."[42]

God's sexual economy and values framework is deep and positive, not full of fearful human rules that work to prohibit specific behaviors. The wonderful Trinity created us in their image; our masculinity and femininity with sexual desires should foster and empower intimate sexual attitudes and interactions. Human sexuality is an important part of God's love story.

Therefore, I don't just blame the more recent Purity Movement for distortions; I see this shallow and distorted sexual morality going clear back beyond the Victorian era to St. Augustine, and flowing from the early church to the present. A sexual legalism evolved with the Church viewing sex negatively as shameful or dangerous with much silence and repression. The church's shallow and ineffective "Carrot or the Stick" approach to implementing sexual values has, in the present Christian culture, destructively turned into a distorted view of chastity and virginity. Because of this emphasis on banning behavior rather than creating lovingly unselfish hearts, in a sad and ineffective way our evangelical Christian singles have come to define chastity one way: *refraining from penis-in-vagina intercourse*. Scripture warns us that rules for regulating behavior can seem godly, but aren't effective unless they're accompanied by the motivation of a right heart.

> *"These rules may seem wise because they require strong devotion, pious self-regulation, and severe bodily discipline. But they provide no help in conquering a person's evil desires (Stupid)."* Colossians 2:23 (NLT)

"Carrot or the Stick" morality is based on if you're a good boy or girl, you get rewarded (a great sex life in marriage) and if you're a bad girl or boy, you get slapped/punished with God's stick (a bad sex life in marriage or perhaps an STD). A sexual culture built on what you're trying *not* to do becomes anxiously fearful, shame-based, and intolerantly judgmental. Myths and distortions abound: "If I, as a woman, don't dress modestly, I'm being a Jezebel and harming my poor Christian brothers." One woman asked me, "Am I required to morally babysit my Christian brothers?!" Or, "Sexual desire and attraction must be avoided, as it always leads to sinful objectification and harmful lust." Or, "Sexual mistakes will ruin any chance of having a great marriage and sex life."

I sadly remember a Christian speaker during the Purity Movement telling teens, "Your sexuality is like a Kleenex. If you let many partners blow their noses on it, it can never be the same." What a terrible metaphor. I view sexuality as this beautiful Monogrammed Handkerchief and God saying, "Precious child, bring your soiled handkerchief to me. I am going to wash it and iron it and restore it in ways you never thought possible."

> *"Where God's love is, there is no fear, because God's perfect love drives out fear. It is punishment that makes a person fear, so love is not made perfect in the person who fears."* I John 4:18 (NCV)

I hope you can see that a morality based on punishment, rather than love, doesn't motivate that well and is seldom effective. Rather than shame and fear, remember from our Inside-Out chapter that God motivates and empowers us through our sense of "belonging" to Jesus and an obedience that radiates from love. This relationship develops our "believing", which can powerfully shape our "behaving." God does create a godly sorrow when you violate his sexual guidelines, but he motivates more often by love and casting a vision of sexual wholeness.

If we look at the true *definition of chastity* we see an inside-out process of heart attitudes and unselfish behavior being called to our attention—going much beyond one physical prohibition and the ineffective carrot or the stick morality.

Jesus called the religious leaders on the carpet in Matthew 5:28 for their sexual hypocrisy.

"You think that not committing physical adultery is the way you keep from sinful sexual interactions, but I tell you that continually looking on and objectifying a person with lustful thoughts also adulterates and contaminates your relationships; your mind and heart have forfeited their sexual integrity." (DER Paraphrase)

"Let there be no sexual immorality, impurity, or greed among you. Such sins have no place among God's people." Ephesians 5:3 (NLT)

Going back to the purity culture's beliefs and practices—am I against purity rings and pledges of chastity? Not really, but I want the pledges not to be solely about achieving the goal of maintaining one's physical virginity. We need to paint a bigger picture of chastity that's not defined by banning one behavior and making it an idol. As Christians, we need to create a sexual values framework that is based on God's character and guidelines and empowered by the Holy Spirit.

"Love is patient and goes slowly, love is kind with a gentle helpfulness, love is humbly self-confident—not having a need to envy or boast; love honors and respects others, love is never selfishly seeking its own gratification, love is understanding and not easily angered, love forgives and doesn't keep a record of wrongs." I Corinthians 13: 4-5 (DER paraphrase)

I tell singles that if their goal is trying not to sleep with their girlfriend or boyfriend, they're in deep trouble. Virginity must radiate from the redeemed heart. It isn't a goal, but a way of life in Christian community. Living out sexual integrity and chastity is a process with many daily choices, not an outcome to be achieved.

The Old Testament Significance of Virginity

The two predominant Hebrew words for "virgin" in the Old Testament are derived from root words meaning "to separate" or "to hide." To separate or hide something was to set it apart as special, unique, or valuable. God created our sexuality with profound purpose and the potential for creating intimacy. The process of separating or hiding was intended to protect and honor its value, much like hiding precious jewelry in a safe. The veils "hiding" the faces of Hebrew women (and now Muslim women) were worn, in part to symbolize this protected chaste status and a woman's inaccessibility to all but her husband (whether present or future).

Our culture's idea of virginity is vastly different. Currently, the culture places a premium on the free expression of erotic love with no restraint. A virgin is someone who at best "hasn't scored yet" or at worst is an outright social outcast.

Virginity with an "Attitude"

As I was working with a team to evolve some of the concepts of this book, we deliberately stayed away from defining three-dimensional soul virginity as a physical act or imposing right or wrong behavior. Our working definition of **sexual wholeness** and three-dimensional **soul virginity** is: **Valuing, Celebrating, and Protecting** your own sexuality and that of your brothers and sisters! Each of these three words were carefully chosen. <u>Value</u>: to honor something with great worth, to treat as special and precious. <u>Celebrate</u>: to revel in and enjoy. <u>Protect</u>: to look after and guard; to shield from danger and keep safe.

Soul virginity is so much more than abstaining from sex. C.K. Chesterton wrote: "Chastity does not mean abstention from sexual wrong; it means something flaming, like Joan of Arc."[43] Joan of Arc had the boldness and courage to counter her culture and live her life as a beacon—even into martyrdom.

> *"God did not give us a spirit that makes us afraid (of our sexuality) but a spirit of (sexual) power and (sexual) love and (sexual) self-control." II Timothy 1:7 (NCV) (parentheses added)*

I hold with highest regard the words "bold" and "courageous" when defining a sexually pure lifestyle. Bold people are willing to be different, and live courageously by their values. Purity is not naive innocence; many bold and courageous choices need to be made in order to be refined and become Christ-like.

Abstinence isn't fearing your sexuality and abstaining from social sexual intimacy. Abstinence is choosing God's way to freedom and sexual wholeness by abstaining from selfish lust and destructive sexual behavior that can hurt our brothers and sisters and contaminates what God desires for us as sexual beings. It's a costly obedience as a single person to choose not to engage in genital sexuality and learn to steward horny wisely.

> *"God wants you to be holy and to stay away from sexual sins. He wants each of you to learn to control your own body in a way that is holy and honorable. Don't use your body for sexual sin like the people who don't know God. Also, don't wrong or cheat another Christian in this way...." I Thessalonians 4:3-6a (NCV)*
>
> *"There's more to sex than mere skin on skin. Sex is as much a spiritual mystery as physical fact. As written in Scripture,*

'The two become one.' Since we want to become spiritually one with the Master, we must not pursue the kind of sex that avoids commitment and intimacy, leaving us more lonely than ever—the kind of sex that that can never 'become one.' There is a sense in which sexual sins are different from all others. In sexual sin, we violate the sacredness of our own bodies, these bodies that were made for God-given and God-modeled love, for 'becoming one' with another. Or didn't you realize that your body is a sacred place, the place of the Holy Spirit? Don't you see that you can't live however you please, squandering what God paid such a high price for? I Corinthians 6:16-19 (MSG)

As single adults, 3-D soul virginity frees up Christian brothers and sisters to focus on pursuing rich Connecting relationships with the opposite and same-sex friends, growing a few of those opposite-sex relationships into mature romantic Coupling and perhaps one of them (in time) into the fulfilling marital relationship of Covenanting and marriage. Soul virginity gives deep meaning to who you are a sexual person. Unlike animals in heat, you can choose to intimately connect with someone. Please realize that in this book that I'm addressing singles with different sexual preferences and direction of attraction. Whether gay, straight, bi, queer, trans or whatever label that you've chosen, God calls his single children to be sexually chaste.

As you steward your erotic sexuality, it's possible to lose your sexual integrity through your thought-life or a heart that has lost its Christ-like power and desire. We sin 3-dimensionally but let's be honest—you often do the most damage when you physically act out sexually and allow your body to engage in sinful Stupid choices. The physical dimension of your sexual personhood will take a special discipline if you want to live out God's loving design for sexual wholeness. Though keeping penises out of vaginas can't be the definition of chastity, stewarding genital sexuality and what to do with sexual desires is critical. You will need God's Passion Power and the help of your community.

> *"Oh, that my actions would consistently reflect your (sexual) decrees! Then I will not be ashamed when I compare my (sex) life with your commands. As I learn your righteous (sexual) regulations, I will thank you by living as I should (with sexual integrity)." Psalm 119:5-7 (NLT parentheses added)*

Can I be a Soul Virgin—Even if I'm No Longer a Physical Virgin?

One young man asked me if he could be one of those "recycled" virgins. Another inquired about becoming a "reconstituted" virgin. Some label a person with a sexual past who returns to chastity as a "secondary" virgin. None of these create the hope and healing God wants to bring to your sexual story. This is why I coined the concept of a "soul" virgin. God calls all of His children to chastity, no matter what their sexual past or identity holds—whether they're single or married. A caring heavenly Father wants to shape your present sexual story and identity.

Regardless of whether you're a physical virgin or not, you can commit to soul virginity by choosing to "hide" or "separate" the more intimate expressions of your erotic sexual behavior from this point forward. This process will also serve to re-create and restore your sense of sexual worth and integrity. Incidentally, married couples are called to be soul virgins, too. Once married, the vow of a soul virgin requires the same attitude, and may be expressed something like this: "I vow before God from this point forward not to give away my gift of true sex to anyone other than my spouse until 'death do us part'." My wife, Catherine, and I are each other's soul virgins. We have vowed to remain faithful to each other until the end of our lives on this earth. No matter your marital status, every Christian can make such a vow to pursue sexual wholeness by choosing a life of sexual purity in their heart, mind and body.

"But when he the Spirit of truth comes, he will guide you into all the truth…" John 16:13a

"Trust in the Lord with all your heart; do not depend on your own (sexual) understanding. Seek his will in all you do, and he will show you which (sexual) path to take." Proverbs 3:5-6 (NLT, parentheses added)

Becoming a Soul Virgin—Some Practical Suggestions

Just because you aren't (physically) a virgin anymore isn't a cause for guilt and despair. This can be an occasion for humble surrender to your heavenly Father with appropriate remorse and a lifestyle change. If this is your situation, and you find yourself plagued by guilt from your past, I encourage you to hang with me until chapter 18. God's emergency room is open for you, and there you'll find hope and healing in the hands of the Great Physician.

Such a visit to God's sexual ER—will not only restore you to God's design for sexuality as a soul virgin, but will also restore your sexual integrity. You can become "separated" once again with a renewed dedication to reserve true sex for your future mate. Though the consequences (STDs, sadness, unwanted pregnancies, etc.) may remain, remember that there isn't a sexual sin that God can't forgive. If you seek the Lord, he will restore your soul virginity and sexual purity.

Many of the Old Testament patriarchs made vows to the Lord and created monuments by which to remember them. These monuments served to hold them accountable to those vows. In a similar manner, you may need to create such a "monument" when making a pledge of soul virginity: "Heavenly Father, I am committed to understanding and following your heart regarding loving sexual intimacy—from this point forward I am choosing not to give away my gift of true sex until marriage to my spouse, or my marriage to Christ at his coming." Perhaps wearing something symbolic, such as a necklace, ring or bracelet, may help you remember your vow and hold you accountable when you're tempted to forget. Ask your community of friends to encourage, pray for, and hold you accountable. Keep remembering your vow to chastity is a way of life you are embracing, not a goal to achieve.

A brief word of caution to those who are Coupling and are currently sexually active: as you choose to become soul virgins, continue enjoying your relationship while wisely disciplining your sexual desires and erotic sexual behaviors. Alter your lifestyle to support godly changes—but don't stop all romantic and erotic relating. I've worked with many couples who completely "turned off" their sexuality during Coupling, only to later encounter great difficulty "turning it back on" in marriage.

Jack and Bridget, though previously sexually active, resolved not to share true sex for the last six months of their engagement. Rather than simply avoiding the temptation by sleeping separately, they chose to continue spending nights together. Jack said he "willed himself" to avoid arousal or to act out on his desires. Bridget was cautious to never arouse Jack. Both basically became asexual to ensure they made it to their wedding night without having sexual intercourse again. They came in for counseling several months into their marriage, revealing they were having trouble reclaiming their erotic feelings for each other. Together, we had to work through their repression and the scars they experienced from it as they discovered sexual intimacy within God's economy.

For God is working in you, giving you the desire and the power to do what pleases him." Philippians 2:13 (NLT)

In this and many other situations, the Holy Spirit can help you follow God's sexual economy and live out the freedom of soul virginity. Couples may need to quit living or sleeping together and still keep the chemistry and connection in a way that Jack and Bridget did not. The kissing and sensual connecting needs to be engaged in while setting healthy boundaries. You can gauge when you're aroused in a romantic relationship or in life in general. Which triggers need to be avoided? Alcohol? Being alone, without any accountability? Your phone or social media? Feeling lonely and looking for intimacy or attention? Let God help you make wise choices to find true intimacy and sexual integrity.

As I was writing this chapter, a young woman with much sexual brokenness allowed me share her story. I thought it a powerful way to end this chapter:

"I grew up around a sex-oriented family. At a very young age my virginity, both my body and my heart, was taken from me. After that, every relationship I had was based on sex. It became so normal to me, as that was all I knew—that in relationship after relationship a piece of me was given away. As I grew older, I was so ashamed of how many people I'd slept with, and thought if anyone really knew me, they would reject me. I'd cry in my room and think, after everything I've done, I 'll never be accepted or loved. At 16, I found out that wasn't true! I gave my life to God, and Jesus accepted and loved me with open arms. I was still ashamed, because I thought I could never be pure since I wasn't a (physical) virgin. One night, God spoke to me and said, 'I gave you that gift of virginity, and even though it was taken away from you, I will restore it and make you like new.' I knew then, that even though I wasn't a (physical)virgin, I could walk in sexual purity, and that God was making me into the woman he always intended me to be."

CHAPTER TWELVE

The Art of Stewardship, Costly Obedience
& the Benefits of Chastity

with Michael Todd Wilson

How exciting that God has given each of us the astounding gift of our sexuality with our masculinity, femininity and powerful sexual desires. And—how awesome that he is personally developing that gift in each of us to be the man or woman He intends, enhancing all of our relationships in unselfishly intimate ways. Sometimes your sex drive, sexual attractions and aches may seem like a curse, but our wise Creator can provide the grace and power to manage your sexuality in a way that enhances your life journey and blesses your brothers and sisters.

> *"Each of you should use whatever gift you have received (especially your sexuality) to serve others, as faithful stewards of God's grace in its various forms."* I Peter 4:10 (parenthesis added)

> *"...in humility value others above yourselves, not looking to your own (sexual) interests but each of you to the (sexual) interests of the others."* Philippians 2:3b,4 (parentheses added)

In developing further the importance and rewards "3-D soul virginity" and the responsibility of stewarding sexual attraction, let's look at one couple's journey. Jason and Courtney have enjoyed getting to know each other and have spent much time one-on-one developing their romance and talking through their expectations for a potential marriage. One Saturday together, Jason disclosed that he sensed God calling him into full-time ministry overseas. This surprised Courtney. After several discussions and some heartfelt prayers, Courtney concluded that she doesn't feel this same call. The two came to the sad conclusion that their paths were headed in different directions. They decided to do the emotionally difficult work of breaking up and hoped to maintain an ongoing friendship.

In a mature and godly manner, Jason and Courtney treated each other as soul virgins—even during their commitment in a Coupling relationship. Each respected that the other might not be his or her Adam or Eve. They cuddled, kissed and enjoyed some erotic behavior, while limiting others, respecting the godly limit of saving true sex for marriage. In showing this concern for each other, they helped each other grow in maturity throughout their relationship.

When Courtney became engaged to Seth a few years later, Seth wanted to invite Jason to their wedding. Courtney was confused. Why would Seth want Jason there? Seth responded that he wanted to shake Jason's hand, and personally thank him for his contribution to Courtney's life. He wanted to express his appreciation for the godly way he had participated in their courtship. He wasn't happy if he thought about them making out and the intimacy they'd shared. But he knew that Courtney was a better woman for having dated Jason. Courtney was touched as Seth shared this and was glad she had saved true sex for Seth.

Jason, Courtney, and Seth refused to allow the opinions of others or the culture in which they lived to define their sexuality. They built their values framework on God's sexual guidelines.

The Art of Stewardship

Learning to be a wise steward of your sexual urges and aches can revolutionize your sexual journey. We don't often use the concept of steward in our modern culture. A steward is one who *manages* and is responsible for something—and often that something is owned by someone else. Effective stewardship involves accountability for the things a person has been put in charge of.

Jason understood Courtney's value as a woman created in the image of God. He also recognized the importance of stewarding that relationship. You may remember the story from Matthew 25:14–30 about the servants who were given various amounts of money to hold while their master was away. Upon his return, each was held accountable for how faithfully and wisely they managed what God had given them. From this parable flow three truths we can apply in living out God's purpose for our lives and sexuality:

1. God created everything and has graciously entrusted things to us.
2. Therefore, God owns everything, yet he makes us stewards of his possessions.
3. God's desire is for us to (someday) return his possessions back to him, having wisely helped them realize their true potential.

This parable employs the example of money. But it certainly applies to other things we're to steward: possessions, time, relationships—and our sexuality. We belong to God and have been bought at a price.

"Don't you realize that your body is the temple of the Holy Spirit, who lives in you and was given to you by God? You do not belong to yourself, for God bought you with a high price. So you must honor God with your body." I Corinthians 6:19-20 (NLT)

Your sexuality—body, mind and heart—belong to God. We are privileged to steward it during the span of our lives. Our hormonal desires, sex organs, emotional longings—indeed, all of our sexuality—belongs to God.

"Do not offer the (sexual) parts of your body to serve sin, as things to be used in doing evil. Instead, offer yourselves to God as people who have died and now live. Offer the (sexual) parts of your body to God to be used in doing good." Romans 6:13 (NCV) (parentheses added)

Let's be more specific. Guys, your penis doesn't belong to you. It belongs to God and your future mate. It's loaned to you to guard, and its size does not determine your manhood. Gals, your vagina and clitoris don't belong to you. They're given to you to wisely manage. How sad in that singles indifferently share this gift with those who don't value them or desire to help them grow into the special sexual person God created them to become.

Sexual theologian Stanley Grenz encourages us not to turn stewardship into a legalistic effort not to do certain things. "Our stewardship moves beyond the negative, beyond mere avoidance of sexual sin, to include the positive aspects as well, for we are to glorify God in our bodies (I Corinthians 6:20). …we are to employ our sexuality to fulfill God's intention, namely, that as sexual creatures we actualize the divine design, reflect the nature of God! And thereby bring glory to the Creator."[44]

Grenz makes an important point. Our loving Creator is less concerned about what you abstain from and avoid; rather he desires to promote the bold *spirit* of abstinence. Our Savior doesn't wants to let his light permeate your life and drive out the darkness—an inside-out process. Wise stewardship reflects God's "divine design" for our sexuality.

God has graciously made provision for you to celebrate and share your sexuality, both socially and romantically. His desire is for you to steward your sexuality to help develop another's true sexual potential as Jason did with Courtney. I prefer the word "steward" rather than "discipline." The concept of "disciplining" our sexuality can seem more like the chore of managing our behavior, while "stewarding" can lift us to a positive place of loving others and promoting intimate relationships.

As you think through the role of a steward and your role in stewarding your sexuality, I've chosen three words to help describe it: *Prize, Protect, and Promote.*

> **Prize**: *A steward values what has been entrusted to him or her and sees that it as unique, important and special. God's gift of sexuality is truly something that should be Prized!*

> **Protect**: *A steward views his or her responsibility for as something precious to safeguard. God has practical guidelines (a sexual economy) that a steward follows to protect this prized gift of sexuality.*

177

__Promote:__ A steward supports and sponsors what he or she has been given, recognizing its distinct significance, and sharing that value with others. God has commissioned you to promote sexual wholeness within your relationships and community.

Can you see the bigger picture of why God created sexuality for you? He wants to show you the importance of love and intimate relationships. Much more is at stake here than horny feelings, recreational sex, or "falling in love." God designed our love stories to tell his great love story (Ephesians 5:21-32). It's the love story of all love stories: The God of the universe pursues his creation with white-hot passion and desires a genuine love relationship with each of us. It's a love story that transcends every human love story pale in comparison.

How should this affect the stewardship of your sexuality? Faithfulness and chastity are the cornerstones, because Christ asks us to remain faithful until he returns for the "wedding feast" (see Matthew 22:1–14; Revelation 19:6–9). True sex between a husband and his wife reflect God's exclusive love for us—pure, priceless, and protected. If marriage is to be a living parable of greater love story, every Christian single should faithfully wait for their future soul mate to engage in "true sex."

As Christian singles, how you live your life has an impact on the quality of what you portray to a lost world—a world desperate for real intimacy. This is yet another reason why soul virginity matters, and why sexual infidelity in the Christian community damages the message of the gospel itself. Jesus taught that all believers are *light* to a culture desperate for his love and enlightenment.

"You are the light of the world. …Let your (sexual) light shine before men in such a way that they may see your good works (sexual wholeness), and glorify your Father who is in heaven." Matthew 5:14a, 16 (parentheses added)

Shoshandra has chosen to keep her relationship to Malik close, but to wait for true sex. William, despite his same-sex attraction, has chosen not to sexualize his friendship with Robert. Jake and Judith have set and reset boundaries in the sexual expression of their romance. Stewardship demands many courageous and unselfish choices! The truth is, the life you live tells some version of Jesus' love story. Will you tell it faithfully in the way you choose to live out your sexually?

Valuing and Protecting Sexual Purity

My precious Christian sons and daughters sometimes exclaim, "Why am I bothering to guard my chastity when my friends – and probably even my future mate – is out there having sex? It's not fair!" My gentle reply is that their frustration is normal, but their attitude is shortsighted. Hebrews 11 relates how Moses chose not to "enjoy the pleasures of sin for a season" as he left Egypt behind and pressed toward the Promised Land. If we believe that God is smart and loving, then we can trust that he wants the best for us.

"I've been painting pictures of Egypt, leaving out what it lacks,

The future feels so hard and I want to go back,

But the places that used to fit me, cannot hold the things I've learned,

And those roads were closed off to me, while my back was turned."

Sarah Groves, Painting Pictures of Egypt

God's not punishing you by asking you to guard your sexuality. If God believed that true sex was meant for relationships apart from the covenantal bond of marriage, he'd have prescribed that for you. Instead, we should feel compassion for those indulging in sex outside of his guidelines, because in making that choice, they're missing God's best. Soul virgins are rewarded by the deeply abiding presence of Almighty God and are fulfilled by a level of intimacy with him that can leave others shaking their heads in confusion.

The Discipline of Soul Virginity and Chastity in Community

Although soul virginity begins in single adulthood, the concept applies in married, single-again, or widowed life as well. This means the pledge of soul virginity is **a lifetime commitment**. Sexual integrity doesn't just occur. This journey requires courageous choices and a devotion to seeking God's will for our sexuality. Oswald Chambers, wisely exhorts, "Purity is not innocence, it is much more. Purity is the outcome of sustained spiritual sympathy with God. We have to grow in purity."[45]

> "But among you there must not be even a hint of sexual immorality, or of any kind of impurity, or of greed, because these are improper for God's holy people. Nor should there be obscenity, foolish talk or course joking, which are out of place, but rather thanksgiving." Ephesians 5:3-4

All Christians should live out their journey of sexual chastity within community. "Chastity, then, is a basic rule of community, but it is not a mere rule. It is also a discipline. Chastity is something you do, it is something you practice. It is not only a state—the state of being chaste—but a disciplined, active undertaking that we do as part of the Body. It is not the mere absence of sex but an active conforming of one's body to the arc of the Gospel."[46] I strongly believe that Christians need to live out their sexuality in community and should confront one another when one falls short of God's best. Sexual integrity and wholeness is a communal goal.

"No discipline seems pleasant at the time, but painful. Later on, however, it produces a harvest of righteousness and peace for those who have been trained by it." Hebrews 12:11

I'm alarmed at the loss of chastity within the Christian community, and our inability to value and protect it. This is especially clear when I see newlyweds who are already having affairs. I asked one young man if he'd ever practiced the discipline of chastity. His reply: "I tried just to sleep with the girl I was dating. Okay, so I cheated a couple of times. I haven't told her, but I really regret the one time I cheated on my fiancée—but I was drunk." I stopped him and commented, "So, what I'm hearing is that you thought that when you got married, God would give you the ability to stay true to your vows?" I explained that sexual fidelity was not something God bestowed when one says, "I do." It's a discipline that he'd never seen the need to practice.

Costly Obedience

When I encourage singles to wait, I know that for some, a godly celibacy is their destination. Not having a lifetime partner can be a costly obedience. A particular population will never marry, because they believe in the biblical theology that genital sexuality and becoming one should be reserved for a man and a woman in the covenant of marriage. We need to create Christian community that will embrace and support celibate singles. God has called some not to wait on their mate, but to remain celibate and fulfilled throughout their lives.[47]

You may be in that population of singles that still hopes that marriage is your destination, but God hasn't brought that covenant lover into your life yet. This, too, takes costly obedience. Stewarding genital sexuality and not to have sex is costly and not easy. God made sexual attraction and arousal exciting. That being said, I think the greater sacrifice in celibacy is not forfeiting orgasms with a playmate. The deeper costly obedience is not having a committed life partner, an intimate lover and friend with whom to share life, romance and sexual fulfillment. That's the relationship most singles long for.

> *"Consider it joyfully meaningful, my brothers and sisters, whenever you face costly trials of many kinds, because you know that this testing of your faith produces courageous perseverance that relies on God's faithfulness. Let this patient endurance complete its work of making you (sexually) mature and whole, not lacking anything." James 1:2-4 (DER paraphrase)*

This brings me back to my conviction that single adults cannot be sexually whole without community and meaningful friendships. Costly obedience isn't meant to consign single adults to a life devoid of intimacy. Singles need fun and supportive friendships to deal with the ache of loneliness. I also believe that some friendships need to be developed into a deeper commitment. Not erotically becoming one flesh, but having a friend that sticks closer than a brother. This may be with one friend, a group of friends, or even a married couple that have made a commitment to a single's well-being—"I have your back."

"There are 'friends' who destroy each other, but a real friend sticks closer than a brother." Proverbs 18:24 (NLT)

Celibacy has a rich, historical tradition in the Christian church. In his essay in *Sanctified Sexuality*, Abraham Kuruvilla depicts how the celibate Christian single has demonstrated his or her commitment throughout history: self-sacrifice, a true God-dependence and a greater eternity-focus. He writes that celibacy offers *biological* freedom from the compulsion to have sex, *provisional* freedom in choosing to allow God to provide for one's needs, *sociological* freedom from the pressures of marriage and family, and *emotional* freedom to demonstrate love more freely in the wider community of fellow believers.[48]

The church needs to recognize how much celibate singles offer to the Christian community. They model sacrifice, endurance and obedience in powerful ways. Without the responsibility of a mate or even children, singles can serve with a dedication and focus that the Apostle Paul applauds in I Corinthians 7. It may seem a little counterintuitive, but sacrificing celibate singles bring a playful spontaneity and joyful creativity that married couples often lose.

The Benefits of Soul Virginity

I've used many words to define the concept of practicing a godly sexual chastity or purity. Though often misused, purity carries with it the concept of avoiding contamination and keeping your sexuality free of selfish sabotage—being more like Jesus.

"Blessed are the (sexually) pure in heart, for they will see God." Matthew 5:9 (parenthesis added)

Chastity and practicing soul virginity communicate living out your sexual journey as you get excited about all God wants to give you. As skeptical, practical and selfish men and women, singles often want the bottom line: how will this benefit me?

I've used the word "benefits" deliberately, rather than list the "rewards" of chastity. What if the benefit/reward of abstaining from sex was not just avoiding an STI or getting pregnant? What if reward of chastity is *becoming more like Jesus*—enjoying intimate relationships that would've been impossible without a godly purity.

The "benefit" of chastity celebrates a sexually fulfilling lifestyle, which involves so much more than a reward for good behavior. Here are some of the benefits I've observed, and I'm sure you could add to this list:

1. Your Christian faith will become more real and intimate as you depend more deeply on God to help you protect your sexuality and build the love relationships He desires. The discipline of "costly obedience" brings the great rewards of freedom, peace, love and contentment. Romantic erotic sexuality will be seen through the Creator's lens of the Covenant of Marriage and how true sex is becoming an intimate One. You'll see a deeper meaning in the metaphor of Christ and the Bride—and Jesus' love for you! If you marry, that covenant relationship will have a much greater capacity for true intimacy and wonderfully connecting sex.

2. You'll be a powerful testimony of Jesus and his ability to transform sexuality into something so much better than what your culture offers. Meaningful sexual chastity and building healthy sexual relationships is evangelistic. Many singles know something is missing in the way they choose to value sex. Ultimately, helping them understand that they were

created with a sexual capacity for intimacy—and honoring what the God desires for them actually works.

3. You'll create meaningful Connecting friendships with the opposite or same sex, rather than using parties and social gatherings to scope out potential sexual partners. Your friendly connecting will be free of selfish sexual practices that use, rather than love each other.

4. You'll treat the opposite and same sex with respect as brothers and sisters in Christ, seeking to build them up with righteous flirting. You'll enjoy three-dimensional intimacy that includes affirming hugs, connecting conversations, and shared ministry within a caring community.

5. You'll enter romantic Coupling relationships without worrying about when you'll get naked or have sex—and you won't experience the shame that comes from the realization that you've disappointed God, yourself, your future husband or wife, and have harmed your sexual partner. There's a lot of joy and pride in knowing you've helped someone's future wife or husband because you chose to set appropriate sexual boundaries.

6. You'll relate with former Coupling partners with respect and joy—free of shame, regret or embarrassment.

7. You'll have a greater appreciation for how God's sexual economy is lived out in community and how your sexuality enriches each relationship. You'll have a better understanding of intimacy and a healthy respect for your sexual urges in ways those who've simply indulged their desires never will. Practicing stewardship of your sexuality will make more sense and grow easier as you practice this skill in community—and

you'll build wonderfully supportive friendships as everyone in your community practices sexual integrity.

8. You'll enjoy well-rounded dating relationships that aren't dependent on the sexual or romantic aspects, but have evolved the social, spiritual, and emotional aspects. You'll be less likely to ride your sexual feelings into a bad marriage due to giving in to sexual passion and shortcuts to intimacy.

9. You'll avoid: the false intimacy of sexual addiction, the sexual distortions of pornography, and the viruses that demolish sexual wholeness.

10. Your thought life will be more productive as you've earned to shift your thoughts away from sexual lust, fantasies and objectification.

11. You'll enter marriage with greater ability to be truly intimate, with less baggage and with a beautiful gift for your partner.

12. You'll enter marriage with the ability to avoid extramarital affairs, because you understand the concept of fidelity and have learned to discipline your sexual urges.

God will bless you in many ways for choosing to value true sex and protect it for your future spouse. Should God bring a spouse into your life, on your wedding night, you'll be able to say with integrity, "I chose to give you something that has cost me—a valuable gift— my soul virginity that I've kept just for you."

> *"I pray that the God who gives hope will fill you with much (sexual) joy and peace while you trust in him. Then your hope (for the benefits of wisely stewarding your sexuality) will overflow by the power of the Holy Spirit." Romans 15:13 (NCV, parentheses added)*

God *will* bless your choice to steward your sexuality and living the life of a soul virgin. He understands the sexual ache you feel, with a desire for pleasure and a longing for intimacy. The Lord will meet you in the midst of your struggle for sexual purity. He'll be with you in the painful moments. Rely on his power!

"Joyful are people of (sexual) integrity, who follow the (sexual) instructions of the Lord. As I learn your righteous regulations (your sexual economy), I will thank you by living as I should." Psalms 119:1, 7 (NLT, parentheses added)

CHAPTER THIRTEEN

Why Am I So Horny?—Understanding Sexual Desire

How do you react to the word *horny*? I've received many different comments, from "I hate that word" to "No other word expresses the way my sex drive seems to run my life." I've asked for synonyms, and received, among others: randy, libido, amorous, charged, hot, sexual desire, sexually attracted, aroused, turned on, and hormonal. I considered not using this word —thinking it emphasized too many unhealthy stereotypes. But I couldn't come up with a better word that describes how men and women feel turned on by their sexual desire—it was too simplistic a word and needed to be unpacked.

Defining Sexual Desire

Sexual desire was created by God to move us toward greater intimacy. Terms like "horny" or "hot" reduce sexual desire to a one-dimensional hormonal charge we must either indulge or ignore. Have you ever thought about all God wants you to experience through horny and sexual desire: to be intimately naked, known and accepted, the thrill of attraction and pursuit, the mystery and excitement of being a man or a woman and the power it gives, the pleasure and play, righteous flirting, the possibility of a profound "one flesh" covenant union.

A healthy view of sexual desire reflects all three dimensions of your personhood: body, mind, and spirit. Michael Cusick, in his thought-provoking book, *Surfing for God*, points out, "Sexual arousal is an accumulation of your experiences, deep needs, and unconscious beliefs. Your heart shares a deep connection to your body parts. The way you are sexually aroused reflects what's happening deep in your soul, beyond your sexual organs. Indeed, sex is as much a spiritual mystery as it is a physical fact."[49]

God created your *bodies* with a complex hormonal makeup that creates desire through testosterone, estrogen and other body chemistry in both men and women. Your brain, nervous system and blood supply get involved in the arousal process as your eyes take in a variety of cues. It's like you're physically surging with sexual arousal. One young woman stated it well: "Certain days of the month, I'm so turned on I whistle back at construction workers!" These sexual desires can get us into trouble if we don't understand their purpose or if we simply try to repress them.

So much of your sexuality takes place in your mind and imagination. The brain and your prefrontal cortex can help you wisely follow through on your values. The feeling and emotional centers of your mind can hijack the thinking parts, and it's often difficult to distinguish between feelings of romantic love and those of lust and horny.

Your *heart* and the spiritual part of your humanity makes you long for intimacy, to be known and desired. This motivates you to create a relationship with our God and a sexual intimacy with a partner. God's design is not for you to connect genitally with multiple partners, but to find fulfillment in mating for a lifetime with an opposite-sex partner in marriage. God also designed both singles and marrieds to enjoy and steward sexual attraction in meaningful righteous flirting, where the erotic is present, but is always carefully protected with healthy boundaries.

Sexual Surging and the Ache

Two concepts that best describe this three-dimensional sexual desire are "surging" and the "ache." The first concept is that of energy or electricity. Sexual *surges* can portray the sexual electricity God placed inside human beings. Like the Energizer Bunny, you're powered by your sexual current, which leads you into all sorts of behavior and intimate relationships. This would be primarily fueled by hormones (testosterone, estrogen, adrenaline, et al.) and your brain (with nerves and feelings and imagination), and your body (with blood flowing into our nerve-rich genitals). God gave you your physical and mental surges to facilitate emotional attraction, interaction and pursuit.

"Surge protectors" (godly boundaries) must also be put into place to discipline this energy in Connecting and Coupling relationships. For example, certain levels of surging may simply indicate loneliness and a need to hang out with same-sex friends rather than run the risk of inappropriate behavior with the opposite sex. Some horny may indicate boredom or stress and a need for self-nurture and adventure.

A second concept stems from the Italian word *amore*. Our English word "amorous" implies feeling turned on (not by mere hormones) but by a desire to sexually relate, a hunger for intimacy, romance and connection. I debated whether to call this concept a hunger, which it is, but thought it needed a more intense word. I like to describe this sexual longing as an ache. Everyone experiences this ache at times—an intense sexual craving or hunger.

Intimacy Needs and the Sexual Ache

The term *sexual ache* reminds us all that our sexual surges aren't just about hormones and engaging in sexual activity. They're urging us to fill a deep longing. Obviously, erotic sexual behavior creates excitement. However, you can trivialize your sexual desire by merely chasing after a hookup or an orgasm. Whether you're consciously aware of it or not, the yearning for intimacy is always pushing you from within. Some singles can become so desperate to silence it that they turn to all forms of compulsions or addictions: drugs, alcohol, work, partying, gaming, "serial" relationships, or a string of casual hook-ups.

In reality, the fundamental nature of this ache stems from a desire to be vulnerable and intimately known by another, revealing who you are at your deepest level of existence. It's a yearning to be unconditionally accepted, without mask or facade. Marital sexual intercourse was designed by God to be the ultimate expression of such "naked and unashamed" vulnerability and intimacy. In fact, Hebrew Scripture uses the word *yada* (to know) as a word for sexual intimacy: "Adam knew his wife Eve, and she conceived" (Genesis 4:1 NKJV). The essence of desire becomes an intimate, experiential "knowing" originating from deep within the heart.

However, only God, through a relationship with Christ, will ever completely satisfy our need to be unconditionally known and accepted. Intimate lovemaking (as good and complete as that may feel) is only a taste of your ultimate love relationship with God. Being truly known can only be experienced in a loving, intimate encounter between an individual and God himself.

The human erotic sexual intimacy God intended to salve the ache can only be experienced through soul virginity (exclusive fidelity) within the safe commitment of a covenant companionship (marriage). So, what should you do with this ache as a single adult? Take a lot of cold showers, settle for false intimacy, or compulsively masturbate? Nope. You must *embrace horny* and discover the purpose for the ache, understanding why such a deep longing exists—and what to do when it comes to the surface.

Embracing Horny and Your Sexual Desires

Seeing the distortions in our culture, the evangelical church has traditionally responded with what initially appears as godly wisdom: "Sex is for marriage—be abstinent." But this statement, without a practical explanation of the meaning of sex within a covenant marriage—sends a disturbing message: "We aren't comfortable discussing what to do with your sexual desires as a single person. If you just abstain from all sexual thoughts and behavior, you won't struggle."

Another unspoken message is: "As a single person, you are asexual until marriage—then you can turn your sexual switch 'on.'" Obviously, single adults are sexual beings and have sexual desires. It seems the Church sometimes views the eternal Creator as throwing up his hands in shock: "Oh no, single adults have sexual feelings and desire, and now they aren't getting married until almost thirty! Wow! This caught me off guard. What am I going to do now?" How ridiculous! God always knows exactly what he's doing. One of Satan's favorite tricks is distorting and destroying something God made beautiful.

I recall being a single Christian man in the sexual confusion of the 1960s and 70s, longing for some guidance for my sexual desire. Imagine the appreciation I felt the day I encountered this story by missionary Walter Trobisch:

"Once upon a time there was a tiger. He was captured and put in a cage. The keeper's task was to feed him and guard him. But the keeper wanted to make the tiger his friend. He always spoke to him in a friendly voice whenever he came to his cage. The tiger, however, always looked at him with hostility in his green, glowing eyes. He followed every movement of the keeper, ready to spring on him. The keeper was afraid of the tiger and asked God to tame him.

One evening, when the keeper had already gone to bed, a little girl got lost in the vicinity of the tiger's cage and came too near to the iron bars. The tiger reached out with his claws. There was a blow, a scream. When the keeper arrived, he found dismembered human flesh and blood. Then the keeper knew that God had not tamed the tiger. His fear grew. He drove the tiger into a dark hole where no one could come close to him.

Now the tiger roared day and night. The terrible sound disturbed the keeper so that he could no longer sleep. It reminded him of his guilt. In his dreams he saw the torn body of the little girl. Then he cried out in his misery. He prayed to God that the tiger might die.

God answered him, but the answer was different from what the keeper had expected. God said, "Let the tiger into your house, into the rooms where you live, even into your most beautiful room." The keeper had no fear of death. He would rather die than go on hearing the roar of the tiger. So he obeyed.

He opened the door of the cage and prayed, "Thy will be done." The tiger came out and stood still. They looked into each other's eyes for a long time. As soon as the tiger noticed that the keeper had no fear and that he breathed quietly, he lay down at his feet ….

After some years the two became good friends. The keeper could touch the tiger, even put his hand between his jaws. But he never dared to take his eyes off the tiger. When they looked at each other they recognized each other and were glad they belonged together and that each was necessary to the other."[50]

Today, sexual issues have only grown more confusing. Keeping the tiger of your sexual desire under lock and key (and even driving it into the deep cave of sexual repression) only serves to intensify its menacing roar in your life. Only when you risk inviting your sexuality into the most beautiful rooms of your house—keeping eye contact as you realize the potential for beauty or harm—will you tame the tiger within.

Common Distortions of Your Sexual Surges and Aches

Taming the tiger of your sexual desires is not simple. Some common attitudes and practices can really sabotage your attempts to wisely steward the surge and ache of horny.

Meat-flavored Candy Bars

We live in a hyper-sexualized culture—one obsessed and saturated with sexual thoughts and images. It's easy to deal with the surge and the ache by simply indulging it. "My sexual 'needs' are unmanageable." "Why am I over 30 and still celibate?" "What if the rapture happens before I've had sex?" "What's wrong with having sex with the person I love?" "Didn't God give us sex for recreation as well as procreation?" Even as a Christian, you may have conformed to the cultural norm of indulging genital sexuality.

Earlier in the book, I explored the illustration of singles and marrieds enjoying different kinds of protein. Singles could be described as vegetarian and feasting on that special type of social sexual protein that doesn't include genital connection. Marrieds relish meat—the tasty steak of being known and making love. But singles often indulge in *steak-flavored candy bars*. Singles want the taste of steak that God designed for marriage, so, they settle for steak-flavored candy bars (hook-ups, etc.). These not only have no nutritional value, but can't provide what God intended lovemaking to express. These candy bars are actually toxic to healthy sexual intimacy. Has Satan deceived you into making unfulfilling choices to deal with your sexual ache? Have you been indulging in steak-flavored candy bars?!

Narcissistic Hedonism and Taking Shortcuts

In Greek mythology, Narcissus was so enraptured with his own beauty that he was doomed to never love another person. He was completely self-absorbed. Today, we define narcissism as, "It's all about me," and hedonism as pursuing personal pleasure as the chief goal in life. Can our management of horny reflect a narcissistic hedonism? Absolutely!

I often tell singles that in this hook-up culture, it's much easier to get naked than to take the time to really get to know someone. Spending hours at a coffee shop getting to know someone takes time, and the effort of active listening that a quick sexual fix doesn't require. I realize that sleeping with a partner is not just narcissistic and hedonistic. But a sexual hookup is a shortcut to true intimacy that will ultimately prove unsatisfying. Even in the context of an ongoing relationship, relying on your sexual connection won't produce the deep knowing that a couple desires. Go to Starbucks and find out what your date is really like. Erotic sexuality is not meant to create intimacy, but to flow out of a committed intimate relationship.

I worry about unmarried couples who sleep together. The sexual intimacy they share creates the illusion that there's more of a connection than there really is. I see couples ignore or blow through real "deal-breakers" for a lasting marriage, because sex makes them feel like everything is great.

A special note for men: you might sometimes feel God gave you more sexual "burn" than necessary, when it seems like half the desire would have gotten the job done. Yet, the Creator uses this seeming "oversexed-ness" to drive men closer to him, to get down on their knees and seek help in stewarding this sexual tidal wave. They can connect with female and male friends, initiate meaningful Coupling relationships—both are great antidotes to lust.

A special note for women: Paula Rinehart makes some wise observations in her book, *Sex and the Soul of a Woman*: "The easiest and most sure way to make a man feel like a man is to have sex. It is the quickest feedback loop, a deep physical dose of masculine validation. The experience of sexual virility is so potent for a guy that his lifelong temptation is to turn it into a god and to make the woman the center of his existence rather than a person herself and his partner."[51] She warns women that in this hook-up culture, they let men remain selfish little boys by hooking up—rather than make them respect their femininity and sexuality.

So then why were these sexual surges and aches given to you as a single adult? Why didn't God design the switch to automatically stay in the "off" position until your wedding night? Without this human capacity to be sexually attracted and aroused—and to celebrate this within relationships—so much would be lost. This still leaves us with a perplexing question: "What do I do with my intense sexual feelings while I wait until I get married?"

CHAPTER FOURTEEN

What Do I Do with All My Sexual Energy?

Have you ever had a meaningful conversation with a friend, or in your church singles group, about what to do when you're feeling sexually charged and don't know what to do with those feelings? We don't address this well in the Christian community. Since we all have sexual attractions and arousal, and if our sexual values mean keeping genital sexual expression for the "oneness" of marriage, then embracing and stewarding your sex drive is a critical part of single sexuality.

A Values Framework: Alternatives and Choices

James K.A. Smith points out that many of the values and internal beliefs that control the choices we make are *unconscious*. He believes that a self-centered culture has subtly taken over our hearts and we now think we can meet our deepest needs and desires by becoming passionate *consumers*.

Smith further writes that selfish consumption can never satisfy our deeper needs and desires. In consumerism, our values and choices are built on two factors that doom us to failure: "the thrill of the unsustainable experience or event, and the sheen of the novel and new…with the necessary disposal of the old and boring."[52] You'll need continual, more intoxicating sexual highs as you indulge your desires, and a constant parade of new partners.

All singles can fall prey to selfish consumerism: a meaningless kiss, oral sex for the buzz, seductive clothing to manipulate, or the ego-boosting hook-up. It's scary to think that Christian singles are *unconsciously* controlled by lust-filled *consumer* beliefs that can almost guarantee living out horny inappropriately. Scripture emphasizes how easily these distorted sexual values distortions can occur.

> *"It is God's will that you should be sanctified: that you should avoid sexual immorality; that each of you should learn to control your body in a way that is holy and honorable, not in passionate lust like the pagans, who do not know God; and that in this matter no one should wrong or take advantage of a brother or sister." I Thessalonians 4:3-6*

> *"For everything in the world—the lust of the flesh, the lust of the eyes, and the pride of life—comes not from the Father but from the world. The world and its desires pass away, but whoever does the will of God lives forever." I John 2:16.17*

We need to think through how each of us (as broken human beings) distort a healthy horny and hurt ourselves and the brothers and sisters in our community. When does Horney cross over into toxic sexual lust that poisons the heart and mind?

- Maintaining attitudes and behavior focused on selfish *consuming* and not loving sacrificial giving (Love can wait to give; lust cannot wait to take.)
- Pursuing immediate pleasure and chasing the sexual "buzz" rather than disciplining for long-term gain—taking shortcuts and eating "meat-flavored candy bars".

- Objectifying another sexually, rather than honoring the sexual capacity God gave you to express love and connection through your sexuality.
- Coveting something that's not yours, rather than being content with soul virginity and protecting another's future husband or wife.
- Adulterating and contaminating your sexual thought-life and forfeiting the ability to experience true intimacy.

Consider that sacred single's ritual: the party. How much fun to be with people who want to lay back, connect and have a good time. But would you agree that sexual attention and attraction will be a part of every party? Can this be a time of healthy social sexuality, righteous flirting, and stewarding horny? Or will toxic lust prevail, with consumerism, worshipping the sexual buzz, coveting what isn't ours, objectifying others and settling for a hook-up?

I wish I could say that lustful, often unconscious, heart attitudes accompanied by stupid, sinful choices and mistakes aren't that big a deal—but there is always a *"cost."* God gracefully forgives but consequences happen when we abuse and distort our sexual desire. When we sin, something always dies. I used to think that if I sinned, God would strike me dead. Now I see that sinfulness does bring death, but often what dies is God's sexual best for our lives and relationships.

"But people are tempted when their own evil desire leads them away and traps them. This desire leads to sin, and then the sin grows and brings death." James 1:14-15 (NCV)

Appreciating and Embracing Sexual Surges

Inside every adult, the sexual ache burns. Sex can be compared to dynamite. It can blast through mountains and create new pathways—or it can blow up one's sexual integrity. Some single adults thrive, finding it easy to make disciplined choices around intense sexual surging, and others are lonely and resentful, or selfishly indulge their sexual itch?

No Christian single comes close to perfection, but you *can* experience consistent progress. Sexual chastity is not a destination, it's a journey with healthy choices and stupid mistakes. God and our friends can help us get back up from our mistakes, dust ourselves off, and continue. We can take comfort in the fact that the Apostle Paul must have felt much the same when he confessed his ongoing struggle with sin. But, with the help of Jesus and the Holy Spirit, he grew into greater spiritual maturity.

> *"I know that nothing good lives in me, that is, in my sinful nature. I want to do what is right but can't. I want to do what is good, but don't. …Who will free me from this life dominated by sin and death? Thank God! The answer is in Jesus Christ our Lord."* Romans 7:18-19, 25 (NLT)

A young man once told me that I was lucky to be married because I was never lonely and had instantly available sex. I responded that we're all lonely apart from God, and that I loved his concept of "instantly available sex." I asked him to please tell my wife, because I didn't think she agreed with that concept.

> *"No discipline seems pleasant at the time, but painful. Later on, however, it produces a harvest of righteousness and peace for those who have been trained by it."* Hebrews 12:11

So, since we don't have a choice as to whether we have all this sexual energy, what can we do about it? Here are some ideas that single adults have found helpful.

The Art of Redirecting and Reframing Sexual Desire and Erotic Needs

As we tried to define horny, we saw that God gave us sexual surges and aches for reasons that went beyond arousal, orgasmic buzzes and having fun in bed. Two practical tools to help steward horny and fulfill some of those deeper erotic needs are *redirecting* and *reframing* them. *Redirecting* takes sexual energy and uses it to engage in other pursuits. An example of this would be the single worship leader who said some of her best songs came when she took her horny feelings and redirected that energy into songwriting. Sublimate is another word we can use, which means to divert desire toward a healthier expression. It isn't that sexual desire is unhealthy, but often God needs us not to indulge them, but to redirect or sublimate them. *Reframing* helps us put a different frame around our sexual desire and value it rather than stay frustrated.

Redirecting and Reframing Erotic, Brotherly, and Unconditional Love

In Greek literature, many words were used for "love." Three prominent words used to describe love were *eros, phileo*, and *agape*. These represented different expressions of love and sexuality. As the root for our English word "erotic," *eros* embodies a passionate love that creates erotic sexual connection. For the Christian who desires to live by God's sexual economy, *eros* or romantic love is intended for marriage and the Coupling relationships leading to marriage.

Phileo is commonly known as "brotherly love"—that is, the friendly warmth and connection you experience with a close friend or your community. It was earlier described as Social Sexuality in which erotic feelings and attractions occur, but we choose to enjoy each other as brothers or sisters. *Agape* represents the intentional and unconditional love God has for us—given with no strings attached and without demanding anything in return.

Redirecting *eros* into *phileo* and *agape* love can make a big difference with horny. When your sexual desire is strongest, your greatest need as a believer is to actively seek a meaningful connection with God and with your brothers and sisters in Christ. Your deepest need isn't for a sexual buzz, but an ache for genuine intimacy. To meet your need for intimacy in healthy and godly ways may mean taking time out to redirect eros into other activities:

- Worship time with God through prayer
- Listening to praise music
- Reading or studying Scripture
- Teaching a Sunday School class
- Talking with a friend, engaging in meaningful conversation over coffee or dinner
- Joining or creating a small group—possibly through your church
- Hugging and touching—never underestimate the need to connect through non-erotic touch
- Creating an relationship of accountability with someone of the same sex, with whom you can tackle the hard questions, sharing and encouraging each other
- Engaging in some fun "righteous flirting" in your singles community
- Throwing a party! Have some serious play time!

Honest same-sex friendships with accountability help absorb sexual energy. A male colleague once told me that he thought good friendships were God's antidote to sexual lust. Sometimes you aren't just horny, you're actually just lonely and bored. Friends supply intimacy which can counter that boredom.

Additional Redirects and Reframes of Horny

Strenuous physical activity increases endorphins and can help you siphon off that erotic energy. My favorite is the college coed who told me, "I put my earbuds in and turn my music up loud—and I vacuum the heck out of my apartment." Here are some other suggestions for venting that sexual frustration or redirecting that energy:

- Get a punching bag or take a kickboxing class
- Learn to dance
- Wash, wax and vacuum your car
- Hike, work out, jog, cycle, swim or other forms of vigorous exercise
- Drive around or take a road trip
- Stand in your apartment and vent your frustration to God
- Find a friend or group of friends that you can moan and whine with about how horny you are and how unfair it is
- Join a team or club like softball, chess, or the Sierra Club
- Socialize and have fun with some mature partying at clubs or friend's homes
- Listen to some live music—take in a concert
- Pursue an advanced degree, take a computer class, learn to speak a foreign language
- Develop a hobby: scuba diving, skiing, cooking or hunting
- Delve into your genealogy

- Find a cause to advocate for and volunteer—like disaster relief, Habitat for Humanity or a homeless shelter
- Go on a short-term mission trip
- Sponsor someone going on a mission trip and vicariously enjoy their experience
- Mentor or disciple a younger believer

Reframing creatively renews your mind, allowing you to seek new definitions and perspectives for old ideas. Like putting a new frame on a favorite piece of art, it helps you see things in the painting you've never seen before. Enjoy the freedom of singleness: seek out exciting adventures, trips and activities; engage in authentic relationships with friends and family. Reframe the idea that enjoying companionship with the opposite sex has to include erotic sexual behavior. Try these activities to help your reframing:

- Step into the chaos of a hurting person's life and take the time to listen and minister to their needs
- Initiate more opposite-sex friendships with the goal of affirming and righteous flirting
- Journal about the life lessons you're learning by disciplining your sexual desires
- Write love letters to your future spouse
- Do something you've never done and be adventurous—take a trip to Ecuador, ski in Wyoming, go to the Chicago Blues Festival, cruise the Caribbean, catch an NFL game
- In your dating life, pursue the goal of helping the person you're dating to become the best man or woman possible—the person God intended them to be
- Build character by intentionally seeing the opposite sex three-dimensionally
- Find ways to unselfishly serve others

Put a bigger frame around your sexual energy, one that allows your ache to motivate you toward compassion, kindness, generosity and depth of character. Consider how agonizing over horny and yearning for intimate connection builds patience and empathy. This place of being single and sexual is often difficult, it can be a time for learning critical skills in intimacy and filling your special role in the Body of Christ. Single sexuality can be recognized and reframed as a place for character building, an opportunity for service, and drawing close to God with a costly but invaluable obedience. Celibacy and dealing with the ache can be a testimony to other Christians and model important virtues within our church communities.

In the book *Costly Obedience* that narrates the stories of celibate gay Christians, the point is well made that "This commitment to a disciplined and costly discipleship is a strength: a gift to others in the church to emulate. ...The lives of gay Christians who embrace this costly obedience, embodying gospel teaching on suffering and grace, provide an outward witness of faithfulness to Christ to the surrounding culture."[53] I deeply believe that as the Holy Spirit permeates singles and the way they live out their sexual narratives, it will add a much-needed ingredient to every Christian community.

> *"We can anticipate a hopeful outcome when we encounter the struggle of dealing with our sexual desires. We know that these challenges help us develop patience and perseverance that will ultimately create sexual character. And, the Holy Spirit will nurture this process and pour into our lives the ability to love intimately." Romans 5:3-5 (DER paraphrase)*

Marriage and singleness both demand the discipline of chastity (soul virginity) because sexual temptation will confront you throughout your life. Six weeks before their wedding date, an engaged couple I'll call Lisa and Greg came to me and with shame and remorse admitted they'd once again crossed sexual boundaries they'd determined to keep. I suggested the following scenario to them: "What if God knew that two years from now, Greg would have a seductive coworker, and that their heavenly Father was helping him learn important lessons in self-control before their marriage?" They may have blown the lesson then, but they had six more weeks to practice self-control before they'd be married.

I hasten to add that erotic sexual fulfillment isn't a "right" but a blessing that God gives, one that should be enjoyed only in a God-honoring manner and context. Reframing this issue in Coupling relationships is an opportunity to learn lessons about self-control and unselfish nurturing important to future marital happiness.

I recall a young man who came to me whining that his wife was having a terrible pregnancy and they hadn't made love for three months. I replied, "Were you never single? Sex isn't a right; it's a privilege. Practice other types of intimacy and nurture your wife." My fear is that he'd never practiced soul virginity or incorporated such disciplines. I don't want you to look at singleness as basic training for marriage, but for those God leads to marriage, your growth as a single person really counts. Learning to reframe and practicing healthy boundaries is great preparation for all of your future relationships, including marriage.

The Ultimate Purpose of Sexual Desire: Enlarging Our Capacity to Love

In *Sex and the Soul of a Woman*, Paula Rinehart puts it so well, "The pain of unmet desire can actually enlarge our hearts. The more we let ourselves long for life, though it brings the ache of incompleteness, the more we are actually able to savor the joy that comes our way. This paradox surprises me on a daily basis. More and more, I recognize this kind of pain for what it is—a ticket to becoming a woman so thoroughly alive that she is afraid of almost nothing."[54]

To acknowledge your sexual surges, allow them to push you toward the mature man or woman God intended. No one else can do this tough but rewarding work for you. Each person must "work out your own salvation [daily walk] with fear and trembling; for it is God who works in you both to will and to do for His good pleasure" (Philippians 2:12–13 NKJV). Soul virgins learn to master the skills for going beyond their sexual longings to gain a greater capacity to love—learning to generously give and to receive in relationships, serve others, build a supportive network of friends, righteously flirting and risk romantic Coupling relationships.

> "Consider it a sheer gift, friends, when tests and challenges come at you from all sides. You know that under pressure, your faith-life is forced into the open and shows its true colors. So don't try to get out of anything prematurely. Let it do its work so you become mature and well-developed, not deficient in any way." James 1:2–4 (MSG)

Your sexual ache is indeed an indispensable part of your life by divine design, helping you build character and connect more deeply with your Christian brothers and sisters.

CHAPTER FIFTEEN
A Theology of Masturbation

Someone once told me, "Doug, you're probably the evangelical Christian expert on masturbation." I thought this a rather dubious honor but appreciated that he was acknowledging my theological wrestling with the topic over the years—and that I wouldn't let this be the elephant in the room that no one addressed. As a fellow Jesus-follower, please let this chapter help you consider important *questions* about this behavior and to find better answers for yourself. Questions like:

- Is masturbation permissible for a Christian? When and how—or never?
- Can you fantasize when you masturbate and not lust?
- Does God allow me a special dispensation, as a single person, to deal with horny by masturbating without having an intimate relationship?
- If a friend felt guilty about masturbating and asked you about his behavior, how would you guide your friend? What questions might you ask? What ideas might you need to consider? What Scripture might shed some answers?

I imagine putting the word "theology" together with the word "masturbation" seems a little irreverent. The word "theology" comes from two Greek words: "theos" (God) and "logos" (a word or teaching). I think it's important that singles construct a theology, godly teaching, about masturbation—both for themselves and to be able to engage others in meaningful conversations around this topic. If you're going to practice sexual chastity and choose not to engage in genital sexuality with another person, then the erotic concept of masturbation has even greater significance to the celibate single adult.

Martha, a single woman in her late 30s, masturbates once or twice a month. She says it diminishes her sexual desire and helps her control her lust when with her male friends. Jim, a single guy in his 20s, believes his efforts to curb his masturbation has helped him discover a deeper intimacy with God and others. Carl thinks the behavior is truly sinful, and has a variety of Scriptures supporting his beliefs, yet struggles with masturbation himself. Alex used to masturbate occasionally, but now that he's seriously dating Ansley, he refrains. He reached this conviction because he was objectifying Ansley in his fantasies, and it was making it harder to control himself when he was with her.

A quick review of Christian literature over the years reveals that pastors, theologians, and Christian writers have very diverse opinions on the subject. A major factor in this range of opinion is the silence of Scripture. We find Old Testament laws (Leviticus 15, for example) requiring a man who experienced a "discharge" of semen to be considered ceremonially unclean until evening. Such ceremonial laws are helpful reminders of how Jewish believers were commanded to practice behaviors that set them apart, but aren't specific teachings on masturbation for Christian singles.

Another passage (Genesis 38:1–10) references a man named Onan's refusal to consummate his (required) marriage to his brother's widow. According to Hebrew custom, if a man died before having children, his brother was expected to marry his widow and produce an heir to carry on the deceased brother's family line. Onan didn't want to split his inheritance between two households (that of his brother's wife and that of his own wife). Therefore, he attempted to resolve his conflict by practicing coitus interruptus—the withdrawal of the penis from the vagina prior to ejaculation—and "spilled his seed on the ground" in an effort to prevent having children with her. This disobedience was devastating, but not a commentary on masturbation.

When I mentioned the silence of Scripture on the issue, one pastor said that I had obviously not read Matthew 6:3b. When I looked up the passage, I quickly knew he was joking, "Do not let your left hand know what your right hand is doing." So, no Scripture directly deals with the topic. I've wondered what it would be like to have a conversation with Jesus about masturbation. I knew how he emphasized heart motivation over debating behaviors. Once when thinking about this topic, the following hypothetical dialogue came to mind:

"Teacher, what do you think about masturbation? Is it always wrong or does it depend?"

"Friend, why do you Christian leaders waste so much time debating masturbation when Satan's deceptions are destroying my gift of sexuality? Have you considered the sexual hypocrisy of your Christian culture?"

"Uh, you're right ... the Christian culture is full of sexual hypocrisy and distortion. I think maybe we debate masturbation because it causes so much guilt and confusion."

"Oh child, what does masturbation mean to you? How does it affect your heart and your relationships?"

"Master, I was thinking a bit more philosophically. I'm trying to develop a theology of masturbation for your Church. Goodness, why do you always get so personal? Now I won't be able to tell them exactly what to do."

"But son, it's your heart that really matters."

Let me take this a step further. You know that when you're masturbating, that God is there, too. I don't think he's looking on in judgment, saying, "You nasty girl (or boy), you shouldn't be engaging in this behavior. You're going to be in trouble if you keep this up." I think a caring Creator is present with concern and love—wisely wanting you to consider some things:

"What needs are you trying to meet and will this really help?"

"Would you let me help you create a meaningful personal theology concerning your masturbation?"

We could endlessly debate the subject of masturbation. I refuse to tell anyone whether it's right or wrong. Here's the place I think we must start: each believer must go deeper to seek and discern God's heart, as loving Trinity helps each person go beyond the behavior of masturbation to discern how it affects their heart, minds and relationships.

Doubtful Things and a Three-Step Process

In the early church, Christians debated whether meat that was offered to idols was okay to eat. Some said that idols weren't real, so why not eat what God created for food? Others stated that it was a bad testimony, and Christians should refrain from eating meat that was tainted by the pagan culture. Christians also debated which day should be the Sabbath—Saturday or Sunday? The Apostle Paul gave the following advice on doubtful things:

> "You cannot judge another person's servant. The master decides if the servant is doing well or not. And the Lord's servant will do well because the Lord helps him do well. ... Some think that one day is more important than another, and others think that every day is the same. Let all be sure in their own mind. If we live, we are living for the Lord, and if we die, we are dying for the Lord. So living or dying, we belong to the Lord." Romans 14:4- 5, 8 (NCV)

Masturbation can be categorized as a disputable or doubtful behavior. Some Christians think it's permissible to relieve some of the built-up sexual tension, where others believe that it's always a sin. God wants us to carefully think through a theology of masturbation. Then, like in Romans 14, we can each stand before the Lord with our own convictions.

> "...The Lord does not look at the things that man looks at. Man looks on the outward appearance, but the Lord looks at the heart." I Samuel 16:7

How do we synchronize our hearts with God's, choosing to apply heart-directed motivation to produce godly behavior? Whether considering masturbation, fantasies, or any other sexual concern, I suggest a three-step process:

Step One: If scriptural guidelines exist that directly address the topic of interest, seek to understand them fully and obediently apply them to your heart, mind, and behavior. Heart-directed morality always begins with obedience to clear biblical teaching.

Example: *"Let there be no sexual immorality, impurity, or greed among you. Such sins have no place among God's people. Obscene stories, foolish talk, and course jokes—these are not for you." Ephesians 5:3,4a (NLT)*

Step Two: If direct scriptural guidelines do not exist, seek to understand and obediently apply passages that indirectly address the issue, or that support any guidelines you found from step one. Since Scripture often doesn't directly address a specific behavior, we need to explore other scriptural principles to guide our hearts, minds and behavior.

Example: *"'I have the right to do anything,' you say—but not everything is beneficial. 'I have the right to do anything'—but I will not be mastered by anything.' " I Corinthians 6:12*

Step Three: For topics still unclear after applying steps one and two, each believer should prayerfully search his or her own heart about the issue. We live out our sexuality in community. Seek wise teachings on a topic, read books, blogs, and church traditions/theologies, and consult those who might have more wisdom.

Example: With masturbation, there is usually a fantasy that helps create sexual arousal and climax. Do your fantasies value and protect your brothers and sisters?

Scriptures that Could Guide our Three-Step Process in Creating a Theology of Masturbation

Below are a number of helpful passages in thinking through your theology. After each, I've posed some questions to help you construct a personal theology of masturbation.

> *"Anyone who even looks at a woman with lust in his eye has already committed adultery with her in his heart" Matthew 5:27-28 (NLT)*

> *"I made a covenant with my eyes, not to look with lust at a young woman (man)." Job 31:1*

The word "adultery" means to pollute by adding a contaminating element. Is masturbation tied to lust? In other words, is the behavior associated with objectifying a brother or sister, or a lustful fantasy about someone?

> *"Even though 'I am allowed to do anything,' I must not become a slave to anything" 1 Corinthians 6:12 (NLT).*

Are you becoming enslaved by or addicted to the behavior? Is it tied in with pornography? If so, it's spiritually harmful for you.

> *"Each of you should look not only to your own interests, but also to the interests of others." Philippians 2:4 (BSB)*

Is the behavior disrespectful to your future mate or to others? Is it selfishly gratifying needs that could be met elsewhere? How is this behavior beneficial? How does it affect your Christian growth, your brothers and sisters in Christ and your community?

"This explains why a man leaves his father and mother and is joined to his wife, and the two are united into one." Genesis 2:24 (NLT) (see also vss.18-25)

Erotic sexual behavior should promote intimacy and move you toward healthy intimate relationships and potential marital sexual oneness. Is the behavior detracting from God's intent? If so, it could be robbing you of what God wants to give to you.

"But if a person believes something is wrong, that thing is wrong for him." Romans 14: 14, 23 (NCV)

Do you believe in your heart this behavior is wrong? Is "true" guilt associated with it? (This is different from "false" guilt, which can result from harmful teaching, immaturity, or abuse.) Pay attention and examine those catches in your spirit.

"Make up your mind not to put any stumbling block or obstacle in your brother's way." Romans 14:13 (BSB) (see also vv.14-22)

Is what you see as your personal freedom to engage in certain sexual behavior causing a brother or sister to stumble? If so, then it's at least inappropriate for you to discuss the freedom you feel regarding this behavior with others who do not feel the same freedom (see v. 22).

By a careful searching of Scripture, you'll find other passages to assist you in determining a godly perspective about masturbation as well as other sexual behavior, such as fantasy and flirting (e.g., Matthew 5:28 warns of contaminating potential relationships with lust, and 1 Thessalonians 4:6 warns against wronging a brother or sister and taking advantage of him or her). Prayerfully allowing

Scripture to reveal the deeper purposes of God where no clear guidelines are given should result in either freedom or conviction about the issue. If your heart is truly intent on pleasing God, you'll receive the wisdom you need.

> *"If any of you lacks wisdom, he should ask God, who gives generously to all without finding fault, and it will be given to him." James 1:5*

> *"But when he, the Spirit of Truth comes, he will guide you into all truth." John 16:13*

Building Your Theology

Sometimes it's good to ask ourselves searching questions with an open mind about the influence of masturbation in your life:

«What would my life be like if I never masturbated again?"

"How is masturbation affecting my life—spiritually and relationally?"

"What needs am I trying to meet through masturbation?

"How does God intend me to steward my erotic sexuality— as a single person—as a single person wanting to sexually become the best lover for my future mate?"

In working through these and similar questions, you may find masturbation to be permissible, needing to be selectively limited, or maybe an unhealthy attempt to satisfy some inner need. God didn't intend for us to resolve non-sexual issues through sexual behavior, like a young man who masturbates himself to sleep every night, or the young woman who masturbates to fantasies of men who find her desirable to bolster her self-image, or the single person who uses pornography and masturbation for the high it gives. Singles can learn to deal with the actual issues in healthy ways that address the real problems or needs, and stop turning to masturbation for a quick fix. Sexual activity should never be a substitute for emotional or spiritual intimacy. It shouldn't be engaged in because you are bored or want a reward for your costly obedience.

Some of you thoughtfully view masturbation as sinful and counterproductive because it's characterized by lustful fantasy, addictive compulsion, and isolation. This type of masturbation, especially accompanied by porn, builds habits around types of arousal that tear at the foundation of true sexual intimacy. To continue with this type of masturbatory behavior will lead to greater sexual distortion, both in your heart now and potentially in your future marital relationship.

Some, like Alex, may have different seasons of singleness with different ways of dealing with this behavior. He especially focused on his thought life. We've already discussed the importance of disciplining your fantasies and guarding your thought life from destructive lust. Your eyes, imagination, and thought life play an important role in your sexuality and relationship building with the same and opposite sex: "*The eye is the lamp of the body. If your eyes are good, your whole body will be full of light*" Matthew 6:22.

These Scriptures do not imply that all mental imagery and fantasy are inappropriate. So much of what happens sexually, occurs in our minds. In Chapters 13 and 14 we thought through being horny and that sexual desire, attraction and arousal were normal. Having sexual thoughts and mental imagery around desire and attraction is also normal. The tricky part is how to use fantasy in masturbation and maintain sexual purity and not contaminate (Matthew 5:28) your sexuality through your thought life.

I've heard a range of opinions on fantasy and sexual wholeness as a single person. From: "Masturbate without having any fantasies." "You can't masturbate without fantasizing so let's think this through." "It's okay if you fantasize about a non-specific male or female person or just fantasize about masculine or feminine parts that are arousing to you." "Don't have one repeated fantasy that is simply about arousal and not at all relational." Etc. Etc.

If masturbation is a "doubtful" issue, then this aspect of mental imagery must be thought through to create a consistent, godly theology. How freeing if we could at least have conversations about fantasy with our brothers and sisters as we ponder all the alternatives and choices with the help of the Holy Spirit.

"The mind of sinful man is death (to God's best sexually), but the mind controlled by the Spirit is life and peace." Romans 8:6 (parenthesis added)

"Trust in the Lord with all your heart, and lean not on your own sexual understanding; in all your ways acknowledge Him, and He will direct your sexual paths." Proverbs 3:5-6 (NKJV, "sexual" added)

Some of you (like Martha) may feel that your own masturbation doesn't violate the heart of the Scriptures we shared. For you, masturbation and solo orgasms may simply represent a legitimate means of dealing with sexual surges and hormonal buildup—helping you live a purer life. If so, please remember that all erotic sexual behavior merely reflects true sex and will always be incomplete apart from covenant lovemaking in marriage. Though the physical part of your sexual desire may be lessened, your inner longing for intimacy will remain and should not be ignored. Masturbation will never resolve loneliness.

Further Musings: Social and Erotic Sexuality and the Three Gift Boxes

If we look at our three "gift boxes" from Chapter 6, there are two very different views on masturbation. Some wonder if perhaps masturbation is where **social sexuality** intersects with **erotic sexuality**. In social sexuality we have erotic sexual feelings that give each of us attractions and the ability for sexual arousal. Could masturbation be a private erotic act, as a special dispensation granted to singles, to intentionally relieve the pressure of erotic sexual feelings (horny) while still guarding lustful fantasies and protecting relationships?

Others, in considering the Boxes, conclude that masturbation goes beyond dealing with the erotic sexual feelings of Social Sexuality and enters into intimate erotic behavior. Therefore, masturbation encroaches on erotic sexuality in unhealthy ways and Christians should refrain from it. Believing that erotic sexual behavior is only appropriate when enjoyed within the correct *intimate* relationship, they would see masturbation (isolating, non-intimate) as an inappropriate behavior in all three of our relationship gift boxes.

Final Observations on Masturbation

Masturbation can alleviate some of the built-up hormonal and physical sexual desire, but will always be *incomplete*. It can take the hormonal edge off, but it won't satisfy the loneliness or emotional needs that God creates through our sexual desire. Only the Lord, community and close friends can accomplish that. Sometimes masturbation can actually increase sexual lusting rather than diminish desire as it moves your mind and body toward a more sexually charged place.

Masturbation may vary with its permissibility, whether you're married or single. In developing your attitude toward this behavior, you're working through God's plan for your sexuality in various seasons of your life. When married couples ask me about masturbation, I say, "Why engage in that behavior?" In marriage, our sexual desires should drive us to our wives or husbands for fulfillment. Masturbation can signal laziness and the lack of a healthy pursuit of intimacy.

One young man, who was getting married in three weeks, asked me if the fact that he'd masturbated every night since he was sixteen in order to go to sleep, would affect his marital sex life. I said, "Of course." His wife's vagina was very different than his hand and he'd created fantasies that weren't about intimate connecting, but simply climaxing quickly.

I would caution that for some, masturbation can be a building block for sexual addiction and shouldn't be engaged in by someone struggling with harmful sexual habits. Porn and masturbation can be a toxic combination. It's also easy to create fantasies that don't promote sexual integrity or intimacy.

We could endlessly debate the subject of masturbation. Maybe someday we'll reach a consensus. But for now, it seems to be a doubtful issue that each of us must each decide before the Lord. Allow yourself to be transparent and engage in meaningful discussion within your community. Those around you will value this opportunity to mutually explore convictions.

"All of us who are spiritually mature should think this way, too. And if there are things you do not agree with, God will make them clear to you. But we should continue following the truth we already have." Philippians 3:15,16 (NCV)

We can discuss, challenge, but not judge our brother or sister's thoughtful decisions. We must decide for ourselves. Always keep in mind that God is less concerned with behavior and more with the heart attitudes that guide your behavior. He gets personal as he inquires, "What does masturbation mean to you?"

"And this is my prayer: that your love may abound more and more in knowledge and depth of insight, so that you may be able to discern what is best." Philippians 1:9–10

CHAPTER SIXTEEN

Porn, The Brain and the Fight for Sexual Wholeness

with Ted Shimer[4]

Let's be honest—all of us have watched porn at some time in our lives. It may have been accidental, infrequent or an addiction. In this sex-saturated culture with cable, the internet and social media, the viewing of pornography is at epidemic levels with toxic effects that often aren't recognized until the damage has been done. A book on single sexuality and cultivating sexual integrity had to include a chapter addressing this destructive tidal wave.

> *"Letting your false sinful nature control your sexual thinking leads to the death of God's best for you. But letting the Spirit control your brain leads to sexual life and peace." Romans 8:6 (DER paraphrase)*

It is worth repeating what has been emphasized in various places in this book. Satan wants to destroy anything that God creates to be beautiful and intimate. His greatest weapon is deception and lies. As you read this chapter, you will see more clearly what a toxic

---

[4] Ted Shimer is the Founder of the ministry The Freedom Fight, an online porn addiction recovery program, and author of the book, *The Freedom Fight: The New Drug and the Truths That Set Us Free.* Ted received his MABS from Dallas Theological Seminary and is trained as a Pastoral Sex Addiction Professional-Supervisor. Since 1991, he has mentored men with the collegiate ministry, Student Mobilization. Ted and wife Amber have four adult children and live in Fayetteville, Arkansas.

effect porn has on sexual wholeness and intimacy—and how to defeat Satan's deception with truth as you take positive steps for fighting through to freedom.

Ted and I, as authors, know that a short chapter on porn isn't enough. But we want to help you start to identify some of the roots of porn addiction, and provide some practical ways of understanding and overcoming its enticements. Know that this is a *fight* you're engaging in and you need to fight for freedom. Your effort is essential, but effort alone is inadequate for lasting freedom. You'll need wise strategies and the help of the Holy Spirit to win. One of these wise strategies is dealing with the roots and not just the behaviors of porn addiction.

So, what are these roots that promote porn addiction? How do you become vulnerable to destructive visual and written sexual content, and end up trapped? What are the truths and the lies about porn, and the influences you need to understand and overcome? How can you put your faith into action as God helps you fight toward sexual maturity, intimacy and wholeness as you apply God's sexual truth to your life. Please, as you read over each of these roots, think, pray and let the Holy Spirit show you how overcoming each of them may be an important part of your fight for freedom.

Root 1: The Sexualized Society

Sex and sexual temptations are everywhere. There are so many triggers, especially easily accessed porn, that your eyes can take in. Social media, the Internet, cable, Netflix, and what's seen as sexually acceptable in the present culture—and the acceptance of porn as normal all contribute to a society virtually saturated with sex and sexual content. Porn comes in through your eyes and senses with what you choose to watch, but it also affects your mind and heart.

"Your eye is like a lamp that provides light for your body. When your eye is healthy, your whole body is filled with light. But when your eye is unhealthy, your whole body is filled with darkness..." Matthew 6:22, 23a (NLT)

The Lies of the Sexualized Society:

So many lies exist: Sexual fulfillment and intimate satisfaction can be found outside of God's sexual guidelines. Being devoted to God's goodness and wisdom could deny some really fun times. Sex isn't about connection and giving, but recreation and consumption. Sexual sins aren't that big a deal, and sexual holiness and integrity are practically impossible anyway.

God's Truth:

Your sexuality is a gift from God, whether single or married. Satan twists and perverts this good gift. Believers can counter the culture and live out an intimate holiness. They can fight for sexual wholeness with the power of the Holy Spirit and follow God's sexual guidelines; guidelines that actually make sense and work. Chastity and healthy sexuality are possible, important and attainable.

"So prepare your minds for action and exercise (sexual) self-control. ...So you must live as God's obedient children. Don't slip back into your old ways of living to satisfy your own (sexual) desires. You didn't know better then. But now you must be holy in everything you do (sexually), just as God who chose you is holy." I Peter 1:13a-15 (NLT parenthesis added)

You can prepare and rewire your brain as you follow God's truth. You can take steps to change your brain from patterns learned from watching porn to living out God's holy design for sexuality. Our loving Creator will always want His gift to produce intimate, unselfish connection—not dopamine buzzes.

The Application Action Steps:

Commit yourself to detox your mind and learn to be aware of your sexual triggers—both externally in the environment, and internally with mental and emotional cues. Find accountability within your singles community as together, you help each other deepen your faith, understand and pursue sexual holiness.

Root 2: The Addicted Brain

This root is especially relevant with all the research that's being done on how the brain is affected by porn. Bottomline: brains are changed and programmed by porn—but the good news is that brains can also build new neurological pathways. Repeatedly using porn creates a porn pathway in the brain, and repetition of new pathways can lead to sexual health and integrity. It's important to note that creating new pathways takes time and repetition. This can often occur in weeks, not days.

Let's dive a little deeper, but still keep it simple. Your brain has a limbic system and a prefrontal cortex (PFC). The limbic system is sometimes called the emotional brain and works to assign value and attach emotions to behavior. When someone encounters a sexual or emotional trigger, dopamine pushes the gas on the limbic system, encouraging the person to take the porn pathway of arousal and eventual pleasure/relief.

The check on the limbic system of your brain is your prefrontal cortex, your logical brain. Your PFC is responsible for executive functions: logic and the ability to problem-solve, determining healthy from unhealthy, understanding consequences, and impulse control. The limbic system regularly overrides the PFC for the sake of survival or one's well-being. When someone sexually acts out, especially as a way to medicate pain, the limbic system begins to treat porn or other unwanted sexual behavior as a way to cure pain. The next time that person feels badly, the limbic system will seek relief and it knows where to find it.[55]

In his book, *Your Brain on Porn*, Gary Wilson gives many sad testimonies of those whose brains have been altered by porn, "As a child, I was highly athletic, smart, and sociable. That all changed around age eleven, when I started watching porn videos and progressed to nearly every type of porn imaginable. I started having severe depression and anxiety. The next fifteen years of my life were miserable."[56] God so wants to help his children conquer all these negative effects of the brain and live in freedom.

The Lies of the Addicted Brain:

Two lies can sabotage those struggling with porn. First, that porn is normal for people to watch and won't have a negative effect on those who watch it. Second, that porn addiction is impossible to change.

God's Truth:

Porn can destructively rewire people's brains, but transformation and freedom are possible by renewing the mind.

"Do not be conformed to the pattern of this world, but be transformed by the renewing of your mind. Then you will be able to test and approve what God's will is—his good, pleasing and perfect will." Romans 12:2

When we discuss the renewal of the mind, it's important to distinguish between "change" and "transformation." Change is a more shallow word, that might imply using willpower to stay off of porn for a season. Transformation takes time and goes deeper—it's rewiring the brain and making dramatic shifts in how you handle your sexuality. Sometimes counselors will distinguish between first-order and second-order change. Second-order change is that deeper transformation that goes beyond behavior to a more three-dimensional paradigm shift with both the heart and the mind altered—reprogrammed.

The Application Action Steps:

You must renew your mind as you build new pathways, especially when you're triggered and tempted. The last part of this chapter will teach the specific tool of the BRACE method to help you build new neurological pathways in your brain. You don't need to simply repress the porn pathway, you must replace it, and that is what the BRACE method will help you do.

Root 3: Isolation

Sex or porn addiction are often classified as intimacy disorders. Your sexuality is intended to enhance and create intimate relationships, but porn can turn your sexuality into an isolating, self-centered activity, unsuccessful in trying to meet your deeper needs. This disconnect and isolation must be recognized, or the susceptibility to the fake, short-cut intimacy of porn will block getting your deeper needs met.

In Surfing for God, therapist Michael Cusick warns, "If we seek on the physical level what can only be obtained on a spiritual level, then we set ourselves up for a never-ending cycle that only leads to desperation, despair, and bondage. ...Your heart shares a deep connection to your body parts. ...The reality is that our heart needs something, and porn promises to meet that need."[57]

Cusick goes on to detail some of the broken promises (lies) of porn that further an isolated selfish sexual existence: "Porn promises sexual fulfillment with relationship, ...promises intimacy without risk and suffering, ...promises power over women without responsibility and humility, ...promises comfort and care without depending on others."[58] Satan uses porn to promote promises and lies that isolate a person and keep him or her trapped.

The false intimacy of porn is tempting. And when a believer resorts to porn, the resulting shame often causes him/her to retreat from vulnerable relationships, which makes the false intimacy of porn even more appealing. A vicious cycle!

The Lies of Isolation:

People believe they can meet their need to be loved and known on their own—and the isolating false intimacy of porn can be satisfying. There's always the Imposter Syndrome of: "If someone truly knew me, they wouldn't love and accept me." And, of course, there's the deception, "I can handle my addiction on my own."

All human beings need each other with deep friendships and authentic accountability. Within community, a person can confess shortcomings and find support and encouragement towards freedom. Pursuing uncontaminated sexual purity together as Christians is critical to breaking those shackles.

"Run from anything that stimulates youthful lusts. Instead, pursue righteous living, faithfulness, love, and peace. Enjoy the companionship of those who call on the Lord with pure hearts." II Timothy: 2:22 (NLT)

The Application Action Steps:

Refuse to isolate. Instead, hang out with Christians who practice sexual chastity. Truly, one of the best antidotes to lust and sexual addiction is a number of close friendships and a loving community. When triggered, seek connection with others. Take the risk of pursuing deeper relationships with God and your brothers and sisters. Welcome accountability and connection!

Root 4: Negative Emotions

Many men and women think an urge to use porn hits them out of nowhere. When they go back and evaluate what first moved them to acting out, it's usually an emotional trigger. Addiction experts tell us that an addiction goes to a deeper level when someone uses the high from a drug (i.e., porn) to medicate their negative emotions (e.g., anxiety, fear, shame, disappointment, frustration, boredom, anger, etc.).

So, if someone starts using porn to numb the stress and negative emotions in their life, then stress and these emotions become the trigger for porn. Dopamine is not only released when they experience pleasure, but it's also released in the anticipation of pleasure. When triggered by stress and negative emotions, the brain releases dopamine to start the craving. This moves you down the porn pathway to experience the temporary pleasure and relief it provides.

Porn becomes the pacifier that people go to in order to feel better. It's critical for us to grow in emotional awareness so we can identify and communicate our emotions. Additionally, we need to grow in emotional intelligence, so we know how to navigate and understand why we feel certain ways and how to process negative emotions instead of medicating them. This is why Freedom Fight ministries created a free App (Google: Freedom Fight) so people can check in daily with accountability partners where they identify their emotions and share how they're doing. Becoming aware of your emotions and learning to process them, can help you see a temptation coming.

The Lies of Negative Emotions:

The belief that suppressing or ignoring one's emotions can help them move on. This lie can distort a healthy anger or caution into a volatile explosion or fearful avoidance—or escaping through porn. Another lie is thinking you can handle your emotions on your own, when they're designed to be processed and experienced in community.

God's Truth:

Emotions are a gift from God that enrich and deepen relationships. Vulnerably sharing, "That hurt my feelings," can deepen intimacy. Friends, a counselor and God can help you sort through your emotions, instead of allowing unprocessed emotions trigger you into using porn.

"Search me, God, and know my heart; test me and know my anxious thoughts. See if there be any offensive way in me, and lead me in the way everlasting." Psalm 139:23-24

Inviting God to help you process your emotions is a helpful step. King David felt anxious and he didn't know why, so he invited God to help him figure things out.

"God did not give us a spirit that makes us afraid but a spirit of power and love and self-control." II Timothy 1:7 (NCV)

The Application Action Steps:

Download the Freedom Fight App and start identifying and sharing your emotions regularly. Become self-aware of and name three or four of the negative emotions that trigger you into using porn. Take the risk and gain the reward of processing your feelings in your relationships. The Freedom Fight App makes this simple. Experience how expressed feelings can create deeper, meaningful intimacy and kill the root of negative emotions.

Root 5: Shame

Steven Tracy, in his touching book, *Mending the Soul*, writes: "I am convinced that shame is the most powerful human emotion. It often overwhelms, directs and transforms all other emotions, thoughts and experiences."[59] We try to distinguish between "guilt" and "shame." Shame is that deep sense of worthlessness. Most books on overcoming sex or porn addiction will emphasize a vicious cycle of abuse: acting out creates shame and shame leads to more acting out to anesthetize the shame. Shame has the power to take over a person's identity as the narrative changes from: I did something bad (guilt) vs. I *AM* bad (shame).

In Chapter 18, you'll see how God has created an Emergency Room for dealing with sexual wounds and brokenness. Confession is a critical part of God's ER! When you find safe confessors and take the risk of sharing your shame—rather than condemnation, you'll find empathy and support. You'll be surprised how that can break the cycle of addition its power over you. You'll replace your sexual shame with an identity in Christ and take a giant step towards freedom.

The Lies of Shame:

It's easy for us, especially if we've been victimized by trauma or trapped in an addiction, to believe that we're worthless. We may think that God's done with us, and are unable to feel his comforting presence. Sadly, we may see our addiction as who we have become, as Satan uses the lie of shame to cripple us.

God's Truth:

God loves you deeply and has created you. All human beings have infinite worth because they're made in the image of God. As Christians, we are chosen, holy and loved—and possess through the Holy Spirit the capacity to love others into wholeness with humility.

"I praise you because you made me in an amazing and wonderful way. What you have done is wonderful. I know this very well." Psalm 139:14 (NCV)

"Therefore as God's chosen people, holy and dearly loved, clothe yourselves with compassion, kindness, humility, gentleness and patience." Colossians 3:12

How cool that that each person who gives their life to God so that he can work his redemption in their lives, can heal and grow into their true selves, because their identity is now shaped and achieved through Christ. He transforms brokenness and shame and gives you the freedom to be all that he intended you to be.

The Application Action Steps:

Satan wants you to live out of what in the New Testament is called "the flesh" or your false self. Whether addicted or not, it's easy to engage in negative self-talk and live in shame. Take time to meditate on your true self in Christ—your capacity for love, integrity, and sexual wholeness. Learn to refute your negative self-talk with new affirmations of your position in Christ. Practice confession and transparency in your friendships—and seek out those affirming, accountability relationships. These action steps can battle all six "roots" of porn addiction.

Root 6: Trauma

Trauma and the wounded child in you often direct how you live out your adult life. Trauma can fuel many negative emotions, like worthlessness, fear, and the unwillingness to be vulnerable.

You can see how trauma can so easily lead to self-medication with porn.

Oftentimes, a person has become so accustomed to living with trauma that they can't even recognize it. Trauma can come in many shapes and sizes. Sexual abuse may have occurred once or many times, but both are tremendously developmentally disabling. Trauma is not only what has been done to you (perpetrated) but is also what has *not* been done for you (neglect).

Trauma experts say that the most damaging and long-lasting impact of trauma is due to the lies the victim believes as a result of the trauma. Lies like "I deserve this". Such lies feed the shame and addiction cycle. Replacing the lies of trauma with truth is an important part in achieving freedom from addiction.

The Lies of Trauma:

Another common lie it that somehow the trauma is the victim's fault. Survivors of trauma often think they could've prevented it somehow or are responsible for what happened. Another lie is that the trauma and subsequent wounds will forever limit their lives and choices. This can shape the core beliefs of how trauma survivors see themselves as without the possibility of change or redemption.

God's Truth:

Isaiah 61 foretells Jesus' ministry and his mission to *"bind up the brokenhearted, proclaim freedom for the captives, release the prisoners from darkness, and restore the places long devastated."* What a comforting promise: that God wants to help you work through the bondage of trauma and the self-medication of addiction.

> *"The weapons we fight with are not the weapons of the world. On the contrary, they have divine power to demolish strongholds." II Corinthians 10: 4*

> *If you continue in My word, then you are truly disciples of Mine; and you will know the truth, and the truth will make you free." John 8:31-32 (NASB)*

God can help his children take negative beliefs captive as he heals the shame and trauma—replacing the lies implanted by trauma with God's truth. He can help bind up the broken, set captives free, and restore those devastated places. At times when, as a counselor, I (Doug) think about the Apostle Paul's words, *"And now these three remain: faith, hope and love. But the greatest of these is love" (I Cor. 13:13)*—I believe that maybe HOPE is the greatest of these for a trauma survivor and an addict.

The Application Action Step:

Begin by identifying the traumatic events in your life. In this process, you'll need to include a helping person. It may be an empathetic friend, or it may take someone trained in trauma therapy. In telling your story as an adult, you're also rewriting your story as you work through a variety of feelings you've probably never processed. Practice healthy self-talk as you refute your negatives beliefs and overcome the strongholds that have held you captive.

When actions steps are connected to deep convictions, they will energize new habits that will become new core beliefs and a new lifestyle. Failing to address these roots of porn and sex addiction will be like mowing a yard full of weeds. It might look great from afar, but if the roots aren't killed, the weeds will come back. Please go back over the roots and their paired lies as well as God's truth. But especially, let God and your friends help you apply the action steps to your life—and addiction.

The BRACE Method

Throughout this chapter, we've given practical suggestions for overcoming some of the roots of sexual addiction and the toxic effects of porn. Let me (Ted) introduce you to a tool that will further help you defeat the effect of porn on your life and help rewire your brain. I've named it the BRACE method to make it easier to remember and practice.

B. Breathe Deeply

Remember when we talked about the brain on porn, and how the (feeling) limbic system can overpower your (thinking) prefrontal cortex (PFC). You can actually learn to train and manage your brain. Navy SEALS are trained to reengage their PFC in the midst of battle, so they can think clearly and make more logical decisions. This is where they practice "combat breathing."

Your 3-D body, mind and heart all have to be engaged in this fight against porn and addictive thoughts and behavior. So, what is combat breathing? Nothing new, really. Many people use this throughout the day to deal with anxiety and stress. It's a slow-you-down, relax your body, deep diaphragmatic breathing that sends more oxygen to the PFC, improving your brain's ability to make wise choices and control impulsive acting out.

Combat breathing: Inhale through your nose slowly for 4 seconds (to be diaphragmatic your stomach should expand). Now hold your breath for 4 seconds. It can be helpful to imagine all your tension is being balled up in your stomach as you hold your breath. Now, slowly exhale for 4 seconds, or however long it takes to completely empty your lungs and allow your stomach to relax. The seconds aren't important. What's important is slowly inhaling (4 seconds), holding your breath as tension is balled up and oxygen goes to brain (4 to 7 seconds), then slowly exhaling, as tension is released, and your body relaxes (4 to 8 seconds). Now, you're ready to move to the next step.

R. Remember the Truth

As a Jesus follower, remembering the truth can remind you of who God is and how he wants to help you find your true identity and avoid the consequences of sinful choices. Thinking on truth helps you reengage your PFC, where higher reasoning and wise choices take place based on godly values.

> *"We demolish arguments and every pretension that sets itself up against the knowledge of God, and we take captive every thought to make it obedient to Christ." II Corinthians 10:5*

Meditating on biblical truth is a great way to refocus your mind on what is genuine and right.

- You were created in God's image and have great value. (Gen. 1:27)

- In Christ, you're dead to (freed from) sin, but alive to all God is. (Romans 6:10-11)

- Those who pursue purity (free from toxic contamination), will experience God in wonderful ways. (Matthew 5:8)

- God is able to give freedom to the captives...release prisoners from bondage (Isa. 61)

After spending thirty to sixty seconds on breathing and reminding yourself of the truth of your identity in Christ, move on to the next step—asking God for help.

A. Ask God for Help

Ask God to help you believe and act on the truths on which you're meditating. Truths won't be effective in altering your thinking if you don't believe them; and in the midst of strong temptation, it's difficult to believe they're trustworthy. This is where the Holy Spirit wants to enter in—ask for God's help. He will provide a way to escape and endure.

"No temptation has overtaken you except what is common to mankind. And God is faithful; he will not let you be tempted beyond what you can bear. But when you are tempted, he will also provide a way out so that you can endure." I Corinthians 10:13

C. Call an Accountability Partner

In order to successfully accomplish this step, you must buy into your need for community. You need to break your isolation by reaching out to someone with a call. You'll also need to have people you trust and with whom you've created a caring and transparent relationship. If you haven't made the easy friendship calls, it'll be almost impossible to make the tough" I need help" calls.

"Flee the evil desires of youth and pursue righteousness, faith, love and peace, along with those who call on the Lord out of a pure heart." II Timothy 2:22

E. Escape the Situation

This is a critical, final step. The quicker you choose to escape the temptation, the more successful you'll be. One young man stated that he had given into temptation and was angry at God for not providing him with a way to escape. However, it was like he'd been on the interstate and God had given him several exit ramps that he'd blown by before he relapsed.

There are many ways to escape after breathing, emphasizing truth, and touching base with your accountability partners. Go shopping or get some coffee. Just getting up and being around others can diffuse temptation. Hang out with your "peeps" and have fun together. Get up and do something—walk, work out, play a game. Often, you'll find that if you can ride the temptation out and distract yourself for about 15 minutes to an hour, you're safe.

How motivating that BRACE doesn't just help you avoid unhealthy thinking and behaving. It can build habits with new brain pathways. Porn addiction hijacks the brain and BRACE is a guide to finding freedom on your sexual journey. Let's summarize:

Old Porn Pathways	New BRACE Pathways
>Repress the Truth	>Remember the Truth
>Rely on You Own Strength	>Ask God for Help
>Seek Isolation	>Call to Break Isolation
>Stay in Tempting Situations	>Escape Tempting Situations

Let me (Ted) close this chapter with a quote from my book, *The Freedom Fight*. "Freedom is possible, and the earlier the believer pursues that freedom, the better. Freedom from porn bolsters faith, increases involvement in the things of God, and strengthens the relationships between God and His people.[60]

Recognize when you need further help to break your addiction. Seek out an online or in-person recovery group, or a helpful counselor that specializes in this area, as you build your accountability network. As a single person, you're reading this book because you want sexual wholeness. Let this chapter encourage you to retrain your brain and BRACE yourself into the freedom of sexual integrity and fulfilling intimacy.

CHAPTER SEVENTEEN

Viruses That Can Destroy Healthy Sexual Intimacy

The scary uncertainty of a virus stirs up fears of something incurable. Relational viruses aren't so much like incurable sexually transmitted infections as they are similar to computer viruses—disruptive and destructive, demanding immediate attention. These viruses can be deleted from your hard drive if you can recognize them and take the necessary steps to eliminate them. Even better, they can be prevented.

> *"So I say, let the Holy Spirit guide your lives. Then you won't be doing what your sinful nature craves. …the Spirit gives us desires that are opposite of what the sinful nature desires. These two forces are constantly fighting each other, so you are not free to carry out your good intentions." Galatians 5:16-17 (NLT)*

I'm glad you are reading this chapter. Take time to think through each virus and set up a good "antivirus protection." Trying to motivate people towards sexual integrity through guilt or fear of punishment isn't very effective. It's a "heart" thing empowered by the Holy Spirit. I'm profoundly moved by the verse,

> *"God blesses those whose hearts are (sexually) pure, for they will see (experience) God." Matthew 5:8 (NLT parentheses added)*

Pure = uncontaminated, virus-free, free to make wise choices, living life fully! Jesus can bring your sexuality into an undiluted, uncontaminated and awesomely *pure* place.

"I the Lord search the heart and examine the mind, to reward each person according to their conduct, according to what their deeds deserve." Jeremiah 17:10

These viruses are subtle and sneak in—avoiding them is always wiser than having to heal your heart and relationships from a particular infection. Satan, the master deceiver, will disguise them as okay or normal. Solomon, the wisest man who ever lived, warned about all the little things that destroy romantic relationships and healthy sexuality. We all need to pay attention to the "little foxes"; those small, toxic sexual influences and choices, that can hurt intimate friendships as well as dating relationships.

"Catch all the foxes, those little foxes, before they ruin the vineyard of love, for the grapevines are blossoming!" Song of Songs 2:15 (NLT)

You may wonder why the following pitfalls are so common. It's because Christian singles have legitimate sexual feelings. Because we're designed for sexual relationships. Because we're sinful, selfish human beings, who prefer shortcuts to intimacy. Because it's all too easy to let strong sexual feelings "trump" godly attitudes and values. Sometimes, you won't be self-aware enough to know identify your deeper need. That's when your friends and community can step in.

There are many more viruses than those we'll explore in this chapter. We've already delved into some of them, like *repressing* your sexuality rather than disciplining or stewarding it—refusing to embrace horny. Something is terribly wrong when sexual interaction is reduced to simple recreation and physical indulgence. God's plan is for sexual *intimacy,* not merely creating erotic highs to satisfy sexual urges. God's sexual verbs are not "score," "get some," or "hook up" but rather, "relate", "connect" and "value." Here are some other viruses that can destroy healthy sexual connecting.

Disrespecting Your Own Sexuality

The Virus: The slang word "diss" emphasizes a person's intrinsic need for justice, value and self-worth. Singles fall into the trap of sexually dissing themselves and their relationships. Unfortunately, the Christian culture is full of myths that diss God's gift of sexuality like the "virginity cult" that bases chastity on just one behavior, or that sexual sin is less forgivable than other sins. All of the following viruses distort and cheapen sexuality, but many are unaware of the traps they can fall into.

I once asked a single woman about her first date: "Did you kiss him?" I knew she'd planned to refrain from erotic behavior in Connecting relationships, and I wondered how she'd handled that temptation. She admitted that she'd kissed him, then defensively stated that he'd given her a great evening and had dropped over a hundred dollars on dinner. I sarcastically threw up my hands and declared, "So, now we're into bartering for your sexual favors?" We both laughed, but she'd gotten the point.

The hook-up culture is full of games and manipulation that devalue God's gift of true sexual intimacy. What kind of games do you unknowingly play that cheapen your sexuality? What myths and distortions have you bought into as a single adult: That you're missing out if you don't have sex? Using your erotic sexuality as relational currency? Perhaps one of the biggest "disses" is thinking that sex should be a part of any ongoing dating relationship, and not really thinking through: "What has sex come to *mean* to me—personally, and in my dating relationships?"

Another "diss": when you can't accept your own body and masculine or feminine sexuality. This actually disses the Creator who made you. A woman colleague told me she'd gotten some advice from an older woman when she was worried that her breasts weren't perfectly symmetrical: "Their sisters, not twins." Everyone worries that the sexual parts of their bodies are "too big or too small" or somehow don't look quite right.

It's disrespectful to repress your own allure as a sexual being. Sometimes this is a result of sexual trauma or a strict, religious upbringing, that fears being seen as sexy. Men, do you enjoy and find strength in your masculinity? A man can disrespect his masculinity by lusting over pornography, which degrades both genders as sex objects. Ladies, are you satisfied with your body image? A woman can easily disrespect herself by comparing her body to the cultural standards of the day. Dissing your body and sexuality is a tough virus to overcome.

God's Antivirus

Maintaining a 3-D soul virginity and honoring God's gift of sexuality are the ultimate antidotes to disrespect. Accept God's declaration that you are "fearfully and wonderfully made" (Psalm 139:14). Your body and sexuality are beautiful to him, and you can take great pleasure in that truth if you accept how much God loves you.

Christian singles can practice affirming each other's soul-sexiness rather than settling for the bartering of sexual favors, big or small. They can also create honesty in relationships and prioritize open communication. Pledge to be held accountable by close friends when you're in a Coupling relationship. Encourage them to give you honest feedback about an area where you may be courting a virus that could destroy your relationship.

Meeting Non-Erotic Needs Erotically— Nonsexual Needs Sexually

The Virus

Each person has a legitimate need for sexual adventure and excitement, to be hugged/touched, to receive comfort, to be affirmed as sexy and special, and to feel deeply valued. These are not erotic, sexual needs. Healthy single adults must find godly ways to meet these pressing needs through appropriate non-sexual means.

After John's mother died, he simply wanted a woman to comfort him. He didn't have any close women friends, so he decided the only way to accomplish this was to find a woman with whom he could become sexually involved. Megan felt unattractive and unappreciated. Sex was a way for her to feel desirable. She was currently having an affair with a married man at work. Andy was bored and created his own little adventures with porn. It's so easy for us to fall into the trap of meeting nonsexual needs sexually.

God's Antivirus

Learn healthy ways of giving and receiving non-erotic physical affection within single friendships. In singles' workshops, I often teach single adults to enjoy healthy touch through the use of conga lines and shoulder rubs. We practice hugging in ways that feel safe and comfortable for both genders. Christian brothers and sisters can give verbal compliments and help each other feel special. I sometimes wonder what happened to holy hugs and kisses that characterized the early church.

"Greet one another with a holy kiss." Romans 16:16

"Holy embraces all around!" Romans 16:16 (MSG)

"Therefore encourage one another and build each other up."
I Thessalonians 5:11

These nonsexual needs can be met in non-erotic ways, but it takes creativity, skill-building, and encouragement within your community. Especially with this particular virus, you can't live out sexual wholeness without brothers and sisters to help you. Plan adventures, hug each other by shaking each other's hands with both of yours, righteously flirt, and affirm each other. This can be such an important and fun part of the Dance of the Sexes.

Hoping Instant Erotic Connection Creates Instant Intimacy

The Virus

Many singles hope that getting naked will create an erotic connection that will meet their need for intimacy. Contrary to Hollywood's portrayal, a magical instant chemistry through having sex neither cements commitment nor ensures long-term passion. God designed romantic eroticism to flow out of intimacy—not be the primary creator of it.. How sad that sexual shortcuts usually sabotage rather than enhance intimacy,

It's not unusual that so many Christian singles who are craving love and to be pursued as someone special, hope sex will provide the quick answer to their craving for intimacy. April loved feeling "in love." She also worried that if she didn't have sex with her boyfriends, they'd abandon her. And so the virus of the quest for instant intimacy became a vicious cycle

"There's more to sex than mere skin on skin. Sex is as much a spiritual mystery as physical fact. As written in in Scripture, 'The two become one.' Since we want to become spiritually one with the Master, we must not pursue the kind of sex that avoids commitment and intimacy, leaving us more lonely than ever—the kind of sex than can never 'become one'." I Corinthians 6: 12,13 (MSG)

God's Antivirus

Sexual shortcuts may temporarily create intimacy and meet some needs—but will always leave something missing. God created humans to be incomplete without experiencing the Father's love and acceptance— and finding ways to share His love with others.

This may seem a simple antidote but single communities must learn to feely give and receive the intimate love God pours into all their hearts. This takes time and intentionality, but what reward to be truly loved.

"For we know how dearly God loves us, because he has given us the Holy Spirit to fill our hearts with his love." Romans 5:5 (NLT)

Turning Intimate Friendships Romantic

The Virus

Asking the question, "Why can't we have sex since we're already friends?" This is a great way to kill a solid friendship. Romance and erotic involvement will dramatically alter a relationship. Companionship should be part of a good dating relationship. But, believing that a great friendship is a predictor of a great romance can lead to disaster. In his singles' Bible study, Dave was one of only three guys among fourteen women. He was attractive and funny, but he was already in a Coupling relationship. He developed some significant friendships in the study and grew close to several women in the group. He thought of these girls as great friends and nothing more—until his girlfriend broke off their relationship.

Dave didn't handle it well. Suddenly his Bible study friends became "dating material." He'd never really wanted to date any of these women before, but several were attractive, and he enjoyed spending time with them. So why not? After only a few months, however, he was on speaking terms with so few in the study that he no longer felt comfortable attending. He hadn't done harm on purpose, but he found out the hard way that it's tough to date several members of a Bible study and remain comfortable in that setting when things don't pan out. This is especially true when your only rationale for dating is the fear of being alone. This is similar to the virus of indulging sexual surges, rather than disciplining them, as we've discussed in previous chapters.

God's Antivirus

Dave was clearly on the rebound and could've used another guy to talk some sense into him. If you decide to pursue Coupling with

252

a close friend, go slow and talk it through early in the process. Many friendships aren't destined for romance and/or marriage. Be intentional and subordinate your erotic desire or loneliness to wisdom and concern for the other person. "Friends with benefits" detracts from genuine intimacy and seldom leads to meaningful commitment.

Spitting into the Wind: Ignoring and Distorting Boundaries

The Virus

It's fascinating how easy it is to fall into the trap of thinking:" If I spit into the wind, I'll avoid the natural consequences." Do you really believe you can hock a goober with the wind in your face and it won't fly back and hit you? Can you speed up a relationship, spend the night at his or her apartment, drink too much, and have sex without any negative consequences?

"Do not be deceived…a man reaps what he sows." Galatians 6:7

Sexually whole singles enjoy the freedom of making wise choices rather than ignoring or testing God's law of sowing and reaping—and the chaos of ineffective boundaries. To say you won't engage in deeper erotic expression unless you're "in love" with someone (whatever that means) is not truly setting a limit. Be honest with yourself about this virus and your tendency to push limits. What creates chemistry and makes you feel "in love"? The desire to find someone similar to or different from your parents? A certain body type? Four margaritas? Loneliness? Feeling horny? Emotions can be fickle—having poor boundaries or blowing right through them can set yourself up for a world of hurt.

A sign of true maturity is the ability to postpone immediate gratification for long-term gain. Every Connecting and Coupling relationship needs healthy stop signs. Set those healthy boundaries and put stop signs in your relationships and not just the vague "in love" rule. The concept of stop signs will be further developed in later chapters, but a healthy stop sign can be an identifiable behavior (such as touching beneath each other's clothing) that you deliberately choose not to do.

Pay attention to those "catches" in your spirit when your conscience kicks in. You know, those inner misgivings that say, "This doesn't feel right." Or, "The last time I did this, it didn't work." God wants to help you keep wise boundaries. Ask for help and courage when your conscience gives you that twitch in your Spirit-directed heart and mind.

> *"So I say, let the Holy Spirit guide your lives. Then you won't be doing what your sinful nature craves." Galatians 5:16 (NLT)*

I feel sad when I hear, "My friends had reservations about this relationship, but I just couldn't hear them." One of our Creator's great anti-viruses is a *loving community* of friends and wiser people who've learned from their own mistakes and can help you avoid heartache. The decision to engage in various erotic sexual behaviors or deepen a relationship should be made intentionally and should be rationally based. Are you working on the assumption of your own values and long-term aspirations or merely acting out in the "heat" of the moment? Let your loving tribe have deliberate, invited input into your developing relationships.

To avoid these common sexual viruses will require a balance of law and grace. Stop signs will need to be thoughtfully placed, and these practical boundaries will serve as a strong antivirus to help protect your relationship from harm.

One final encouragement—remember that as Christians we should live out our sexuality within community. Each of us has the Holy Spirit renewing our hearts and minds. Please have the love and courage to *confront* that friend in your "tribe" who's on the slippery slope of falling prey to Stupid. Have those tough conversations can help your friends avoid these destructive viruses.

"To learn, you must love discipline; it is stupid to hate correction." Proverbs 12:1 (NLT)

"But encourage one another daily…so that none of you may be hardened by sin's deceitfulness." Hebrews 3:13

"And let us consider how we may spur one another on toward love and good deeds, not giving up meeting together… encouraging one another…" Hebrews 10:24,25

CHAPTER EIGHTEEN

God's Sexual E.R.

There's a girl in the corner
With tear stains on her eyes
From the places she's wandered
And the shame she can't hide
She says, how did I get here?
I'm not who I once was.
And I'm crippled by the fear
That I've fallen too far to love.

But don't you know who you are,
What's been done for you?
You are more than the choices that you've made,
You are more than the sum of your past mistakes,
You are more than the problems you create,
You've been remade!

You Are More — 10th Avenue North

Suppose you woke up one morning and said to yourself, "Today, I'd like to make some people uncomfortable; I want to watch them react with shock and revulsion." Unfortunately, there are some easy ways to accomplish that: confess a secret sexual sin, admit that you were sexually abused, acknowledge you've had more than ten sexual partners, or talk about how often you watch porn.

Josh felt his church was more likely to forgive and accept him if he told them he'd killed someone in a fit of rage than if he told them about his struggle with homosexuality. Katie slept with many guys in college, was date raped, and had an abortion. Jeannie and Tim are close friends – both were molested by their moms' boyfriends. Jordan fights sexual addiction and the urge to expose himself. April entered her Christian marriage two months' pregnant. How tragic that sexual mistakes and brokenness create such reactions of judgment, condemnation, and confusion among Christians—the very group Christ commissioned to reach out to the lonely and broken-hearted with a message of hope and healing!

Christian sex therapist Cliff Penner once told me that he views single sexuality as a hand grenade in the Church—mostly ignored, but ready to explode. Guilt runs rampant. Inconsistency exists between our stated Christian values and our actual Christian behavior. Penner fears that much of our single Christian leadership has been lost because of sexual sin and guilt, and the inability of the Church to effectively address it.

In the story of the prodigal son, the father embraced the shamed and dirty son while the older brother looked on in judgment (see Luke 15:11–32). Similarly, our heavenly Father grieves over sexual sin and longs for reconciliation with us. Why does sexual sin seem to create a special kind of guilt and shame?

The Uniqueness of Sexual Sin

It shouldn't be surprising. Sexuality in general—and sexual sin in particular—isn't often addressed in the Christian community. Consequently, it seems scary, shameful, and weirdly perverse. Many in the Church judge the sexually hurting. I wonder if it's because they fear being found out themselves. Most Christians don't reflect Christ's compassion for the wounded sexual sinner.

Jesus wouldn't have flinched or condemned the chronic masturbator, a practicing gay man or woman, the voyeur, sex addict or promiscuous college student. He'd have gently brought his redemptive touch to bear as he asked, "Why don't you tell me about it?" He'd have listened to the story of the sexually molested or raped with empathy.

One reason sexual sin carries more weight is from misunderstanding of God's sexual economy. Because he made us to reflect Himself, sexual sin touches a part of us few other sins do. Even the most casual sexual encounter violates something deep within.

> *"Flee from sexual immorality. All other sins a person commits are outside his body, but whoever sins sexually, sins against their own body. Do you not know that your bodies are temples of the Holy Spirit, who is in you, whom you have received from God?" 1 Corinthians 6:18–19*

The consequences of sexual sin affect us more deeply than lying or being impolite. Our sexual sin affects our total personhood (body, mind and heart) and can destroy true intimacy. And often, the consequences affect more than the sinner, as many of you who've been victims of another's sexual brokenness can testify. Something that was meant to be valued is shared with casual indifference. Promises are broken, beauty is distorted, and trust is betrayed.

Tragically, Christians confuse the greater consequence of sexual sin with the need for greater judgment on those who struggle with it. God recognizes our identity in Christ and is able to separates who we are from our sinful mistakes. He doesn't pass out scarlet letters for sleeping with your high school girlfriend, struggling with same-sex attraction, having an abortion, or compulsive masturbation. A rewarding part of my ministry as a Christian sex therapist is seeing God's restoration. Sexual sin isn't less forgivable than other sins. In God's eyes, sexual restoration is an opportunity for building a testimony of Christ's redemptive power and love. He graciously invites us to his emergency room for healing.

The Necessity of the E.R. Experience

Have you ever been to an emergency room? I remember when my ladder (propped up on wet leaves) dropped me onto a stone walkway. My hand bled profusely, and my bruised ribs made breathing difficult. How glad I was for a place focused exclusively on restoring me to health!

Remember the story of the woman caught in adultery (John 8:1–11)? She also needed a physician of sorts, because she was about to be stoned to death. Fortunately, the Physician on duty that day made house calls. He brought the E.R. to her. Her story is one of the most captivating passages in all of the Gospels. It tells of a woman's miraculous encounter with Christ. She didn't deserve his mercy and care, yet he gave it anyway. Of particular interest is the "prescription" he gave her. Jesus told her accusers they were free to stone her for her sin—but only if they were without sin. Of course, none were. One by one, they left the scene. Jesus asked her if anyone still condemned her. She answered, "No one."

He then administered his healing antidote:

"Then neither do I condemn you...Go now and leave your life of sin." John 8:11

Jesus prescribed an inside-out lifestyle change, a transformation consistent with God's will for her. However, he first performed a "spiritual transplant" by giving her the spiritual power necessary to accomplish a change in her behavior: his forgiveness. "Neither do I condemn you." Jesus's lack of condemnation was the spiritual power needed to break through her shame, enabling her to live out God's desire for her.

This is what God's sexual E.R. is all about. When your sexual self becomes distorted or broken, the Great Physician wants to give you a heart transplant that transforms your mind and life—empowering you through his forgiveness and presence. But you also have a part in this process. Tough choices must be made to focus on healing. You'll also need humility to ask others for help. Time alone doesn't heal, but time with the proper treatment can bring healing, relief from guilt—and restoration. Surrendering to God and allowing him to perform spiritual surgery and transformation *his way* is vital.

The ER Treatment

God didn't panic when Adam and Eve's sin distorted his beautiful creation. Neither does he do so with us. Instead, he makes a way to *"bind up the brokenhearted, to proclaim freedom for the captives… to comfort all who mourn and provide for those who grieve"* (Isaiah 61:1–2). Instead of shame and disgrace, *"everlasting joy will be theirs"* (v. 7).

When we're wounded and hurting, especially sexually, we can come to God's emergency room. His E.R. is equipped with the treatment options necessary to heal our distorted and broken sexuality. Let's look at a few of the more common interventions in the Emergency Room. They include: confronting, grieving, confessing, repenting, forgiving, making amends, accountability, and becoming whole.

Confronting

"Correct, rebuke, and encourage—with great patience and careful instruction." II Timothy 4:2

"But exhort one another daily...lest any of you be hardened through the deceitfulness of sin." Hebrews 3:13 (NKJV)

The Apostle Paul knew that life in this fallen world would require Christians to hold each other accountable for growing and avoid becoming trapped by sin's deceitfulness. We live out our sexuality within community and we *should* be in each other's sexual business. Sexual sin appeals to our selfish desire and is exciting. We should all be encouraged to look out for our fellow Christian brothers and sisters. We should confront when we see behavior or attitudes out of line with God's sexual economy.

We should model our confrontation after Christ, who *"is able to deal gently with those who are ignorant and are going astray"* (Hebrews 5:2). We know there's a lot of sexual sin we can fall prey to. We can help each other confess and repent, grieve and change.

In confrontation, it helps to sandwich your correction with encouragement. "You have such a great small group to disciple you. Why don't you run your relationship with your boyfriend by them? God is doing some amazing things in your life." Sandwiching suggestions or confrontations between affirmations creates less defensiveness and is likelier to encourage change.

We have to care enough to confront. I think that one of the reasons Jesus didn't let the religious rulers throw stones at the woman taken in adultery is because they didn't love her enough to correct her. We have to have someone's best interest at heart—to really care about them—in order for confrontation to be an effective part of God's emergency room.

Grieving

"Blessed are those who mourn, for they shall be comforted."
Matthew 5:4 (NKJV)

"Come close to God, and he will come close to you. Wash your hands, you sinners; purify your hearts...Let there be tears for what you have done. Let there be sorrow and deep grief. ...Humble yourselves before the Lord, and he will lift you up in honor." James 4:8-10 (NLT)

Because we live in a broken world, we must learn to grieve. Grieving can take many forms, but it's often filled with cleansing, healing tears as we work through denial, anger, confusion and hurt. We may grieve what we've suffered, or we may feel genuine remorse over how we've dishonored God's gift of sexuality.

Although tears aren't always necessary, admitting the truth, feeling painful feelings, and letting go of things are all critical. God knew we would need to grieve to help heal our three-dimensional selves in this messy world. He promises his comfort.

Kyle and April were in God's sexual E.R. because they planned to get married, but neither had set effective sexual boundaries in their previous romantic relationships, or with each other. They were engaged when April got pregnant. As a result, April began fears Kyle's abandonment (such fears had motivated her sexual behavior in the past). Kyle became honest about using his previous girlfriends for his own selfish sexual gratification. Both grieved over what they'd lost over the years as they moved toward healing. Once April allowed herself to grieve, it wasn't just over what she'd forfeited with Kyle—lots of distorted and hurtful relationships with men came flooding back, including an inappropriate relationship with her dad.

As with April and Kyle, our grief may be over a whole collection of wounds. A present loss may trigger grief over previous losses that haven't been properly addressed and healed. Grieving isn't a process that can be worked through alone. You'll need others to share the process with you, holding and encouraging your wounds, as you cry tears of release.

"For the kind of sorrow God want us to experience leads us away from sin and results in salvation." 2 Corinthians 7:10 (NLT)

True guilt (or godly sorrow) is a catalyst for a healthy grief that drives us toward needed change, and back to God's purpose for our lives. Without it, we'll likely miss out on his best. If we ask the Holy Spirit's guidance to convict us of sin, he'll lead us straight to God's emergency room. Such conviction helps us see where we've violated God's values, and will motivate us toward healthy grief, confession, and repentance.

In grieving, you'll experience a variety of emotions: sorrow and tears, anger, depression, guilt, and fear. Our emotions will serve us well if we allow them to motivate us toward godly change. Use anger, sadness, fear and guilt as catalysts for transformation, seeing them as God's tools for mending the losses in your broken places. Anger can signal that something that happened was wrong. Sadness helps us feel what we've lost. Guilt and shame turn us toward needed change. Fear can motivate you to seek help. Accepting and dealing with emotions is a key part of E.R. work.

Confessing

What's your darkest secret? What skeletons are in your closet that you desperately hope no one discovers? I would guess that most of them are sexual in nature. Healing confession of sexual brokenness is a gift we don't often receive in the Church. I remember Jordan, a client who struggled with sexual addiction and exhibitionism. One day, we were discussing how great it would be if he could find a mature couple in his church to mentor him. He'd confess, "I'm struggling with exhibitionism," and they'd reply, "Dear brother, we're so sorry. That's a tough sin to wrestle with. Tell us more about your struggle, and we'll come alongside you and love you toward greater sexual wholeness."

We both burst out laughing: "Yeah, right! Do those kinds of people even exist?" Believe it or not, they do. Jordan was able to find compassionate, godly people to love and accept him. But I won't lie to you. They're not always easy to find.

"People who cover over their sins will not prosper. But if they confess and forsake them, they will receive mercy." Proverbs 28:13 (NLT)

Confession brings secrets to light, draining their power. Satan operates in secrecy and darkness. The secrets we hide fester and gain greater destructive power. When we bring them to the light, God gives us his perspective on them. The one who confesses his lust for someone else often finds his attraction greatly diminished. As we confess our secrets, Satan is robbed of his condemning, enslaving power—giving us hope and perspective to make necessary changes.

"Confess your sins to each other, and pray for each other, so God can heal you. When a believing person prays, great things happen." James 5:16 (NCV)

Confession also allows God and a caring person or community to see our ugliness and love us anyway. Humble confession and taking ownership of one's mistakes is a discipline every community of singles should practice. It stops us from feeling that we're imposters. In our previous examples, April, Kyle, and Jordan experienced the healing power of confession when they trusted enough to risk revealing their secrets. We can let go of guilt and shame as we separate what we've done from who we are. We can move from imposters to redeemable sinners.

Confession is a life-changing gift to the confessor *and* the one who receives the confession. The confessor exposes his wounds and ugliness; bravely trusting, painfully grieving, and accepting love and care from the one receiving his confession. The one receiving the confession covers the confessor with grace-filled acceptance and forgiveness, practicing confidentiality, and isn't repulsed by the sexual sinner or pass judgment on him or her.

Seeking out appropriate confessors isn't an easy process. Men need other men to hear their confessions—men who'll encourage them and hold their feet to the fire without overreacting. Women need a girlfriend with whom they can unload, feel understood by, and be exhorted toward maturity. Both men and women need safe people in their lives who truly care about them. At times you'll need to both give and receive this gift of confession, as you mature in your soul virginity.

Repenting

Repentance is a central element in Christian change and redemption. It demonstrates that you recognize and accept responsibility for your wrong thoughts and behaviors—that difficult process of *owning*. You must then choose to make necessary changes as God breaks the destructive power of sin and encourages growth in your life.

> *"[The Lord] is patient with you, not wanting anyone to perish, but everyone to come to repentance." 2 Peter 3:9*

> *"Godly sorrow brings repentance that leads to salvation and brings no regret." 2 Corinthians 7:10*

Repentance is putting feet to your remorse, making dramatic, at times 180-degree changes in life. The Greek word for repentance (metanoia) means to change your mind and way of thinking. Remember that we sin three-dimensionally with sinful actions, selfish thoughts and feelings, and a heart that's unloving. We must therefore repent 3-dimensionally. With the Holy Spirit's power and enlightenment, repentance affects our total 3-D personhood as we mature in sexual purity.

> *"Produce fruit in keeping with repentance." Matthew 3:8*

> *"Do the things that show you really have changed your hearts and lives." Matthew 3:8 (NCV)*

Some of you have already encountered serious sexual mistakes and trauma. Please know that God is no more repulsed by you than a doctor who sees a trauma victim in the E.R. However, his compassion for your condition motivates our Savior to use his healing touch to bring you back to health. This can include confrontation, grieving, and a confession that brings repentance. Your humble presence in the ER is all that's required.

Katie (whom you met at the beginning of this chapter) was sexually involved with many guys in college. Three of them were casual hookups when she was drunk. She felt some shame over this behavior, but thought it was just a normal part being single. But when Christ entered her life, she felt cheated and ashamed by what she'd done and by what had been done to her. This godly sorrow began a process of character change in her life and will require many ongoing choices in her lifetime.

We must actively search out the destructive thoughts and behaviors that damage our sexuality in order to change them. Identifying them, making initial changes, and then continuing to change is the only way sexual healing and growth take place. But take heart in Scripture's promise:

"The God who started the great work in you [will] keep at it and bring it to a flourishing finish on the very day Christ Jesus appears" Philippians 1:6 (MSG)

An important part of sexual repentance is breaking the unseen hold sinful relationships have on us. We sometimes call these "soul ties." When two people have sex outside marriage, they become "one flesh" (1 Corinthians 6:16); an intimacy has been established. Here's a practical step many have found helpful: specifically recall each person you've shared a sexual relationship with and ask forgiveness from God. Further ask him to break any bonds that may still exist between you. This could include fantasies, continued inappropriate contact or guilt. In the E.R., we trust the Creator's power to bring a surprising makeover.

Forgiving

Kari came to me, weeping that she'd ruined her honeymoon. Though her wedding was still three weeks away, she wasn't a physical virgin and feared her sexual past had "totally destroyed" any chance of a meaningful honeymoon. I asked if she felt God and her fiancé had forgiven her. She replied that Jeremy had amazed her with his understanding, forgiveness, and acceptance of her. Of course, God had also forgiven her.

I helped her understand that her past wouldn't ruin her honeymoon. It was her inability to forgive herself that might damage the gift God wanted to give her in her marriage to Jeremy. As Christians, we're not given an option to forgive—we forgive because we've been forgiven. Jesus taught us to forgive "seventy times seven" (in other words, as many times as it takes), not because our offender deserves it, but because we remember how great a debt we owed that was canceled by God himself (Matthew 18:21–35). To refuse to forgive another's offense is to mock God's own gift of forgiveness to us.

"Make allowance for each other's faults, and forgive anyone who offends you. Remember, the Lord forgave you, so you must forgive others." Colossians 3:13 (NLT)

Like Kari, we sometimes find ourselves the most difficult person to whom to extend grace. Whether for others or ourselves, restoration in God's E.R. comes from letting go of condemnation and allowing God to apply his healing salve of grace and forgiveness.

"The Lord is compassionate and gracious, slow to anger, abounding in love... He does not treat us as our sins deserve." Psalm 103:8, 10

God knows we desperately need his grace. His forgiveness enables us to offer the same to others—and to ourselves. We must learn to master forgiveness as one of God's healing arts. Some initial steps might include:

1. Confess your sins to yourself, to God, and to a trusted Christian brother or sister (this could also be a minister, spiritual director, counselor, or accountability partner). Allow this other person to help you separate what you've done from you are as God's child, and to demonstrate God's loving acceptance and forgiveness to you. (See 1 John 1:9)
2. Thank God for his mercy and forgiveness as you embrace it with your head and your heart. Consider praying through Psalm 51 or Psalm 103.
3. Ask God to help you grieve your losses and release the shame, so you might see the wonderful "hope and future" he has for you (Jeremiah 29:11).
4. Make needed behavior changes and *restitution* to clear your conscience and reconcile your relationships.

Making Amends (Restitution)

After his own confession and repentance, Zacchaeus told Jesus he would make amends to those he had cheated as a tax collector: *"If I have cheated anybody out of anything, I will pay back four times the amount" (Luke 19:8).* Christ saw evidence of true repentance in his action. Zacchaeus needed to make those amends to experience deeper healing.

Other words for making amends are *restoration* or *restitution*. Making amends involves taking ownership for your offenses and reinforces a change of heart. It also helps restore trust and intimacy in your relationships, promoting further growth and healing. Kyle and April decided that part of their amends to each other would be to set aside time and money for counseling.

Attending a support group, getting counseling, and offering to right wrongs to those you've offended will all move you toward wholeness. Mentor teens in your church, so they'll avoid making the same mistakes you did, or contribute to a nonprofit working to stop sex-trafficking are examples of an indirect amends.

> *"Just see what this godly sorrow produced in you! Such earnestness, such concern to clear yourselves...You showed that you have done everything necessary to make things right." II Corinthians 7:11 (NLT)*

Understand that making amends differs from confession. Making amends is taking actions steps to mend relationships: "I've sinned against you; what can I do to make this right?" Though it stems from godly sorrow and remorse, this is an active process beyond a simple, "I'm sorry." Healthy communities need this restoring process.

Be careful—all amends aren't necessarily healthy. In the Twelve-Step model of recovery, Step Nine says, "We make direct amends to people when possible, except when doing so will injure them or others."[61] It's not just about your need to make things right. To unearth an issue that has been dormant for 20 years, or to bring up a hurt previously unknown to the other person isn't always healing. Seek out a mature friend for advice before undertaking such amends.

In some cases, amends may need to be indirect (sharing helpful lessons learned with others) rather than directly dealing with the offended party.

Personal and Community Accountability

Throughout this book I've emphasized that single adults need a loving community in order to thrive. This is especially true of the E.R. processes. You'll need good friends and a caring community to "keep you on your toes" as you become more like Jesus—the ultimate model of sexual wholeness.

> *"So watch your step, friends. Make sure there's no evil unbelief lying around that will trip you up and throw you off course, diverting you from the living God. For as long it is still God's Today, keep each other on your toes so sin doesn't slow down your reflexes. If we can only keep our grip on the sure thing we started out with, we're in this with Christ for the long haul." Hebrews 3:12-14 (MSG)*

Be humble as you invite others into your life to help you live out God's sexual economy. Accountability starts with your vertical relationship to God, as you build that godly value structure to guide your sexual journey. Then, you can create horizontal accountability by inviting some good friends and your community to come alongside and help you live out your vertical values. Your accountability network will only be as good as your active pursuit in reaching out to others for help—boldly confronting you as you practice confession, repentance and forgiveness.

I rarely see Christian communities hold each other accountable. The early church seemed to do better. Yes, I know these are tough conversations, "Are you spending the night at your girlfriend's apartment?" or, "Is that TV show (or social media) good for you?" We are indeed our brother and sister's keeper, and some healthy accountability, lovingly practiced, is a much- needed skill.

"Dear brothers and sisters, if another believer is overcome by some sin, you who are godly should gently and humbly help that person back onto the right path. And be careful not to fall into the same temptation yourself." Galatians 6:1 (NLT)

Sexually Whole: Our Father's Heart and the Process of Growth and Restoration

Once your wounds are bandaged, the Great Physician gives you the responsibility for overcoming your immaturity and making wise choices. Put simply, he expects you to grow up and engage in some healthy "Adulting." Reading this book and finding other helpful tools will go far in overcoming obstacles and incorporating new heart attitudes. Creating your healthy sexual narrative is a lifelong process of choices and growth toward maturity.

A Complex Journey of Growth

Through a tough time of maturing in God's E.R., Josh realized that becoming more Christ-like was a healthier goal than simply striving to "become straight." His lack of soul virginity was deeper than his struggle with same-sex attraction. He needed to better appreciate his masculinity and to heal his mother and father wounds. He recognized his need to make friends with women who valued and encouraged it, rather than treating him as "one of the girls." He wanted a man who he wouldn't objectify. He was also becoming more aware of his struggle with isolation and sexual addiction.

Do the consequences of your sin haunt you? Do new relationships unearth old memories of sexual brokenness you'd like to forget? Like Kari, are you worried that you've ruined your future honeymoon? Recall the story of the prodigal son:

"So he got up and went to his father. But while he was still a long way off, his father saw him and was filled with compassion for him; he ran to his son, threw his arms around him and kissed him." Luke 15:20

Restoring What's Lost—The Years The Locust Ate

A striking aspect of our Father's heart is revealed in the book of Joel. Israel was often spoken of as a woman who, in her attempt to follow the gods of the nations around her, "played the harlot," spiritually speaking. Scripture frequently records God discipline of Israel for her spiritual adultery, often by allowing a neighboring nation to take her captive and exile her from the Promised Land. But by his mercy—God promised to restore her losses, if only she'd exhibit true remorse, confession, and repentance over her sin.

"The Lord says, 'Even now, come back to me with all your heart. Fast, cry, and be sad.' Tearing your clothes is not enough to show you are sad: let your heart be broken. Come back to the Lord your God, because he is kind and shows mercy...and he has great love. ...I will restore to you the years that the swarming locust has eaten.'" Joel 2:12–13, 25 (NCV, NKJV)

Of course, some consequences of your sin may remain, such as an STI, haunting memories, the loss of innocence, the loss of physical virginity, or an aborted child. However, in marvelous ways God can heal the past and make things new. In thinking through the process God takes you through to restore the "locust-eaten" events in your life, five steps are important:

1. Create a deeply meaningful love relationship with God through Jesus—that is the beginning place.
2. Allow God to heal your guilt and shame, through forgiveness; as you live fully in the present, rather than continuously grieving the past or fearing the future.
3. Recognize that God has always been with you, and he can change your perspective from one that was ravaged by locusts, to seeing that his loving presence buffered you from even greater sins.
4. Know that God can always trump Satan, and that there were valuable life lessons learned in the midst of your pain which God used as a catalyst to bring you closer to him.
5. Take the new you, and the lessons you've learned, and build healthier future relationships to experience an intimacy you've never had.

The E.R. can help you become a living testimony to God's ability to forgive, heal, grow and restore. Please begin your own personal journey into healing, because it takes two *whole* people to create *whole,* healthy and intimate sexual relationships.

CHAPTER NINETEEN

Is This a Date?

with Vickie L. George[5]

Jodie came to counseling, wondering if it was possible for her to have good friendships with men. Unless they saw a potential girlfriend, they didn't seem to want to connect. She longed for compliments from men, a listening ear and talk from masculine perspective—and in time, a "boyfriend." In Josh's last two relationships, the women quickly "fell in love" with him, when he simply wanted to be friends—at least early on. He was also frustrated that his community assumed that because a man and a woman were spending time together, they were classified as an "item."

All successful Coupling relationships begin as Connecting friendships—even blind dates and online matches. Making romance or erotic attraction the focal point of a new relationship, without first establishing a genuine companionship, all but guarantees you'll flame out when the intoxicating feelings fade. So, why don't these fulfilling opposite sex friendships occur more frequently? Possibilities include:

---

[5] Vickie George (M.Ed., MS) is a Licensed Marriage and Family Therapist, Licensed Professional Counselor, Certified Sex Therapist and Approved Supervisor. Besides her private practice, Vickie had supervised the next generation of therapists for 30 years. She has taught graduate classes, interviewed hundreds of missionary candidates for the mission field and spoken at numerous conferences. She was in practice with Doug for over 20 years.

- Initial awkwardness and a hesitation to risk a misunderstanding
- Avoiding natural sexual feelings rather than valuing and stewarding them
- A fear that one of you will fall in love, but the feelings won't be mutual
- A belief that spending one-on-one time together makes you a couple, rather than enjoying the friendship
- Distorted connecting relationships over the years
- A lack of information about the sexual difference between men and women
- Not enough DTRs (Define the Relationship conversations)

In Chapter Eight, I emphasized the importance, and often absence, of that skill of DTR'). We worked through the three critical skills of DTRs: Constancy, Compassion and Clarity. Constancy in occurring frequently and intentionally; Compassionate in "speaking the truth in love" as we guide a relationship; Clarity, speaking and acting with transparency and honesty.

Distorted Connecting Relationships

Of the three types of relationships—Connecting (friends), Coupling (becoming an item), and Covenanting (marriage)—we spend most of our time in Connecting friendships, whether we're single or married. But from an early age, many experience significant distortions in both and opposite-sex intimacy. All of us learning about Connecting relationships on, most often from observing others. Parents, stepparents, peers, and extended family all play a large part in our early understanding of same-sex and opposite-sex relating—for good or for bad.

Some lessons are verbally spelled out; others are more caught than taught. A young girl whose stepmom takes the time to watch her dance recital, quickly learns she has something special to offer. Yet, a girl whose uncle molests her, may learn to yield sexually to please the men in her life. A young boy whose grandfather teaches him to fish or catch fireflies, learns how mutually enjoyed activities create meaningful relationships. Yet, he quickly learns to hide his feelings from others when, after he scrapes his knee, his mother warns, "Big boys don't cry."

The schoolyard is a notorious source for negative messages related to Connecting. Within peer groups, mean-spirited rejection from other children cut deeply into a child's sense of self. For many, fearfulness in same-sex or opposite-sex Connecting has its roots in these formative years. Having never been taught to connect in healthy and respectful ways, many rely on trial and error as their primary learning tool.

Through much relational drama, some will successfully learn to connect with the same and opposite sex. Others will be scarred by pitiless rejection or manipulation. Lessons of unhealthy sexual identity are often carried into adulthood and haunt many for life: a fear of women, a hatred of men, narcissistic male dominance, erotically manipulative femininity, and putting up walls in any intimate relationship. Others will isolate themselves with Internet porn or sex chat rooms, favoring pseudo-relationships, rather than risking the pain of more complex relationships in the real world.

Let's be honest—as adults, your past has left its scars. If you feel the weight of that baggage, you may need help to let it go. Most people aren't objective enough to work through it on their own, and others don't recognize the walls they put up. Current and future Coupling partners can be healing. It often takes a successful new relationship to heal from an earlier hurtful one. It is also helpful is enlist a mentor, pastor, Christian counselor, or a a healthy singles community to help you understand how to leave your past behind and embrace heal a healthier present.

Misunderstanding the Sexual Differences of Men and Women

Too often men are sold short with comments like, "All he thinks about is sex," or "He's a man; no wonder he sucks at relationships." The truth is, men often want an emotional connection, can be sensitive, and thrive on friendship and social sexuality. Women are often cast as too emotional, and either uninterested in sex or come on too strongly. The truth is that though women's and men's sexuality differ, it will often be more similar than different.

Men and the Sexual Dance

Men are as fascinating as women —not as complex, but equally interesting in his contribution to the dance. The following demonstrates some of the ways many men differ from women in their sexual style.

Assertive

With more testosterone and the absence of menstrual fluctuation, men generally possess a more consistent and assertive sex drive. They typically have sexual thoughts more often than women. Men can enjoy initiating, whether in friendship, playful flirting, or erotic sexual behaviors. (Unfortunately, much of the broken masculinity in Western culture has been in this area, with men reverting to passivity in great numbers—and not initiating, for a variety of personal and societal fears and reservations.)

Simple and Eternal Adolescents

The need for adventure permeates masculinity. Physical activity is the most common way men affirm each another. Men also experience affirmation from women through physical affection.

Erotic connection often makes a man feel like everything's okay in his relationship with a woman. Men are more predictable in what arouses them. With an "eternal adolescence" and a childlike curiosity, guys experience more immediate enjoyment of sexual cues and can neglect the emotional connecting women need.

MEN:

Physical intimacy >

      connects the heart >

            leads to emotional closeness

Visual with Mental Imagery

Women notice men and create mental imagery. However, this can differ dramatically from the male process. Men zoom in visually on female parts and curves. They're much more specific in their mental imagery—breasts, booty, navel, legs, and so on. Erotic arousal happens quickly.

Men often see a sexual cue and run with it. His fantasy life is off and running unless he exercises the discipline to rein it in. Female fantasy tends to create sensual pictures, tends to focus on the whole person, noticing things like his smile, voice, and emotional response.

Women and the Sexual Dance

Rom-coms, reality shows and many movies unrealistically portray women as casual about sex, and suggest, often with a subtle pressure, the need to be more aggressive and less modest. Rarely is sexual connecting linked to an expectation of an exclusive emotional commitment and truly intimate relationships.

When the modern woman attempts to separate erotic behavior from loving tenderness and the feeling of being cherished, she loses out on becoming who God created her to be. A woman should never abandon these God-given desires to be known, pursued and special!

<u>WOMEN:</u>

Emotional closeness >

    connects the heart >

        open door to physical intimacy

Chantal's favorite memory with Tyson was a long walk on the beach—hanging out, talking, and holding hands by the salty air and surf. For her, kissing and caressing may follow the walk. But Tyson's physical advances before such emotional connecting may seem pushy and intrusive to her.

Women take in a man's character, tone of voice, communication style, and personality. My wife, Catherine, likes my dimples and hairy legs. But she says my optimism, sense of humor, and gentle spirit are what really turn her on.

Slow and Special

Women usually like to begin the dance slowly. Slow and more romantic characterizes the feminine approach. She he may then enjoy more direct sexual pursuit and romantic involvement. Feeling valued is so important for women rather than simple being viewed as a sex object. But don't think that women don't have sexual feelings and can be as attracted and aroused as their male counterparts.

The female sexual dance is to a variable beat. Men try to anticipate a woman's next move or the direction of the relationship, but this often doesn't fit with the complexity of women's sexuality. Successful relating to a girlfriend or spouse won't conform to a formula. Men might need to prepare plans A through E (or maybe Z!), and learn how to gracefully shift from plan to plan without getting defensive or pouting . Instead, they should simply enjoy the moment in the dance.

Ladies, you may need to provide some honest coaching on the nuances of your responses. Men want to man-up and be the "knight in shining armor" for the women in the dance with them.

The Relationship Continuum Bridge

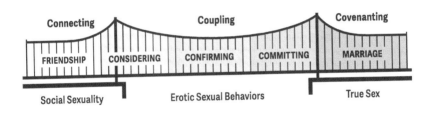

Skill-building in Connecting Friendships

As we look again at the Bridge Continuum, single adults can judiciously steward their Connecting relationships with healthy Social Sexuality to prepare for future Coupling and Covenanting intimacy. This season of singleness is a time to learn relational *skills* that will help you move toward a great marriage. We've explored some of them, like righteous flirting and managing horny. Here are some additional strategies singles have found helpful as they move from friendship to romance.

List-Making (Non-Negotiables and Desirables)

When you connect with a member of the opposite sex, you have the opportunity to explore the characteristics you're looking for in a future partner. What's her faith background? Is he introverted or extroverted? Does she like to hike or is she more of a homebody? Is he organized or more spontaneous and carefree? What are her personal strengths and weaknesses? Could you deal with his or her idiosyncrasies in a marital relationship *if he or she never changed*?

Qualities such as integrity, respect, attractiveness, responsibility, and trustworthiness are those most of us would want in a potential mate. You may desire other qualities as well, such as a sense of humor, intelligence, outdoorsy, playful, steady, adventurous, artistic, outgoing, challenging, or has a desire to travel. But I can't downplay the importance of chemistry. This box must be checked for a great marriage.

Observing these character traits up close – before the interference of serious romantic involvement – is advantageous to learning about yourself and the kind of person you're ultimately seeking. At the online relationship website eHarmony.com, Dr. Neil Clark Warren uses two categories: "Must Haves" and "Can't Stands." Similarly, we suggest you create your own list of ten to fifteen non-negotiables (things you either couldn't live with or couldn't live without in a Covenanting partner) and another list of ten to fifteen desirables (things you would love to have, but won't be deal-breakers if you don't find them). Whatever the method, it's important to clarify what you're looking for before getting into a serious romantic relationship. Once the flames of romance are ablaze, objectivity disappears. But it's important to recognize that there are no perfect relationships or matches.

I (Vickie) made a list of things I was looking for spiritually, emotionally, physically, intellectually, and vocationally. I used this as my overall framework, then filled in specifics as I learned more about myself and what I wanted. For instance, under "emotionally" I included such characteristics as warm, a good listener, sensitive toward others, and having a servant's heart. As a married woman, looking back, I'm still amazed at how my husband fits the characteristics on my list. Of course, it took twenty years to find him, but he was worth the wait!

Letters to Your Future Mate

An interesting exercise while you anticipate a future mate while keeping Connecting friendships in proper perspective: buy some stationery and write letters to your future mate. Write about your dreams and struggles, your sexual ache and the anticipation of its fulfillment, and the things you hope to someday share together. Write about the character traits you desire and admire most. Think about how you'd help your mate reach his or her true potential. Be open with your feelings and expectations. Keep your letters private from your Coupling relationships until your Covenanting partner finally arrives.

Tracey Casale, a friend, allowed me to share an excerpt from one of her own love letters: "You cross my mind frequently, and often I pray for your beloved soul. I've been learning to love you faithfully, even before I know your name. I will do my best to love you fully and live in such a way that I have a full self to give you. I'm reminded as I sit under the stars tonight, and as I hear the waves brushing gently against the shore, that you're the one I will make a full gift of myself to, only you. You will have my whole heart, mind, and body. Please know that for now, writing is the only way I know to love you, to give you my love now. Love, Tracey."

Writing letters such as Tracey's can bring many benefits to your Connecting friendships. They may:

- assist you in developing a model for what you desire in a future mate
- help you maintain your perspective in Connecting relationships, and not rush into Coupling
- strengthen your resolve to protect your soul virginity during Coupling
- aid you as you practice a transparent style of communicating your feelings and desires (will serve you well in developing meaningful friendships and preparing for a future marriage)
- prepare a one-of-a-kind gift to be read by your future spouse

Searching for Mr. or Mrs. Right

What we've mentioned thus far illustrates the importance of same-sex and opposite-sex friendships. Through them, you'll lay the groundwork for a significant secondary benefit of Connecting: finding those of the opposite sex you'd consider marrying. Of course, finding that person can be exasperating. With so many unhealthy and immature men and women to sift through, where should you look to find the godly mate of your dreams?

The local bar isn't likely to have what you're looking for as a Christian single. However, there are good alternatives to consider. For example, I (Vickie) met my husband at a gym that was part of our church. We knew each other as friends for four years before our first date.

Even if at first sight you find someone sexually attractive, pursuing a friendship first will allow each of you to know the other more fully before exploring each other as potential lovers.

Singles Groups at a Local Church

Many Christian singles enjoy a singles group of at medium- or large-sized church. While this is a valid place for finding a quality mate, ensure to carefully examine your motives. Too many singles attend a church with an active singles group for the sole purpose of finding a mate. The purpose for a local church community is to provide a spiritual family for each believer, where you can mutually serve each another with your spiritual giftedness (see 1 Corinthians 12:18). If you merely select a church based on its potential to help you find a spouse, you'll likely bounce from church to church, and miss the greater benefits of a stable, supportive church community.

Online Romance

Online dating has become increasingly popular among Christian singles. The success of such websites comes from their ability to remove some of the guesswork in finding a potential mate by screening out candidates who don't fit your standard of attractiveness, personality or values. They allow single adults to meet people (either locally or across the globe) who never would've met otherwise. But a word to the wise: don't always believe everything you read in someone's online profile.

Too many Christian singles have "fallen in love" with an online persona only to feel differently when meeting them in person. If your heart gets involved before you being to really know them, your brain will fill in the gaps with how you want them to be, rather than the way they really are. Face-to-face time is critical for building intimate relationships. Less than ten percent of communication involves the words we say (or share through social media); much more critical is the way we say them (voice inflection, pitch, volume—things you can only interpret by hearing); and more than half of any communication is non-verbal (hand gestures, looks, facial expressions—things you can only see in person).

If you're pursuing an online relationship, do yourself a favor: get to know the other 90 percent of the person as quickly as possible before you decide he or she is the partner of your dreams. If you prefer moving more slowly, then by all means do whatever is necessary to protect your heart from becoming involved too quickly. Solomon, in the Song of Songs wrote these words to lovers:

"Promise not to awaken or excite my feelings of love until it is ready." Song of Songs 8:4 (NCV)

There's one more pitfall to online dating. Their stated goal is to create Coupling relationships. However, such relationships work best if you put this goal and allow the relationship to begin as a Connecting friendship. The Connecting process is too often bypassed. When you match with someone of interest, *resist getting on the bridge of Coupling too soon.* Linger on the "Connecting" side and focus on building non-romantic companionship.

The "Friends and Family" Plan

Think of the people who know you best. They have a network of people they know, too. Could they possibly help you take some of the guesswork out of finding a suitable soul mate? Many single adults neglect this potential networking gold mine. One group of girlfriends started having "share the wealth" parties and invited all their male friends.

Many singles look for a common interests and a heart to serve. Becoming involved in something you care passionately about (overseas missions, singing in the choir, mentoring children, working on a political campaign, etc.) will allow you to rub shoulders with others who have similar interests.

These are but a few ideas for finding quality Christian singles. If you want to get married someday, actively (not desperately) seek a quality partner, and allow God to help you mature into your attractive best. *"He who finds a wife finds a good thing"* (Proverbs 18:22 NKJV). Of course, the same holds true for finding a husband.

More than Just Friends: "Considering" as Preparation for Coupling

Throughout life, you'll develop many Connecting friendships with the opposite sex. Some of these will spark an undeniable chemistry. At some point, you'll make the decision to begin "considering" something more than a friendship. This typically begins when you go out on "dates," which we define as two people who get together for the purpose of sharing an activity to get to know one another better.

The Relationship Continuum Bridge takes you from the solid ground of single (Connecting) to the solid ground of married (Covenanting), with "Coupling" in between. However, we've put "considering" under both Connecting and Coupling. What distinguishes Connecting from a Coupling is having a DTR to intentionally define the relationship. In Connecting, no defined relationship exists other than friendship, and there's no commitment to romantic *exclusivity*. When there's a serious consideration of marriage and exclusivity has been agreed upon, you're proceeding on the bridge to Coupling.

What about hugging, kissing, or handholding while Considering in a Connecting friendship with romantic interest. Rather than legislating specific behavior, we offer two questions to consider: (1) What's the purpose or meaning behind the behavior? (2) Does it express appreciation and a beginning romantic interest, or "Erotic Sexual Behavior" that's more conducive to lovers than friends?

John feels kissing Suzanne goodnight after their dates is his way of expressing his attraction to her and thanking her for a wonderful evening. To Suzanne, a kiss moves them to a more sexual place. For her, a hug is a better expression of friendship and gratitude. Some of her feelings come from previous history of making out with guys she'd just started dating, or had an interest in. The kiss was more about the sexual excitement than about developing real intimacy. This illustrates the importance of DTRs.

Erotic sexual behavior is given intimate meaning (and boundaries) in a Connecting or a committed Coupling relationship. This protects newer relationships from cementing too quickly, with little or no commitment. Only when a couple is committed enough to define an exclusive relationship—both parties are willing to consider the possibility of marriage—can such erotic behaviors be engaged.

Below are some tips for remaining in a Connecting relationship while feeling attracted to each other, and considering, but not quite ready to move on to exclusive Coupling:

- monitor erotic activity, allowing touch, but ensuring that it's more about appreciation that romantically passionate
- less time alone as a couple—spend time together with your friends (and listen to their observations)

- limit daily contact, including texting and checking out each other's social media accounts
- allow self-disclosure to occur naturally as the relationship develops   •

God's Culturally Radical Approach to Finding a Soul Mate

In Chapter Three, we discussed the importance of having a godly values framework in your relationships. These values become the lens through which you view your sexual story and dating life. Scripture reveals God's perspective on finding the man or woman of your dreams.

> *"It is God's will that you should be sanctified: that you should avoid sexual immorality; that each of you should learn to acquire a wife in a way that is holy and honorable, not in passionate lust like the heathen, who do not know God; and that in this matter no one should wrong his brother or take advantage of him." 1 Thessalonians 4:3–6 (alternate translation)*

The word "sanctified" means holy (literally, "set apart") and is similar to the Hebrew word for virgin in the Old Testament. God's purpose for you is a holy one. This means practicing a sexual integrity that chooses to wait.

As a Christian, acquiring a wife (or husband) in a holy and honorable way is a radically different process. The world's perspective on this is selfishly pursuing a desirable person in selfishness and "passionate lust" with little consideration for the emotional (and other) consequences.

The Christian's pursuit of a spouse should be distinctly different from this. We're called to avoid wronging our brother (or sister) or taking advantage of them. What does this mean? As a believer, you must assume the other person does not belong to you—that he or she may ultimately belong to another, future spouse. Until marriage vows are exchanged, there are no guarantees—even if your relationship is headed for marriage.

You should operate as if you're getting to know another man's future wife or another woman's future husband. Treat them with the respect you hope someone would show your future spouse and avoid "sexual immorality"—that selfishly takes advantage of what may rightly belongs to someone else.

In the pursuing your future mate, Scripture also encourages that we marry only other Christians, (2 Corinthians 6:14) pursue relationships with honesty (1 Peter 2:1), encouragement (Ephesians 4:29), forgiveness (Ephesians 4:32), and a servant's heart (Matthew 23:11). It also teaches us to pursue unconditional love, which expresses itself in patience, kindness, protection, trust, hope, and perseverance; and avoiding envy, boastfulness, rudeness, selfishness, and anger. (1 Corinthians 13:4–7).

When two people know each other well, have chemistry, and have discussed the possibility of spending a lifetime together, they should have another one of those crucial DTRs—in which they dedicate themselves to an exclusivity. They prayerfully pledge to seek God's will in exploring a possible lifetime commitment. In short, they choose to define themselves as a couple, and move toward Covenanting. An exciting and passionate new pursuit begins.

CHAPTER TWENTY

Coupling: The Wheel and the Bridge

Falling in love, getting married, and creating a great sex life sounds exciting and can be a compelling goal. Tim Keller comments, "Here's what it means to fall in love. It is to look at another person and get a glimpse of the person God is creating, and to say, 'I see who God is making you and it excites me! I want to be a part of that. I want to partner with you in the journey...'"[62]

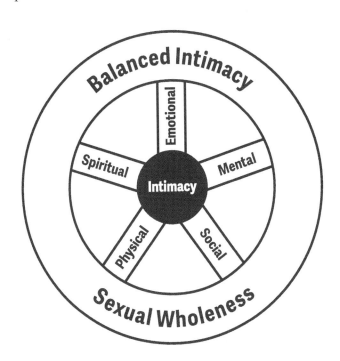

The Wheel and Spokes of Balanced Intimacy

Couples have the responsibility and privilege of helping their partner mature into all that God intends. Keeping a balanced intimacy helps achieve a meaningful dating experience (ultimately) and a wonderfully satisfying marriage.

A wheel with five spokes is a helpful way of illustrating a healthy courtship. This balanced intimacy will include spiritual nurture, emotional warmth, intellectual stimulation, social playfulness, and arousing physical touch. When properly maintained, each spoke of the wheel will move the couple deeper in love and connection. Every human being has a God-given desire to be heard, to be known, to be pursued, to be loved, to be chosen. Each spoke of the wheel helps meet these profound needs.

As a sex therapist, I've learned that a great sex life in marriage is built on the foundation of an intimate companionship with real connection in all five spokes of this wheel. Your sexual expression will definitely be physical, and that's a part of the wheel I want to address: sexual chemistry and attraction. Your sexual attraction should include aspects of the other four spokes if you want to achieve a sexually whole, balanced intimacy. You'll desire spiritual connection, want to share your feelings, exchange ideas, and talk for hours.

Sometimes, couples will struggle with certain spokes more than others. This may be due to trauma, one's family background, personality preference or other factors. Please note that when one spoke gets longer (more developed) or shorter (neglected) that the wheel gets out of balance and will clunk along for an ineffective ride to a balanced intimacy.

Spoke #1: Spiritual

Spiritual intimacy refers to building a personal relationship with God. This process includes many of the suggestions made in Chapter Ten and living inside-out. Couples may be a bit startled to find themselves sexually surging after praying together or enjoying a particularly moving worship experience. Sharing hearts and enjoying God's presence together will create a special closeness couples must guard.

Spoke #2: Emotional

Though women tend to respond more emotionally than men, neither gender finds it easy to be consistently emotionally expressive. Real emotional intimacy lets the walls down to become "naked and unashamed". Building trust and safety are important factors. Strong feelings (anger, fear, jealousy) may emerge at times as a couple works through conflict. Most adults have a skill deficit in this area. Depth of intimacy grows in proportion to your ability to express your feelings. This requires practice and taking the risk to be vulnerable with each other.

Spoke #3: Mental

Mental intimacy is often overlooked. However, neglect this spoke, and your intimacy wheel will certainly be out of round. As three-dimensional people, our minds are so important. Examples of mental intimacy include dreaming about and planning for the future, humor, making deliberate choices as a couple, setting healthy boundaries, and engaging in stimulating discussions on topics of mutual interest. Playful banter, surprisingly, is an intellectual exercise. Renewing your mind (Romans 12:2) and changing unhealthy thought patterns can help ensure growth in this area.

Spoke #4: Social

I remember a client who asked if he could bring his girlfriend to a counseling session. I asked how long he'd been seeing this girl. He replied, "three weeks." I responded that meeting his therapist was far too intimate an experience for such a new relationship (I also told him I hoped he hadn't introduced her to his mom yet, either). Bypassing the process of getting to know someone isn't wise. When a couple doesn't have enough social intimacy to be comfortable passing gas together, but are sexually active, something's wrong. You need to see your dating partner in a variety of social settings (with friends, at a wedding, getting a traffic ticket, interacting with mom) to really get to know him or her.

Another part of social intimacy is the ability to talk about everything—this includes honest conversations about sex. Married couples live years without learning this skill and their marriages suffer because of it.

Spoke #5: Physical

God created us with bodies that express our desires and feelings. Physical intimacy involves much more than just erotic touch. Non-erotic touch also enhances physical intimacy. Three levels of sensual zones exist in the body, and all can be erogenous (that is, erotically stimulating). The lighter Level One zone is the skin of the entire body, which is obviously sensitive to touch. Level Two zones have more nerve endings or are near the erogenous zones of the genitals or nipples. Level Two zones include the mouth, neck, tummy, inner thighs, backs of the knees, lower back, and most places on the head. Level Three zones are the genital areas of the penis and clitoris, which are capable of stimulation to create orgasms (beware that some level two zones can stimulate orgasm for some, too).

Because we all need physical touch, physical intimacy can be developed generously in connecting relationships through Level One hugs, pats on the back and shoulders, and non-erotic caresses of the arms. Those in Coupling should prayerfully consider which Level Two zones are safe for them, while protecting Level One zones.

The Bridge and Exclusivity

In the previous chapter, we described the difference between Connecting and Coupling. Coupling is about being up front and honest about your interest in a future relationship. In this manner, Coupling becomes "basic training" for Covenanting, or marriage. Only those who are truly intentional are ready for Coupling.

The process of constructing a wise Coupling relationship and a great marriage parallels the planning and construction of a building. The different stages within Coupling reflect the critical importance of following a blueprint.

> *"Suppose one of you wants to build a tower. Won't you first sit down and estimate the cost to see if you have enough money to complete it?"* Luke 14:28

How will you know when you're ready to move from Connecting to Coupling? Below are a few questions to consider:

- Are you ready to commit to an exclusive relationship?
- Have you begun to establish a successful friendship with this person?
- Are you willing to define the relationship before and during Coupling?

- Is your goal to get a married at this time? If this person turns out to be all you'd hoped, are you prepared to marry them?
- Does this person pass the test of your non-negotiable? Is there genuine chemistry and a 3-D attraction?

If you can answer yes to each of these questions you're ready for Coupling.

Here's another of my observations. Adolescents are generally unprepared for the responsibility of caring for a family. They're focused on school, friends, and establishing independence. They're also still tethered to their family financially and, most likely, unable to provide for the needs of themselves or another person. Only adults are ready for Coupling or Covenanting.

Erotic sexual thoughts and behavior are intended by God to move a relationship toward marriage, revealing a more complete reflection of intimacy. Logically, then, these are not intended as a part of Connecting. As you might expect, a great deal of difference exists between a couple in their early stage of exploration and a couple preparing to walk down the aisle. The three stages of Coupling help us explain this.

The Relationship Continuum Bridge

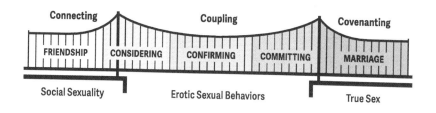

The Three Stages of Coupling

To better grasp the typical progression along the Relationship Continuum Bridge, consider Bill and Tina. They met when Bill first visited Tina's church. At that time, they began Connecting as friends with no real consideration of anything further. They talked at church on Sundays, joined other church members for activities, and served alongside each other on a mission trip to Mexico.

However, a few months ago, Bill began to think about Tina a bit differently. He'd always thought she was attractive. But as they've come to know each other better, Bill has become impressed with her spirit, love for life, and desire for Godliness. They also have many interests in common, including reading, attending concerts, and enjoy hiking and the outdoors. So, Bill asked Tina to attend a local Christian concert, an invitation Tina eagerly accepted.

Considering

With this step, Bill and Tina have transitioned from merely Connecting as friends to considering—but still as a Connecting friendship. They won't pursue each other physically, other than a hug goodbye or a casual kiss; and they won't feel any pressure to figure out what to do sexually. The reason is simple: they're both aware of the Relationship Continuum Bridge, having discussed it on their first date. Each is clear on the "rules of engagement" and they've agreed to respect each other. They simply desire to know each other in a deeper way by spending more time together.

Considering isn't just about hanging out or doing activities together. Getting to know another person takes some planning and forethought. If you always see movies together, you'll only get to know the other person's preference in film. You need to be collecting data from a variety of settings that can reveal each other's character and compatibility. If you're want to get to know someone better, consider "the Five Fs":

Food. Share a meal, especially one where the restaurant isn't too noisy for conversation. Ask relevant questions, from surface questions such as, "What's your favorite restaurant?" or "Where are you from" to more personal questions such as, "Tell me about your family?" Or, "If you could do anything in your life over again, what would it be?" Such curiosity not only reveals helpful information, but also gives you a glimpse into their ability to carry on "below the surface" conversation.

Fun: Invite the other person to do things you enjoy. Find out what sports, hobbies, and interests he or she enjoys and share them together. Not only will you learn about the other person, you'll also have fun—and maybe even find a new hobby. This time can include some physical interaction with handholding, appropriate kissing, and that looking into each other's eyes.

Friends: Invite him or her to join a small group of your friends. Observing how they behave when they're with a group helps you see their "true colors." The group might try tackling a project together, such as yard work or a community cleanup effort.

Future: What does he or she want to accomplish in the next year? Five years? Twenty years? How would he or she answer that question with regard to career, family, children, friends, where to live, how to spend his or her leisure time, and interest in serving? These questions can reveal much about your relationship's long-term potential. Different visions for the future will eventually yield divergent paths.

Faith: Does he or she profess a Christian faith? Does his lifestyle confirm or betray his profession? What does she believe about church, Scripture, and a daily walk with God? If one of you holds faith as central to daily life, and the other merely provides lip service, your relationship will only go so far. Value differences are deal breakers in Coupling. Don't fool yourself into thinking you can change another person. People must choose to change. They can't be manipulated into it, no matter how tenderly it's done. Such spiritual differences are okay in a Connecting friendship. Perhaps your godly influence will encourage him/her to seek a relationship with God. However, allowing your emotions to lead you into Coupling is a poor decision. This truth forms the backdrop for Scripture's warning not to *"team up with those who are unbelievers"* (2 Corinthians 6:14 NLT).

Defining the Relationship and Creating Healthy Boundaries. After two months of delightful dates, Bill is more impressed with Tina than ever. He suggests their next date be at a quiet restaurant where they can talk, followed by a walk around a nearby park. His intention is to have a discussion about the future of their relationship, and whether she's as interested as he is in an exclusive Coupling relationship.

At dinner, he tells Tina his desire —choosing not to date anyone else—and to date someone else from this point on would only be acceptable after a joint decision to return "considering" to return their Coupling back to Connecting. Tina agrees, then they openly discuss what this new stage of their relationship will look like.

Choosing to take a relationship towards marriage takes commitment with some risk involved. Exclusive dating, through the Considering and Confirming stages, is heading towards Commitment/Engagement. Remember that choosing to back off the Bridge may also be wise when Considering and Confirming helps a couple recognize some real deal-breakers.

Here's a helpful suggestion that I've seen dating couples use. Commit to a three-to-six month process with a lot of food, fun, friendship, talks about the future and faith. Have transparent conversations about feelings and needs—defining the direction of your relationship, and what marriage would look like. Risk letting your heart get engaged, so you can discover if this is your life partner.

Couples should be intentional not only about the direction of their relationship, but also its boundaries. In a manner of speaking, "good fences make good couples." We might think of fences as restricting, but you can also look at a fence as keeping damaging influences out of the beautiful garden you're growing as a couple. With expectations discussed up front about social media and friendship/family interactions, couples can relax and enjoy their relationship, knowing what they each feel is appropriate. In fact, if you're presently Coupling, share this book with your coupling partner. Reading it together can create an opportunity for dialogue about becoming more intentional. Perhaps you need your own DTR.

What areas should couples define? In addition to defining the relationship as exclusive, couples need to place limits on specific erotic behavior, recognizing the godly need for avoiding all forms of intercourse, mutual orgasms, and selfish thoughts (Hebrews 13:4; Matthew 5:28). No other issue has the power to ruin a good relationship as having poorly defined sexual boundaries (for more on this, see chapter 21).

Helpful boundaries are important in all the spokes of the intimacy wheel in moving a Coupling relationship forward during the Considering stage. Here are a few examples of areas in which to exercise caution, so you don't move too fast during the Considering stage:

- Sharing time by yourselves in worship, and holding hands and praying together after 10 p.m.
- Introducing your partner to parents, your children (for those single-again), or your close friends; inviting your partner to a wedding; inviting your partner to your church (especially if it's small); seeing each other daily
- Choosing to disclose your childhood abuse and its effect on you; saying "I love you"; watching certain (especially R-rated) movies together, and crying in each other's arms
- Discussing sensitive topics (politics, parenting, etc.); talking about STIs, mental illness or substance abuse issues; sharing future goals and dreams; engaging in sexual banter and flirting

You're becoming a couple. Confirming is where more of these deep conversations and social interactions will take place.

Confirming

Bill and Tina have now been Coupling for over six months, and it's getting serious. They've talked about a possible future together. They pray for God's discernment, together and individually. Now each must risk full disclosure with the other. This is the often-neglected stage of Coupling known as Confirming.

At this point, an official announcement of engagement does not occur. Some have called this stage of Coupling "engaged to be engaged"—a time when each partner willingly places all their cards on the table, and risks abandonment for a chance at a relationship in which they are fully known. The couple wades into the deeper emotional waters of genuine emotional intimacy. Any secrets thus far held from the other need to be shared at this stage. To the degree secrets are held back, fear will exist on the part of the secret-holder and (if it's ever discovered) mistrust on the part of other. Keeping secrets is a lousy way to start a lifelong commitment.

A couple may need to plan a day trip (or several such trips) somewhere quiet to create a safe place for discussion. Of course, this depends on how much they've already disclosed. No question should be off limits: prior sexual relationships; STIs; same-sex attractions; abortions; debt and financial instability; expectations about children, parenting, the level of involvement of their in-laws, the frequency of sex; mental illness, denominational preference; and gender roles in marriage. If it's important to one partner, it's important for the couple's future survival to bring it into the open for honest discussion.

Moving from Confirming to Committing—or engagement—shouldn't take place until each partner has fully disclosed everything and is satisfied the other has done likewise. Confirming is also the best time for premarital counseling from a pastor or Christian counselor. Confirming couples allow the idea of being married to settle on them as they actively sort through the future joining of their lives. Premarital counseling presents a great opportunity for the counselor to teach them skills, affirm their strengths, and expose weaknesses in their relationship. When premarital counseling is prioritized at this stage of the relationship, the couple has time to either work through the issues or call off the relationship without the undue burden of social or family pressure.

For example, a discovery, through counseling, reveals a partner's former substance abuse or struggle with same-sex attraction, allows for more conversation about these issues than waiting until the Committing stage—after the invitations have been mailed and the wedding plans are finalized. Delaying such discovery not only will place undue pressure on the couple ("Do we postpone the wedding? What will we tell our guests?") and may cause irreparable damage to the relationship.

The Confirming stage should also involve the couple's family and support network. One premarital counseling model involves parents/stepparents with the couple in a session, formally asking them to bless their children and to help launch the couple into their new commitment. My marriage to Catherine came after a painful divorce. This time around, I got everybody's opinion—including my parents' formal blessing.

One final thought about the Confirming stage: just because a couple takes this step doesn't mean they should feel obligated to become more physically intimate. On the other hand, some couples may have legitimate reasons for making a calculated move toward greater physical intimacy while posting new, clearly marked stop signs for the more intimate erotic behaviors (see chapters 17 and 18). I sometimes worry that if couples aren't having trouble keeping their hands off each other, perhaps they'll have trouble with sexual chemistry. But lustfully indulging an erotic buzz differs significantly from an unselfish desire for true intimacy.

If you're a couple struggling in this area, consider the discipline of erotic fasting. In immature Coupling, increased physical intimacy often leads to decreased verbal intimacy. Too much emphasis on the physical also leads to the neglect of other important dimensions of the relationship. Couples miss out on getting to know each other and enjoying social interaction in a more well-rounded sense. Too much emphasis on the physical also leads to less objectivity about the developing relationship. Fasting from specific or all aspects of physical intimacy for an agreed-upon period of time is a valuable tool in Coupling, when used for the purpose of maturing a relationship. Respecting a more conservative limitation on physical intimacy for a time may benefit your coupling relationship in a number of ways:

- You might discover a new depth of love for each other (that is, you might find reasons you love your partner besides the erotic).
- You might discover your relationship feels so empty without the erotic behavior that you're forced to work on improving the other areas (mental, social, emotional, and spiritual intimacy), making it healthier and stronger.
- You may decide to reconsider your relationship itself. The erotic intimacy may be the only thing holding it together. In this case, the relationship should prayerfully be dissolved (either temporarily or permanently).

Erotic fasting in a romantic relationship also serves as a reminder to depend upon God to meet your deepest need for intimacy. He is the only source for this, anyway. Real intimacy is more than erotic physical expression. Remember, Coupling is basic training for marriage.

Deliberate and unintended erotic fasting also occurs even in marriage (due sickness, post-childbirth, physical separation, periods of disagreement). Voluntary periods of premarital erotic fasting help you prepare for such occasions in marriage. Fasting from erotic behaviors will not only teach you to delay gratification, but will also reveal if the person you're considering marrying can delay gratification as well. What a great character quality to know about your partner before getting married!

Committing

Having become familiar with each other's strengths, faults, failures, goals, and dreams, Bill and Tina realized that they each held assumptions about their future marriage of which they were previously unaware. Thankfully, they'd pursued full disclosure prior to a formal engagement, allowing them the extra time to work through their issues. Though it wasn't easy, they're convinced that this time gave them not only a deeper appreciation for each other, but also a head start on their first years of their marriage.

Because much of the difficult relational work has already been done, their engagement will only need to be as long as necessary to coordinate the wedding plans—sending invitations, selecting dresses and caterers, planning their honeymoon, and so on. This shorter engagement provides a significant benefit for couples who've already done the hard work in the Confirming stage. Having discussed what their marriage will look like, the Committing stage is all the practical steps of joining two lives together: opening a joint checking account, initiating steps toward merging two households, and the like.

The Committing stage is also a time when priority should be placed upon "grieving and cleaving." No, this is not a typo. Men, especially, have a genuine need for grieving the loss of singleness. Reduced independence and potentially reduced financial freedom are real losses that must be grieved to successfully "leave" the benefits of singleness and "cleave" to the good (but different) benefits of marital partnership.

For women, this grieving is typically a bit different. Women may grieve the reduced opportunities for and differences in their friendships with women. Their single friends may view them differently, back away, or even become jealous. Couples will benefit from talking with seasoned married couples who can share their own experiences.

Please be aware that the references to time spent in each of the three Coupling stages by Bill and Tina are simply their experience and are in no way meant to set a precedent. Every relationship is unique in its progression. However, following our model for Coupling should reduce the time required for the Committing stage. It also should significantly reduce your risk of a broken engagement, and the likelihood of an unhealthy marriage by heading off problematic romance before the "point of no return." In addition, such intentional progression in Coupling encourages the biblical view of your impending marriage, leading to a greater sense of love, trust and desire. Bless you in this journey.

CHAPTER TWENTY-ONE

Virginity, The Bikini Boundary and "How Far Can I Go?"

with Michael Todd Wilson

Okay—now we get down to some tough alternatives and choices. How far do you think you should go as a couple in love with a lot of sexual attraction? All of us would like an easy Christian formula to guide our erotic sexual behaviors. You may be frustrated because this book and chapter won't give you a legalistic, cookie-cutter approach to sexual purity. Sometimes, it depends and is a 3-D soul thing, based on your inside-out values framework and your unique relationship.

If you've read the chapters leading up to this one, I hope that by now you understand that "how far can I go?" isn't the right question to ask. It reveals the selfish, immature nature of your heart. A better question is, "How do I grow, stay pure, and help my partner become more sexually whole—building a solid foundation for great lovemaking in a future marriage?"

But, the questions behind "How far can I go?" are still important to consider. While it's true that Christians live under grace (from a heart motivated by godliness), we still need a measure of law/boundaries (i.e., "How far can I go?") to keep our sinful, selfish hearts on track.

Law, Grace and Asking the Right Questions

When looking at the biblical concepts of law and grace, we often err in thinking that they're opposing concepts. With regard to our sexuality, if we focus too much on the "law" side of things and abstaining from certain behaviors, we'll find ourselves consumed with rules and regulations, and will miss the heart of the issue. On the other hand, if we become too focused on the "grace" side of sexuality, we may become too permissive and fall into potentially Stupid (sinful) thoughts and behaviors that ultimately won't help us value, celebrate and protect our sexuality.

Part of the vision for sexual wholeness is seeing law and grace as two currents in the same stream of God's desire for us as sexual beings. Ultimately, God wants to move us forward into a healthy vision of sexuality. In this vision, His sexual economy provides us with healthy guidelines and boundaries so we can stay safe, while God's grace reminds us that it is not about rules, but about seeking the heart of our Father and modeling after Jesus.

"How Far Can I Go?" versus "How Can I Grow Healthy Sexual Intimacy?"

In seeing our sexuality as a heart issue, we have to challenge the meaning of the questions we often ask in regard to our sexuality. Frequently, I hear a question like "We're heading towards marriage, how far can we go sexually without sinning?" On one level, this question makes sense: there's a desire to know the appropriate boundaries. But on a deeper level, it misses the heart of the issue. In my view, it's a bit like asking the question: "Forget about guard rails, how close to a cliff can I get without falling over?"

Instead, I challenge you to ask questions like "What does

healthy sexuality and a godly intimacy look like?" Can you see the difference between the two? The first question is about what you can get away with without suffering any consequences, while the second question asks what is good for us as we enter a romantic, sexual relationship.

"And athletes cannot win the prize unless they follow the rules." II Timothy 2:5 (NLT)

The Tension between Law and Grace

Join us on an imaginary trip. It's November, and you're on your way from the East Coast to a reunion with a friend in Colorado. Dog-tired, you've seen enough of Kansas and Interstate 70 to last two lifetimes—when suddenly you realize you're significantly exceeding the speed limit. What should you do?

You're ready to be done with this tedious journey, and you're on a deserted stretch of highway with few speed traps. As a mature Christian, though, you choose to slow down because you know the speed limit is there for your own good. You don't want to run the risk of hurting yourself or another motorist regardless of whether the cops are out. Right?

Wrong! The pedal's to the metal. This story illustrates a common dilemma. We need guidelines and limits to be safe and flourish. Unfortunately, we often need law enforcement to help us keep them. Otherwise, our human hearts have a tendency to behave immaturely and engage in irresponsible Stupid, even when our sexual values framework is modeled after God's sexual economy. But here's the catch: when it comes to our erotic sexual behaviors in adult relationships, the "sex police" aren't out. Laws (God's regulating principles) related to sexuality can't really govern your behavior unless they're self-imposed and internally motivated by your mind, will, and heart. They're guidelines you can choose to follow—or not. I am reemphasizing the importance of an Inside-Out approach (Chapter 10) with a love of Jesus and a transformed heart being the motivating starting place for valuing and following God's rules. Internally appropriated guidelines and not externally imposed laws.

"Happy are those who keep his rules, who try to obey him with their whole heart." Psalm 119:2 (NCV)

The Rules without the Heart

Mark and Tiffany fell in love their sophomore year of college. They both grew up in conservative homes where sex was not discussed. The intensity of their erotic surges somehow seemed wrong. So, they constructed rigid boundaries around their erotic behaviors. They thought they were doing well as they followed the guidelines set up in their former youth group—light kissing and handholding only. In fact, everything was great until Christmas vacation, when Mark went over to Tiffany's before heading back to school. They spent lots of time together that night and to their dismay, they went much further than either had anticipated.

After that night, they resolved to shift back into the safe rules of the past. But when they were together, the rules seemed to fly right out the window. The cycle repeated itself again and again. By the following spring, their disillusionment with their lack of discipline brought them in for counseling.

After listening to their story, I made several observations.

Their relationship clearly had the virus of disrespecting their normal sexual desires. In their upbringing, rules had been set without any explanation of their deeper purpose in protecting God's gift of sexual intimacy. Mark and Tiffany repressed their erotic sexuality rather than embracing horny and practicing a healthy self-discipline and stewarding of their sexual surging.

The Heart behind the Rules

The fact that Mark and Tiffany repressed their erotic sexuality doesn't necessarily make all their boundaries wrong. Scripture encourages us to set godly rules/boundaries around inappropriate behavior. Laws are designed to pinpoint counterproductive behavior and encourage us to see the heart of God and his plan for us: "Through the law we become conscious of sin...I would not have known what sin was except through the law" (Romans 3:20; 7:7).

Being wise stewards requires a couple to understand the spirit behind God's sexual guidelines that can help motivate (Inside-Out) the discipline of godly sexual behaviors. Building mature attitudes based on the spirit of the law is different from simply outlawing certain behaviors and legalistically following the rules. Chastity isn't keeping a penis out of a vagina, but "valuing, celebrating and protecting" sexuality.

A sign of adult maturity is the ability to keep rules and postpone immediate gratification for long-term gain. Teens often think having sex will make them more adult, when the opposite is actually a truer test of mature adult character. Mark was surprised at how quickly sexual immaturity took over when they didn't relate deeper heart principles with their sexual rules. Scripture speaks to this: "Such regulations indeed have an appearance of wisdom... but they lack any value in restraining sensual indulgence" (Colossians 2:23). Simply outlawing certain behavior won't stop your sexual thoughts and behaviors from going outside the lines.

Pursuing the spirit of the law, I told Mark and Tiffany that I preferred the term love-touching for sexual caressing. Romantic affection involves more than the rush of being pursued, the excitement of indulging horny or wanting to be accepted and loved. Love-touching is a 3-D soul thing that guides behavior with an attitude of respect for the other person and the relationship—incorporating tenderness, patience, consideration, self-discipline, and a desire to be connected and intimate. Such a viewpoint holds us accountable to a different ideal than petting, fingering, hooking up, getting some and other demeaning terms our culture uses for sexual behaviors.

Mark and Tiffany appreciated the idea of love-touching but were still discouraged at their ability to violate their desired boundaries so easily. I reinforced the difficulty most singles have in being governed by the spirit of the law instead of the letter of the law. Sex police wouldn't miraculously appear, order them to stop, give them a ticket, or revoke their license—although that certainly might seem warranted at times. A sexually mature courtship needs to combine law with the deeper reasons for that law. That kind of motivation only comes inside-out from the heart and a deeper understanding of God's desires for genuine sexual intimacy.

The Heart without Costly Obedience of the Rules

Then there's the opposite problem. Keith and Traci's voices resonated with shame as they shared their pain. They'd been together at her apartment until 2:30 a.m. the night before and had once again been sexual in ways both knew were counter to their values. They

314

asked for each other's forgiveness and had already sought forgiveness from their heavenly Father.

After listening to their story, I challenged them: "You've done some good work in setting godly boundaries. You also understand and believe in the reasons behind them. You're simply choosing to disobey them. You aren't allowing your boundaries to do their job because you deliberately ignore them." They had a lot of *alternatives and choices* they weren't making.

Keith quickly replied, "But we're keeping better boundaries than we used to." Traci followed with, "We struggle with wanting to make better choices. We're just so in love." "Nice try, guys," I responded, "but you're in my office because you're fearful of harming your relationship. You must choose to make some bold changes. Maturity isn't kissing passionately at 2:30 in the morning in her apartment. You aren't consistently observing your stop signs."

The Wisdom of Stop Signs

Although I believe that sexual wholeness is fundamentally a heart issue, it doesn't change the fact that we still need practical boundaries to keep our behaviors healthy. In dating relationships, I call these "stop signs." Like road signs, if we follow their directions, they'll keep us from dangerous behavior. For some couples, their stop signs may include avoiding certain physical behaviors, or not being at each other's apartment alone or past a certain time of day or night. It may involve avoiding certain sexual expressions that may lead in unhealthy directions: keeping clothing on, or keeping touch outside the "bikini boundary" (anywhere the fabric of a bikini would cover).

This might mean choosing to "fast" or refrain from physical interaction (caressing, kissing, or touch) as you focus on develop a healthy social friendship, explore each other's thoughts on important topics, express your feelings with empathy, or deliberately nurture each other's spiritual formation and growth

True Sex was given as a picture of the complete, exclusive intimacy between Christ and his Bride, the Church. As such, all expressions of erotic sexuality should honor and derive their meaning from marital lovemaking. The expression of erotic sexual behavior in premarital relationships will always end in dissatisfaction, because it's incomplete – it's the preamble meant to result in consummation. And though true sex in marriage completes the earthly metaphor, it too remains an incomplete and "dimly reflected" mirror of the ultimate intimacy our souls truly long for—a deep need that will be fully satisfied only by God himself at the end of the divine love story in heaven (Revelation 21:1–7).

Posting Stop Signs—and Reinstating Stop Signs

A stop sign is any behavior you choose, by the deliberate act of your will, not to engage in until you've reached a certain level of commitment in your relationship. This "symbolic behavior" will help you discipline your erotic desire. Examples of stop signs might be no erotic sexual behaviors until Coupling, no kissing after midnight, no hands under clothing, or no making out after a romantic movie—or the Bikini Boundary which I will discuss further.

The journey into mature sexuality is complex. Couples must firmly post and respect stop signs. Understand that stop signs alone are ultimately powerless without your mutually heart-driven choices—that's the respecting part. You'll need to develop character and three-dimensional intimacy (body, soul, and spirit) while still respecting the need for law to serve as guideposts. In marriage you will still maintain many stop signs (healthy boundaries) to protect the sacredness of your sexual relationship.

The Song of Songs beautifully tells the story of maturing Coupling and Covenanting. It also illustrates the wise use of an erotic stop sign. Three times in this story Scripture emphasizes the importance of not "awakening" or "stirring up" erotic passion before its time (Song of Songs 2:7; 3:5; 8:4). Single adults need to discipline their erotic surges by setting limits throughout the different stages of Coupling.

Guard against being too simplistic in thinking through your stop signs. For example, you might be one of those single adults who chooses to wait until your wedding day to kiss, believing that kissing creates too much sexual intimacy in Coupling. But if you're cuddling on the couch, watching a romantic movie and wondering how to ignore his erection, your choice not to kiss isn't helping you discipline your other erotic feelings and behaviors well. Sexual maturity recognizes the complexity of sexual response in Coupling and the need for a variety of behavioral boundaries. The stop signs you post should reflect your deeper heart attitudes and must be chosen wisely for them to be effective in disciplining your sexual surges.

Merely posting a stop sign isn't enough (though it's a good start). You must also choose to obey your stop sign. It will accomplish nothing if you're going to treat it as a rolling stop. You've got to apply the brakes before you get to your posted stop sign. Otherwise, you'll find yourself sitting in the middle of the intersection by the time you actually come to a complete stop.

Like Marl and Tiffany and Keith and Traci, you as a couple may need to reestablish certain stop signs you have blown through recently without even a "rolling" stop. Forgiveness and repentant change is a part of any great relationship as you reinstitute stop signs. Make sure you understand the protective spirit of your stop signs so you don't just ban behaviors but work inside-out.

The Bikini Boundary—Stop Sign

In God's sexual economy, all erotic behavior is modeled after and builds toward true sex. As Christians, we don't want to mirror a society that places such emphasis on genitals and orgasms even in premarital relationships. Instead, our values and behavior need to reflect God's truth that the only true sex we'll find fulfilling is with our Adam or Eve in marriage. As you further sort through stop signs that will enhance and protect your Coupling relationship, I suggest the bikini line.

This valuable stop sign applies throughout all stages of Coupling and helps preserve soul virginity. The bikini line principle says that the parts of the body covered by a bikini (genitals and breasts) should be reserved for Covenanting. Yes, this eliminates any type of mutual orgasms, whether manual or oral, under clothing or on top of clothing (sometimes known as "dry humping").

So what does the bikini line do for couples like Mark and Tiffany and Keith and Traci? Hopefully, it gives them freedom and safety, serving as a guideline/map for their Coupling. You need to maturely recognize that if your hands or mouth stray over the bikini line (or some other stop sign you've posted), a type of erotic arousal is stirred up that frequently results in moving to mutual orgasms and intercourse—a place that can violate the spirit of valuing, celebrating and protecting your wonderful gift of sexual attraction and healthy intimate connecting.

Here's another viewpoint on the bikini stop sign: imagine that having true sex as a single is like falling off a cliff into the Grand Canyon. The "How far can I go" question then becomes, "How close can I get to the edge of the Grand Canyon and still not plunge to my death?" Immaturity and selfishness are all about getting as close to the edge as possible without falling over. The bikini boundary calls you back from the edge to maintain a reasonable margin of safety— while still being able to enjoy the view.

Connecting and Coupling are invaluable preparation for marriage. Posting stop signs (and keeping them) will help you build the necessary skills of patience and self-discipline. Intercourse won't always be available in marriage, and God is teaching you in your Coupling relationship how to love erotically without true sex. An alarming number of couples have extramarital affairs their first few years of marriage because they've never learned covenant faithfulness. Soul virginity applies even after you say "I do."

The Biblical Stop Sign of True Sex and Virginity

Part of the reason you're reading this chapter comes from your desire to see what God says about erotic sexual activity, especially sex outside of marriage. Many of you are already having sexual intercourse or experiencing mutual orgasms with your partner. Because of the great confusion among Christian singles on this subject, we want to walk you through a simple (okay, so it's a bit complex) journey through Scripture to help you see why true sex belongs only within the Covenanting relationship of marriage.

To help you understand why we're so firm on this particular stop sign, let's go back to the three-step model developed in chapter 15 around the behavior of masturbation. The steps presented for understanding God's will about any specific issue begin first with applying biblical passages that directly address the issue (Step One). If none exist, then apply biblical passages that indirectly address the issue (Step Two). If, after all this, the issue of virginity/celibacy still remains unclear, then, seek out Christian writings and traditions, as well as godly mentors to help you understand some of the Christian teachings or biblical passages you find—or even to help you find them in the first place (Step Three). Each believer must prayerfully settle the issue for themselves, consistent with their hearts and internal values. However, unlike the Bible's silence on masturbation, Scripture has much to say about inappropriate erotic behavior in premarital relationships.

A Direct Biblical Understanding of Sexual Immorality (Step One)

Hebrews 13:4 says the marriage bed is to be kept pure. It specifically mentions two groups of people who violate the purity of marital sexual intimacy: adulterers and the sexually immoral. When God's design for sexuality is distorted, strong words like adultery and sexual immorality emphasize how deeply the Father's heart is grieved. "Adulterers" refer to those who break their wedding vows by engaging in sexual intercourse with anyone outside their own marital relationship. Jesus expanded adultery in Matthew 5:28 to include a person's thought life and emotional affairs—not just physically acting out. Our English phrase "to adulterate" means to corrupt something pure by adding a contaminating element. Always remember, God created human sexuality to help us understand genuine intimacy and to demonstrate his exclusive covenant relationship with his people.

> "Marriage should be honored by all, and the marriage bed kept pure, for God will judge the adulterer and all the sexually immoral." Hebrews 13:4

As for sexual immorality, the original Greek root word used in Scripture is *porne*, from which we derive our English word pornography. The New Testament interprets this Greek word with any of the following English words: sexual immorality, prostitution, or fornication. Unlike adultery, sexual immorality is a broader term that is used for any inappropriate sexual behavior outside the commitment of marriage. It is also used regardless of an individual's marital status.

> *"Drink water from your own cistern (of private sexual memories), running water (of erotic pleasure) from your own well. Should your (sexual) springs overflow in the streets... let them be yours alone, never to be shared with strangers. ...may you rejoice with the wife of your youth. ...may her breasts satisfy you always, may you ever be intoxicated by her love." Proverbs 5:15-19 (parentheses added)*

Therefore, Scripture is clear that we shouldn't commit adultery or engage in inappropriate sexual behavior outside of marriage. This clearly includes sexual intercourse, but may include a variety of other erotic activities as well. This is Step One of the inside-out model.

Sexual Immorality through the Broader Scope of Scripture (Step Two)

We now seek to apply Step Two, examining passages that indirectly address the issue. So how else does Scripture speak of sexual immorality and true sex outside of marriage?

Isaiah 1:18–23; Ezekiel 16:1–63 — These passages refer to Israel's abandonment of their worship of Jehovah God (whom they'd made a covenant to serve) to become a spiritual "prostitute" by serving other gods. In sexual terms, this would amount to sharing with someone else those sexual things that are intended only to be shared within the context of a covenanting relationship.

Genesis 34:1–31 (especially v. 31) — This passage portrays is a heart-wrenching story about a woman's rape. Her family became so angry at the perpetrator (and rightly so!) that her brothers accused the rapist of treating their sister "as a prostitute" (v. 31), using the same root word used for "sexually immoral." In their view, Shechem (the offender) took something that didn't belong to him. Their sister's virginity was intentionally set apart for her future husband. It didn't matter that Shechem was attracted to her (v. 3), even attracted enough to request that his father "get me this girl as my wife" (v. 4). His future desire, intention, and even possible future marriage to her didn't matter. At the time of the incident, neither she nor her sexuality belonged to him.

1 Corinthians 6:12–20 — The apostle Paul warned the Corinthians that when they engaged in erotic sexual interaction with a prostitute, they weren't simply getting "their needs met." Sexual intercourse united them with that person on a deeper level—as if they were married, or "one flesh" (v. 16). On the surface, Paul is talking about sex with a prostitute. Yet a deeper admonition is clear: Don't engage in any inappropriate erotic sexual activity—especially "true sex" — outside of a committed marital relationship.

Ephesians 5:25–33 — Becoming sexually one in marriage mirrors the covenant relationship Christ has with his bride, the Church. Sexual intercourse is both a metaphor for this spiritual reality and a physical sign that seals the earthly covenant of marriage. A person becomes part of Christ's bride with a deliberate decision to pledge his or her life to Christ. In the same way, the covenant of marriage pledges two people to one another, making them "one flesh" and sexually uniting them in true sex.

To summarize the above Scripture references, sexual immorality has at least the following characteristics: (1) erotic sexual behavior (2) between two people who aren't married to each other (3) that at least includes the lovemaking behavior of sexual intercourse (true sex). Also, (4) neither being "in love" nor having a future intention or pledge to marry seems to affect Scripture's perspective.

In this chapter we have detailed Scripture that confirms God's sexual guidelines that True Sex is designed for marriage.

Here's another comment I frequently hear from singles: because of their love and commitment for one another, they believe they're already "married in the eyes of God"—even if they aren't yet legally married. This is terrible logic designed either to quiet guilty consciences or perhaps to ease their fear of commitment. If you're a couple serious about lifelong commitment, then honor your relationship as sacred: exchange your covenant vows publicly in marriage and allow your family and friends to celebrate and hold you accountable for your promise to one other. Remember the important Commitment Post of the Relationship Continuum Bridge.

Allowing God's Heart and Christian Community to Guide (Step Three)

You're probably still wondering, "What behavior, besides sexual intercourse, are considered 'sexual immorality'?" Even after all of these Scriptures, I still haven't defined other specific behaviors that can be so destructive to your Coupling relationship. Maybe you're saying to yourself, "So, we'll do our best to make good decisions. Right?"

Well, not exactly. You must still live a life that's consistent with God's heart as expressed in Scriptures such as "Serve one another in love" (Galatians 5:13) and "'Everything is permissible for me'—but not everything is beneficial" (1 Corinthians 6:12). Just because the Bible has no direct (or indirect) teaching on a particular sexual behavior, doesn't mean that engaging in it is healthy, godly, or even wise. As we said earlier, "How far can I go?" isn't a mature and loving question. When asked by itself, it's usually based on selfish motivations.

You also can profit from what Christians in community have thought through and written about sexuality over the history of the Church. There are many wise teachings on celibacy, the body, and single sexuality—many of the works I have quoted in this book.

This lack of clear direction doesn't necessarily mean that all erotic sexual behavior before marriage are harmful. A variety of sexual behaviors may be appropriate for certain couples (kissing, deep kissing, love-touching, etc.). For behavior neither directly nor indirectly addressed in Scripture, you'll need to prayerfully search your heart and have many long conversations with your lover. This is what applying Step Three of the inside-out model means, as you profit from your community. And remember, you are valuing, celebrating and protecting each other's gift of sexuality.

The Importance of Personal Responsibility

As you've probably figured out by now, I'm not going to tell which specific erotic behavior is appropriate or inappropriate for your own Coupling relationship. I don't want to play judge and jury where Scripture isn't clear. True sex—which at least includes intercourse (oral, anal, vaginal) and mutual orgasms—is scripturally out of bounds before marriage. I also highly recommend the bikini boundary as a premarital stop sign. For everything else, the line you need to draw depends on your heart and what the behavior means to you and/or your partner as you intentionally respect, value and protect each other sexually.

Personal Responsibility

I ask you, dear Christian, to sincerely pray for the Lord's guidance on your sexual expression within committed romantic Coupling. Ask yourself, "How does this behavior affect me and my relationship both with my coupling partner and with God—now and in the future?" Once you've prayed it through, sought godly counsel (if necessary), and discussed it thoroughly with your Coupling partner, confidently and playfully engage in the behaviors you've agreed upon without guilt or doubt.

> *"Blessed are those who do not condemn themselves by doing something they know is all right. … If you do anything you believe is not right, you are sinning" Romans 14:22–23 (NLT)*

You must take personal responsibility for whatever decisions you and your Coupling partner ultimately make. Also, beware of needless comparisons with others. What may be counterproductive for you may be appropriate for your friends, or vice versa. Often depending on your heart attitude of selfish or unselfish, the same behavior may be a sin on one day and not on another.

Practicing Godly Stewardship

In an effort to be as practical as possible, let me give you a few final questions to ask yourself as you work through, "How far can I go?" If you're honest, these questions will likely encourage you to draw "the line" more conservatively than you might otherwise want.

1. Because you aren't yet married, assume your future spouse is going out on a date with someone else. Where would you want that man or woman to set the erotic behavior limits with your future spouse? Many singles haven't thought of such a question. Yet it only makes sense that wherever you want the line drawn for that person (in terms of erotic behavior), you must be willing to accept this same limit for yourself. For the remaining questions, think of a specific erotic behavior you're concerned about and ask yourself the following:

2. Will you regret having engaged in this behavior if your current Coupling relationship doesn't end in marriage? Could you remain friends with this person without feeling guilty?

3. Does this sexual behavior shift the focus of your relationship from encouraging sexual integrity and loving intimacy? Is *intimacy* the focus, or are you merely indulging sexual buzzes and hormonal surges?

4. At the moment you engage in this behavior, does it stimulate you to want to carry your erotic expression to its ultimate conclusion—sexual intercourse? If so, it may be too arousing for you in Coupling and, therefore, too risky.

5. Are you "falling into" physical expressions of intimacy because the relationship is lacking in the area of sharing spiritual, emotional, social, and mental intimacy?

Each of these questions may yield red flags you'll want to pay attention to, as your soul virginity may be at risk. Bless you, friend. Erotic sexual intimacy brings many dilemmas and tough choices for couples who truly desire to honor God's sexual economy. However, your heavenly Father wants you to create a fun, safe, and soul-satisfying intimacy that may one day lead to beautiful covenant lovemaking for a lifetime. Getting there will require many deliberate choices to keep your intimacy in balance and your relationship moving in a healthy direction—and never forget that the Holy Spirit will help you live out your stop signs and your values framework.

"Joyful are the people of (sexual) integrity, who follow the (sexual) instructions of the Lord. As I learn your righteous (sexual) regulations, I will thank you by living as I should (sexually)!" Psalm 119:1,7 (NLT parentheses added)

CHAPTER TWENTY-TWO

Single & Sexually Whole: The Seven Pledges

To summarize God's strategy concerning sex, whether single or married, I'd encourage you to try something you've (likely) never done. A pledge is generally defined as an inner promise to believe in and follow through on something, like the Pledge of Allegiance. In conclusion I'd like you to consider the following seven pledges:

1. I pledge to make the invisible visible and the visible invisible.

2. I pledge to ask God to help me live out my faith and sexuality from the Inside-Out.

3. I pledge to join and help build a (sexually) supportive community where God has placed me— one open to righteous flirting.

4. I pledge to develop and celebrate all three dimensions of my sexuality and personhood.

5. I pledge to embrace sexual desire (horny) and steward it wisely.

6. I pledge to run to God's sexual ER with my sexual trauma and mistakes.

7. I pledge to fight my desire to watch porn and fight Satan's destructive viruses, and to intentionally create a godly values framework.

1. I pledge to make the Invisible Visible and the Visible Invisible

The Intimate Trinity isn't physically sexual. The Father, Son and Holy Spirit needed a way to help us understand how they value relationships and love intimately. Though operating in the invisible spirit realm, they created men and women to love and form deep, complex, intimate connections—like Life in the Trinity. Scripture tells us that God made his invisible qualities known through us — a three-dimensional people with a body, mind and heart—in the material world.

> *"For since the creation of the world God's invisible qualities—his eternal power and divine nature—have been clearly seen, being understood from what has been made." Romans 1:20*

> *"So God created human beings in his image. In the image of God he created them. He created them male and female." Genesis 1:27 (NCV)*

> *"The Son is the image of the invisible God, the firstborn over all creation." Colossians 1:15*

Jesus came to earth and entered humanity, with the typical sexual desires, for thirty-three years before he ascended to heaven. This should reassure us that he understands single sexuality. Jesus was the ultimate example as he lived out his single life with purity, righteous flirting and intimate same-sex and opposite sex friendships.

> *"For our high priest is able to understand our weaknesses. He was tempted in every way that we are, but he did not*

sin. Let us, then, feel sure we can come before God's throne where there is grace. There we can receive mercy and grace to help us when we need it." Hebrews 4:15,16 (NCV)

You may feel uncomfortable when you realize, "God sees me naked in every way." We know that because he isn't physically sexual, he isn't voyeuristically observing everything we do—but he's always present. He created the beauty of masculine and feminine bodies. He created with the ability to be sexually attracted and aroused. He wants us to righteously flirt and engage in social and erotic sexuality.

"Now we see things imperfectly, like puzzling reflections in a mirror, but then we will see everything with perfect clarity. All that I know now is partial and incomplete, but then I will know everything completely, just as God now knows me completely." I Corinthians 13:12 NLT

Remember that you, as men and women, reflect, imperfectly, some aspect of God in your sexuality. Though partial and incomplete in this present world, the Loving Trinity gives you the privilege of mirroring their love through sexually intimate relationships as your physical sexuality (visible) displays God's character (invisible). Your sexual journey can increasingly make *visible the invisible* and be testimony to God's intimate love.

2. I pledge to ask God to help me live out my faith and sexuality from the Inside-Out.

As a Christian, everything good in your life starts with a personal relationship with God through Jesus, and the Holy Spirit as it empowers you. God must be at the center as you create intimate relationships with Jesus and your Christian brothers and sisters; then work inside-out with your and heart attitudes shaping your "behavior."

"Don't become so well-adjusted to your culture that you fit into it without even thinking. Instead, fix your attention on God. You'll be changed from the inside out" Romans 12:2 (MSG)

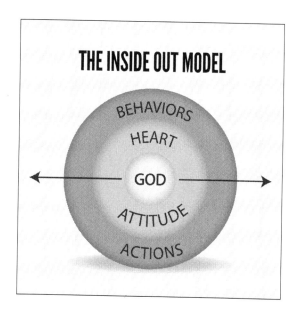

Starting with abstaining from certain sexual behavior (outside-in) doesn't work well. Letting God create in you an unselfish value system can be truly transforming. Jesus-values that internally direct your sexual journey, are so much more powerful than externally imposed rules. That's why an Inside-Out approach is such good news: *A heart surrendered to God produces godly behavior directed by God.* If the attitude of your heart is to please God, surrendering ownership of yourself and your sexuality to his plan will become your desire.

"Work hard to show the results of your salvation, obeying God with deep reverence and fear. For God is working in you, giving you the desire and the power to do what pleases him (sexually)." Philippians 2: 12b, 13 (NLT parenthesis added)

"But the Holy Spirit produces this kind of fruit in our lives: sexual love, sexual joy, sexual peace, sexual patience, sexual kindness, sexual goodness, sexual faithfulness, sexual gentleness and sexual self-control." Galatians 5:22 (NLT, "sexual" added)

3. I pledge to join and help build a (sexually) supportive community where God has placed me—one open to righteous flirting.

As I've emphasized many times in this book, you can't accomplish sexual wholeness as a single adult without the help of a supportive community. You need their affirming touch and words. You need to be with others who aren't afraid to embrace horny and are learning to set healthy boundaries with plenty of righteous flirting. You need the accountability that a community practicing chastity can provide. You need a place to serve and have fellowship. You need people who have your back—intimate friendships where you can enjoy giving and receiving love.

With this pledge, like Hercules on his journey of 12 Labors, there are some difficult tasks ahead of you. Finding a truly supportive community isn't easy. In fact, you may need several communities in different life stages. Creating a support group in your church, if one doesn't exist, won't be easy, either. Start with your pastoral staff, and be persistent, like the widow who wouldn't take "no" for an answer. (Luke 18:1-8) Do some research and make some helpful suggestions. Start a group, then take the risk of developing deeper friendships as you create the community that you need.

> *"A friend is always loyal, and a brother [or sister] is born to help in time of need."* Proverbs 17:17 (NLT)

> *"And let us consider how we may spur one another on toward love and good deeds, not giving up meeting together, as some are in the habit of doing, but encouraging one another…"* Hebrews 10:24-25a

Building your communities into a *sexually supportive* community can also feel like a Herculean task. It may start with making opposite-sex friendships that are fun and safe. Defining and enjoying same-sex and opposite-sex righteous flirting will be essential. Putting into sexual chastity and purity with accountability will be a communal process of valuing, celebrating, and protecting each other's sexuality. God created us to thrive in community. Pledge to be persistent in this quest, as you find the love and support that can help you and others flourish.

4. I pledge to develop and celebrate all three dimensions of my sexuality and personhood.

You are a body, you are a mind, and you are a heart. God has given you a three-dimensional personhood of body, mind and spirit to help you develop as an intimate sexual being.

"Offer your bodies as living sacrifices...be transformed by the renewing of your mind...[appreciate] the measure of faith God has given [to each spiritually]." Romans 12:1-3

In developing your body dimension, you probably need to work on a better body image and appreciate your unique qualities. It's easy to fall into the mindset of "I'm too big" or "I'm too small." God wants you to be comfortable in your own skin. Exercise helps bodies function better. Use your body to express emotions and love—practice physical affection, laugh loudly, cry with your friends, wave your arms in excitement, and look with appreciation into a friend's eyes.

You're "soul sexy." All three dimensions of your personhood help express and celebrate your sexuality. Your masculinity or femininity can be demonstrated and enjoyed in so many ways. This is what makes righteous flirting come alive. Sometimes you'll need to focus on your soul sexy mind and heart—not just your body.

Your mind has many false ideas about yourself and about sexuality. Reading helpful books can dispute some of these myths. Healthy dialogue in your community can bring healing to your sexual traumas. Developing the right attitudes is so important.

Your sexually effective values will often come from a changed heart. The Holy Spirit can help you to be kind and patient in living out your 3-D sexuality. He can instill a wisdom that will guide your sexual journey. He wants to help you give and receive love freely from an open heart.

"For we know how dearly God loves us, because he has given us the Holy Spirit to fill our hearts with his love." Romans 5:5 (NLT)

God uses each of your three dimensions to bring you to sexual maturity and wholeness, especially your hearts and minds. What an encouragement that Jesus can create a redeemed mind and heart expressed through our bodies. Hebrews 8:10 tells us that Jesus has made a new Covenant with his people and that things will be different now. This time it's not just about behavior and sacrifices. This new covenant is be based on a changed heart and renewed mind.

> *"But this is the new covenant I will make..., says the Lord: I will put my (sexual) laws in their minds, and I will write them on their hearts. I will be their God, and they will be my people." Hebrews 8:10 (NLT)*

God gives you the ability to love and have sexual integrity with a redeemed heart and mind. Honor this important pledge of developing and celebrating all three dimensions of your personhood.

5. I pledge to embrace sexual desire (horny) and steward it wisely.

In the word "embrace" I hope to convey a different concept than "repress or casually indulge." Repressing sexual desire is often composed of refusing to deal with your sexual feelings, identifying them as bad, and white-knuckling it as you try to abstain from certain behavior. Casually indulging is conforming to the present cultural belief that chastity is old-fashioned and that we should be sexually active. Neither of these work well in writing a healthy sexual story as a Christian single adult.

Embracing sexual desire means more than merely accepting that God created you with the ability to be sexually attracted and aroused. It means finding meaning, confidence and fun in sexual desire. God can give you the ability to control your sexual desire as you make wise choices.

In Chapter 14, I provided lists for stewarding horny and two practical tools to fulfill those deeper erotic needs: *redirecting* and *reframing*. *Redirecting* takes sexual energy and uses it to engage in other activities. Sublimate is another word for redirect and means to divert your desire toward a healthier expression. An example of this would be a strenuous hike in the great outdoors. It isn't that sexual desire is unhealthy, but God often needs us to refuse to indulge, and instead redirect or sublimate them.

Reframing sees into the deeper meaning of sexual desire, allowing this perspective to inspire one to greater wholeness. Like the way a new picture frame can transform the way we view a work of art, our heavenly Father can help us put a different frame around our sexual desire, and value it rather than stay frustrated. An example of reframing would be seeing the advantages of single sexuality. You still have the energy of sexual desire and the possibility of attraction and pursuit, the mystery and excitement, and the power of gender interaction righteous flirting and so much more!

Embracing "horny" and stewarding it is a central pledge for Christian singles. This is where transparency, dialogue and accountability within a loving community is so vital.

6. I pledge to run to God's sexual E.R. with my sexual trauma and mistakes.

Most of you reading this book have some sexually traumatic event or events that has happened to you and have also made some inappropriate sexual choices. This why you must pledge to seek out

God's sexual E.R. when your sexual self is distorted or broken. Jesus, the Great Physician, wants to transform your heart, mind and life—empowering you through his forgiveness and redemptive presence in your life.

But you also have a part in this process. Difficult choices must be made to enter the E.R. and focus on healing. You'll need humility to ask for help. Time alone doesn't heal, but time and the proper treatment can bring healing, relief from guilt, and restoration. Surrendering to God and allowing him to perform spiritual surgery his way isn't easy. And don't try to undergo this process alone. You need God and the *community of your Christian brothers and sisters* to accomplish the Emergency Room healing.

God's E.R. is equipped with many treatment options and interventions:

- Confronting- facing brokenness honestly as you admit necessary changes
- Grieving- crying and working through your many emotions
- Confessing- taking ownership of your mistakes
- Repenting- acknowledging your need to make changes
- Forgiving- living fully in the present without being haunted by the past or fearing the future
- Making Amends- the appropriate confession and restitution for sinful mistakes as you help those you've offended
- Becoming Whole- the ultimate task of achieving sexual maturity in your sexual journey.

The prophet Isaiah described what the Messiah would bring to a (sexually) broken world. That he would "bind up the brokenhearted, proclaim freedom for the captives… comfort all who mourn and provide for those who grieve" (Isaiah 61:1–2). Instead of shame and disgrace, "everlasting joy will be theirs" (v. 7). Choosing to run to God's E.R. can dramatically transform your sexual story.

7. I pledge to fight my desire to watch porn and fight Satan's destructive viruses, and to intentionally create a godly values framework.

Writing involves many components—and Satan will try to deceive you to live out of a false self and identity. Developing a comfortable sense (gender identity) of how to live out your gender is another quest. You may still be sorting out to whom you're attracted.

SEXUAL IDENTITY

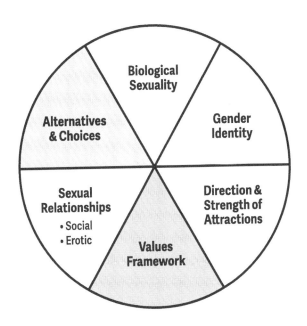

The key foundation to build upon in guiding your sexual journey will be your *values framework and the choices* you make based on those values. This is the grand finale to your seven pledges—pledging to fight Satan's attempts to sabotage your sexual story!

"Do not let anyone fool you by telling you things that are (sexually) untrue…live like children who belong to the light. Light brings every kind of (sexual) goodness, right living, and truth. So be careful how you live. Do not live like those who are not (sexually) wise, but live wisely. So do not be (sexually) foolish but learn what the Lord wants you to do."
Ephesians 5: 6a,8b,9, 15-17 (NCV Parentheses added)

Many singles begin their journey to sexual wholeness hoping for minor changes, only to realize they need a completely new map—a radically different way to reach the destination of sexual integrity and intimacy. Dear Christian reader, more than you realize, your values are what help you live out what you believe, but often the values shaping your belief system come from a distorted culture, not godly wisdom.

Creating a new understanding of sexual wholeness is about discarding ineffective thinking and creating new heart attitudes and a healthy sexual culture. How sad that our selfish, immature culture has so warped and idolized sex. I challenge you, as you read this book to ask God to give you a new map for your single adult sexual journey. You need a new road map of godly principles that will have an impact on your total personhood – that will *revolutionize your hearts, minds and your behaviors*

WORKS CITED

1   Christopher West, Theology of the Body for Beginners: A Basic Introduction to Pope John Paul II's Sexual Revolution, Westchester, PA: Ascension Press, 2004, p.5.

2   Gary Thomas, Devotions for a Sacred Marriage: A Year of Weekly Devotions for Couples, Grand Rapids, MI: Zondervan, 2005, p.31.

3   Lauren Winner, Real Sex: The Naked Truth About Chastity, Ada, MI: Brazos Press, 2005, p.124, 126.

4   Hill, p.108

5   Wesley Hill, Spiritual Friendship: Finding Love in the Church as a Celibate Gay Christian, Ada, MI: Brazos Press, 2015, p.52.

6   Timothy & Kathy Keller, The Meaning of Marriage, New York, NY: Dutton, 2022, p.110-133.

7   Oswald Chambers, Daily Thoughts for Disciples, Ada, MI: Discovery House, p.32.

8   Brendan Manning, Abba's Child: The Cry of the Heart for Intimate Belonging, Colorado Springs, CO: NavPress, 2015, p.17.

9   Thomas Merton Quotes. (n.d.). BrainyQuote.com. Retrieved May 15, 2022, from BrainyQuote.com Web site: https://www.brainyquote.com/quotes/thomas_merton_387047

10 Juli Slattery, Sex and the Single Girl, Chicago: Moody Publishers, 2017, pp. 25, 40, 78, 91.

11 Paula Rinehart, Sex and the Soul of a Woman: The Reality of Love and Romance in an Age of Casual Sex, Grand Rapids: Zondervan, p. 173.

12 Stasi & John Eldredge, Captivating: Unveiling the Mystery of a Woman's Soul, Nashville: Thomas Nelson, 2010, p.?.

13 Wendy Shallit, A Return to Modesty: Romance in an Age of Casual Sex, Grand Rapids: Zondervan, 2004, p.46.

14 Rinehart, p.?

15 Rosemary Basson, A Model of Women's Sexual Arousal, Journal of Sex & Marital Therapy, 28 (2002). p. 17-28.

16 Stanley J. Grenz, Sexual Ethics: An Evangelical Perspective, Louisville, KY: Westminster John Knox Press, 1990, p.195.

17 Ibid., p.218

18 Rolheiser, R. (1999). The Holy Longing: the Search for a Christian Spirituality, Doubleday, p. 192, 193.

19 Christopher West, The Theology of the Body for Beginners, North Palm Beach, FL: Blue Sparrow Books, 2018, p.8.

20 David Benner, Care of Souls: Revisiting Christian Nurture and Counsel, Ada, MN: Baker Books, 1998, p.13.

21 Ibid., p.22

22 Chambers, p. 117.

23 Ibid., p. 140.

24 Christopher West, Our Bodies Tell God's Story: Discovering the Divine Plan for Love, Sex, and Gender, Ada, MI: Brazos Press, 2020, p.5.

25 Dallas Willard, Renovation of the Heart: Putting on the Character of Christ, Colorado Springs, CO: NavPress Publishing Group, 2002, p.33.

26 Curt Thompson, Anatomy of the Soul: Surprising Connections between Neuroscience and Spiritual Practices That Can Transform Your Life and Relationships, Carol Stream, IL: Tyndale Momentum, 2010, p.29

27 Ibid.

28 Keller, K., Keller, T. (2011). The Meaning of Marriage: Facing the Complexities of Commitment with the Wisdom of God. United States: Penguin Group US. p.95.

29 James K.A. Smith, You Are What You Love: The Spiritual Power of Habit, Ada, MI: Brazos Press, 2016, p.7

30 Ibid., p.9

31 Craig Barnes, Pastor as Minor Poet: Texts and Subtexts in the Ministerial Life, Grand Rapids, MI: Eerdmans, 2008, p.46.

32 Chambers, p.247-248

33 Manning, B. (2015). Abba's Child: The Cry of the Heart for Intimate Belonging. United States: NavPress. p.61, 61.

34 C.S. Lewis, The Weight of Glory, San Francisco, CA: HarperOne, 2001, p.26.

35 Smith, p. 19.

36 Smith, p. 61.

37 Rolheiser, R. (2014). The Holy Longing: The Search for a Christian Spirituality. United States: Image. p.192.

38 Sandra L. Glahn and C. Gary Barnes, eds., Sanctified Sexuality: Valuing Sex in an Oversexed World, Grand Rapids, MI: Kregel Academic, 2020.

39 Abbie Smith, Celibate Sex: Musings on Being Loved, Single, Twisted and Holy, Colorado Springs, CO: NavPress, 2013, p.138.

40 Harvey Cox, The Secular City: Secularization and Urbanization in Theological Perspective, New York, NY: Macmillan, 1966.

41 Rachel Joy Welcher and Scott Sauls, Talking Back to Purity Culture: Rediscovering Faithful Christian Sexuality, Colorado Springs, CO: NavPress, 2020.

42 Manning, B. (2015). Abba's Child: The Cry of the Heart for Intimate Belonging. United States: NavPress. pp. 59, 62.

43 Chesterton, G. K., (1920). Tremendous Trifles. Accessed through the Gutenberg Project: https://www.gutenberg.org/files/8092/8092-h/8092-h.htm

44 Grenz, p.52.

45 Chambers, p.144.

46 Winner, p.124, 126.

47 Mark Yarhouse and Olya Zaporozhetz, Costly Obedience: What We Can Learn from the Celibate Gay Christian Community, Grand Rapids, MI: Zondervan, 2019

48 Glahn and Barnes, pp.168-172.

49 Michael J. Cusick, Surfing for God: Discovering the Divine Desire Beneath Sexual Struggle, Grand Rapids: Thomas Nelson, 2012 pp.15-16.

50 Walter Trobisch, I Loved a Girl: A Private Correspondence, Bolivar, MO: Quiet Waters, 2001, pp. 75–76.

51 Rinehart, p. 173

52 Smith, p.51.

53 Yarhouse and Zaporozhets, p.193.

54 Rinehart, p.148.

55 Ted Shimer, The Freedom Fight: The New Drug and the Truths That Set Us Free, Houston, TX: High Bridge Books, 2020, p.143.

56 Gary Wilson, Your Brain on Porn: Internet Pornography and the Emerging Science of Addiction, Beverly, MA: Commonwealth Publishing, 2015, p.38.

57 Cusick, pp.15-16.

58 Ibid., pp.19-23.

59 Steven R. Tracy, Mending the Soul: Understanding and Healing Abuse, Grand Rapids, MI: Zondervan, 2005, p.74.

60 Shimer, p.71.

61 Alcoholics Anonymous World Services, I. (2013). Alcoholics Anonymous, Fourth Edition: The Official "Big Book" from Alcoholic Anonymous. United States: Alcoholics Anonymous World Services, Incorporated.

62 Keller and Keller, p.121.

Douglas Eugene Rosenau

Douglas Rosenau was born June 25, 1947, 100 yards from where his father was born in French Equatorial Africa. Born to second generation missionary parents, Doug grew up in Africa with his parents and siblings, Vernon and Anna Kay, until coming to the United States in his teens for High School. Doug received his Master of Theology from Dallas Theological Seminary before pursuing a doctorate in Counselor Education (Ed.D.) from Northern Illinois University. It was there he raised support to study sex therapy at Loyola University.

Doug became a licensed psychologist, marriage and family therapist, and certified sex therapist, setting up practice in Atlanta, Georgia. As a therapist, he helped countless individuals, couples and families, providing over 50,000 hours of expert counseling and compassionate care.

While in Atlanta he met and married his wife, Cathy. Together they raised their daughter Merrill and his granddaughter Caitlyn, who was truly the apple of his eye. All you had to do was ask about her and his eyes sparkled! He was a kind, caring, loving and gentle husband and father to Cathy and Merrill.

Doug carried on his family's missionary history by becoming "a missionary for sexual wholeness," developing a vision and passion for cultivating a sexually healthy church. Through his gentle spirit, jokes, and love for Christ, Doug became a respected voice encouraging the Church to deal with sexuality. He authored *A Celebration of Sex* in 1994 (revised in 2002), *Soul Virgins: Redefining Single Sexuality* (2006/2012), *Total Intimacy* (2014), and several others. He was a frequent speaker at national conferences and loved teaching singles and couples in churches and seminars.

SEXUAL WHOLENESS

In 2000 he joined with three other Christian sex therapists to found Sexual Wholeness, Inc. Through this ministry he taught hundreds of counselors, therapists, pastors, and educators in healthy sexuality and sex therapy. He was a professor at multiple graduate schools including Richmont Graduate University, Dallas Theological Seminary, Reformed Theological Seminary, and Denver Seminary. Doug called many to join him in being a "missionary for sexual wholeness" and today there are hundreds of students and supervisees who carry on his passion and legacy.

Dr. Doug went to be with his Lord on Palm Sunday, April 10th, 2022, at the age of 74. He is sorely missed by his family, friends, and colleagues who had their lives enriched by his presence.

May you catch a glimpse of his spirit in this book.

Made in the USA
Columbia, SC
22 November 2024